Queer Troublemakers

Bloomsbury Studies in Critical Poetics

Series Editor: Daniel Katz, University of Warwick, UK

Political, social, erotic, and aesthetic – poetry has been a challenge to many of the dominant discourses of our age across the globe. Bloomsbury Studies in Critical Poetics publishes books on modern and contemporary poetry and poetics that explore the intersection of poetry with philosophy, linguistics, psychoanalysis, political and economic theory, protest and liberation movements, as well as other art forms, including prose. With a primary focus on texts written in English but including work from other languages, the series brings together leading and rising scholars from a diverse range of fields for whom poetry has become a vital element of their research.

Editorial Board:
Hélène Aji, University of Paris Ouest-Nanterre, France
Vincent Broqua, University of Paris 8–Vincennes/Saint Denis, France
Olivier Brossard, University of Paris Est Marne La Vallée, France
Daniel Kane, University of Sussex, UK
Miriam Nichols, University of the Fraser Valley, Canada
Peter Middleton, University of Southampton, UK
Cristanne Miller, SUNY Buffalo, USA
Aldon Nielsen, Pennsylvania State University, USA
Stephen Ross, University of Warwick, UK; Editor, Wave Composition
Richard Sieburth, New York University, USA
Daniel Tiffany, University of Southern California, USA
Steven G. Yao, Hamilton College, USA

Titles in the series include:
A Black Arts Poetry Machine, David Grundy
Affect, Psychoanalysis, and American Poetry, John Steen
City Poems and American Urban Crisis, Nate Mickelson
Lyric Pedagogy and Marxist-Feminism, Samuel Solomon

Queer Troublemakers

The Poetics of Flippancy

Prudence Bussey-Chamberlain
Royal Holloway, University of London, UK

BLOOMSBURY ACADEMIC
LONDON • NEW YORK • OXFORD • NEW DELHI • SYDNEY

BLOOMSBURY ACADEMIC
Bloomsbury Publishing Plc
50 Bedford Square, London, WC1B 3DP, UK
1385 Broadway, New York, NY 10018, USA
29 Earlsfort Terrace, Dublin 2, Ireland

BLOOMSBURY, BLOOMSBURY ACADEMIC and the Diana logo
are trademarks of Bloomsbury Publishing Plc

First published in Great Britain 2019
Paperback edition published 2021

Copyright © Prudence Bussey-Chamberlain, 2019

Prudence Bussey-Chamberlain has asserted her right under the Copyright,
Designs and Patents Act, 1988, to be identified as Author of this work.

For legal purposes the Acknowledgements on p. vii constitute
an extension of this copyright page.

Cover design: Eleanor Rose
Cover image © Getty Images

All rights reserved. No part of this publication may be reproduced or
transmitted in any form or by any means, electronic or mechanical,
including photocopying, recording, or any information storage or retrieval
system, without prior permission in writing from the publishers.

Bloomsbury Publishing Plc does not have any control over, or responsibility for,
any thirdparty websites referred to or in this book. All internet addresses given
in this book were correct at the time of going to press. The author and publisher
regret any inconvenience caused if addresses have changed or sites have
ceased to exist, but can accept no responsibility for any such changes.

A catalogue record for this book is available from the British Library.

Library of Congress Cataloging-in-Publication Data
Names: Bussey-Chamberlain, Prudence, author.
Title: Queer troublemakers: the poetics of flippancy / Prudence
Bussey-Chamberlain, Royal Holloway, University of London, UK.
Description: London; New York: Bloomsbury Academic, 2019. |
Series: Bloomsbury studies in critical poetics |
Includes bibliographical references and index.
Identifiers: LCCN 2018058496 (print) | ISBN 9781350079359 (hb) |
ISBN 9781350079366 (ePDF) | ISBN 9781350079373 (eBook)
Subjects: LCSH: Flippancy in literature. | Experimental poetry, American–History
and criticism. | American poetry–20th century–History and criticism. |
Gays' writings, American–History and criticism. | Stein, Gertrude, 1874-1946–Criticism
and interpretation. | O'Hara, Frank, 1926-1966–Criticism and interpretation. | Myles,
Eileen–Criticism and interpretation. | Nelson, Maggie, 1973–Criticism and interpretation.
Classification: LCC PS310.F55 B87 2019 (print) |
LCC PS310.F55 (ebook) | DDC 811/.509353–dc23
LC record available at https://lccn.loc.gov/2018058496
LC ebook record available at https://lccn.loc.gov/2019980030
Edit

ISBN: HB: 978-1-3500-7935-9
PB: 978-1-3502-1542-9
ePDF: 978-1-3500-7936-6
eBook: 978-1-3500-7937-3

Series: Bloomsbury Studies in Critical Poetics
Typeset by Integra Software Services Pvt. Ltd.

To find out more about our authors and books visit
www.bloomsbury.com and sign up for our newsletters.

Contents

List of Figures	vi
Acknowledgements	vii
Introduction	1
1 The Poetics of Flippancy	11
2 'He Cannot Understand Women. I Can': Gertrude Stein and the Camp Butch	33
3 'There's Nothing Metaphysical about It': Frank O'Hara's Flippant Manifesto and the Poetry of Tight Trousers	69
4 'Who Are These Idiots Writing These Poems?': Eileen Myles' Pornographic Tone and Mutable Categories	101
5 'Was Harry a Woman? Was I a Straight Lady?': Tensions of Heteronormativity, Assimilation and the Second Person	139
Conclusion	165
References	187
Index	193

List of Figures

1. Eileen Myles author attribution – *Inferno (A Poet's Novel)*. 104
2. Eileen Myles reading from text – *Inferno (A Poet's Novel)*. 105
3. Eileen Myles reading from text – *Inferno (A Poet's Novel)*. 106

Acknowledgements

Aspects of the work presented here were initially explored in other critical writing. 'The Inheritance of Irony and Development of Flippancy', which appeared in *Feminism, Influence, Inheritance: New Essays in English* (eds. Emily Hogg and Clara Jones), explored the relationship between the two linguistic strategies in relation to contemporary feminism. Both *The Poetry Review* and *Culture Matters* have given me the space to review Eileen Myles' *I Must Be Living Twice* and Maggie Nelson's *The Argonauts*, respectively. This space was invaluable for celebrating and enjoying the poets' work alongside writing about them critically. Finally, a piece on Eileen Myles, porn movies and *Step Up: The Streets* has recently appeared in *Versopolis Journal*.

There have also been a number of conferences and discussions germane to my thinking. *Frank O'Hara and Friends* (2016), organized by the North American Poetics Network of CHASE, was an exciting space in which to celebrate the poet. The Contemporary Poetry Research Seminar allowed me to present a paper on Maggie Nelson, Eileen Myles and the pornographic, considering the resonances between the two poets' sex writing. Being invited to talk about Myles at *Women, Community & Tradition in the Avant-Garde* at Kent University also entailed a day of discussion around exciting contemporary women writers. Finally, Royal Holloway's *Modernism Lecture Series* facilitated an extended discussion of Stein, with a paper entitled '"All This and Not Ordinary": The Radical Re-orientation of Objects in Gertrude Stein's *Tender Buttons*'.

A number of my colleagues have been very supportive through the process of writing. I would like to thank Professor Redell Olsen for introducing me to Frank O'Hara when I took her Poetic Practice module and then allowing me to study his writing further through the Poetic Practice MA. Professor Kristen Kreider has been influential to all of my thinking and encouraged me both towards Eileen Myles during my PhD and towards lightness more generally. Professor Robert Hampson and Dr Will Montgomery released a brilliant book on Frank O'Hara which challenged my thinking on the poet. Discussing O'Hara and flippancy with both Robert and Will has been invaluable to the political aspects of this book. Professor Bob Eaglestone kindly took the time to read through my proposal (again), for which I am very grateful.

I would also like to thank the students of First Person for their interesting discussions on cross-genre writing and memoir. The second year poets (who will always be known as such) – thank you for your love of O'Hara, bringing him into seminars so that I didn't have to. Thank you, too, for being all-round rabble-rousers in both seminars and the lyric. The third year poets, I really appreciate your discussions on Myles and Nelson over our two years of poetry together.

Finally, thanks Marj for all of the reading and discussions. I will always appreciate your levity and what you have to say about the poets, gender or anything else. KB, my own queer troublemaker, thank you for my first editions, for listening to the revelation moment and for your own brilliant brand of dark-humoured flippancy. Kit Ziggy, we can't wait for the trouble you'll bring.

Introduction

Flippancy began with Frank O'Hara. First reading his *Lunch Poems*, the lightness of foot as he traversed New York was an irreverent kind of movement, concerned with lovers, friends, the city and art. This characteristic levity was further reinforced by O'Hara's 'Personism: A Manifesto', which rejected didacticism in favour of celebrating the movies and the telephone over the poem itself. Unfortunately, my light reading coincided with a critical movement in the opposite direction, in which the poet was being rehabilitated as a figure of seriousness. In *Frank O'Hara Now* (2010) Will Montgomery and Robert Hampson outline a strenuous project of identifying the dark, political and highly experimental within the poet's work, prioritizing heaviness over the usual lightness. Similarly, in 'Frank O'Hara Drives Olson's Car', J. Duncan claims that 'contrary to predominant interpretations, [O'Hara] is not being flippant' (2010: 77) in his *Lunch Poems*. Rather, he is exploring a deep anxiety related to selfhood and his place within commodity culture. While these are just two examples of scholarship deliberately moving away from a light reading of O'Hara's writing, they demonstrate that the critical reception of the poet's work has perhaps focused on an easily accessible levity, as opposed to the greater complex seriousness of his more experimental writing. Interestingly, Mark Silverberg attempts to create a relationship between these two aspects of the poet's writing. In *The New York School Poets and the New Avant-Garde: Between Radical Art and Radical Chic*, he writes that there is a 'widely encompassing program hiding behind O'Hara's typically flippant and whimsical prose' (2010: 47). It could be argued, then, that flippancy itself is a point of tension, in which the lightness always engages with a greater sense of seriousness. The unbecoming levity clearly demonstrated through the work does not betray depth or politics, but rather creates a more dynamic relationship with radicalism that demands gravitas and commitment. Flippancy, certainly in O'Hara studies, might not do the poet a disservice of lightness, instead creating a dialogue with seriousness that resonates through queer politics.

O'Hara scholars are not the only critical thinkers to struggle with the flippant and serious dynamic. As I explore later in this book, Susan Sontag retrospectively revisits her writing on camp to bemoan the lack of seriousness in culture at large. She reports that she might not have celebrated camp's levity in the same way had she realized that its characteristics were going to become so widespread. Once more, seriousness seems to have been decimated by the existence of levity, rather than Sontag allowing for the two to coexist in a productive uneasiness. This might relate, more generally, to how flippancy itself is difficult to situate. It is not an identity, nor can it be understood as an affect, and while it is partly a performance, it can be realized through tone and posture. In the case of the queer troublemakers I survey here, flippancy has to be perpetuated through the text, performed among a series of juxtapositions in which lightness is made apparent through its contrast to context. As such, I see flippancy itself as elusive, but nonetheless operating as a queer strategy that mobilizes the text in its consideration of politics, identity and assimilation. At some points, flippancy can be read as a self-defence strategy, enabling the poets to react to their contexts without becoming entrapped or enmeshed. It is a useful means by which to take on pre-Stonewall America, Modernist Paris, hetero-patriarchies and American culture at the time of Prop 8. In these instances, flippancy creates a disconnect with the seriousness of the context, so that the poet can be seen to reject the normative politics of their own time. At other points, flippancy is simply a lightness of foot or surface movement, facilitating the speaker in the creation of space and therefore freedom. That the poetics emphasizes non-commitment allows for each of the poets to move between multiple subjects, creating exit routes through extreme juxtaposition.

It is for these reasons that a poetics of flippancy necessarily extends beyond O'Hara. While O'Hara's work might be the point of origination, the poetics themselves operate in multiple ways, manifesting differently throughout a lineage of queer, experimental writing. The four writers I have chosen to discuss here are part of a self-selecting lineage, all creating links of influence with one another. Gertrude Stein, Frank O'Hara, Eileen Myles and Maggie Nelson accrue and accumulate chronologically, with the Modernist ultimately impacting on the youngest, New York and Bay Area–inflected poet. The temporality of the book then extends and compresses, mapping Modernism through O'Hara's writing in the 1950s and early 1960s to resolve in the contemporaneity of Myles and Nelson. Myles and Nelson are in fact so closely situated in both temporality and locale that they have become friends, even dedicating books to one another. I see Stein as the matriarch of this line of flippancy, distant from the other three poets in regard to her geography, as well as time. Situated in Paris, she does not have the same New York-inflected walk as O'Hara, nor the Bostonian accent that resonates so strongly throughout Myles' work. While I will not be focusing on national identity here, it is interesting to note that all the writers discussed in relation to flippancy are American, even if one of them lived an expatriate life in Paris. Although the Modernist is often attributed with having influenced the Language school more than any other American experimental strand of writing, O'Hara was also very interested in Stein's work. As an undergraduate, the poet had written an essay on Stein's *The Autobiography of Alice B. Toklas*, describing it in a letter as 'one of the most interesting things I've ever read' (Mikkelsen 2011: 151). O'Hara was also known for disappearing to buy the newest Stein whenever they appeared in the bookshops, and he even used her name in the title of 'Poem (À la recherche de Gertrude Stein)', which was written in celebration of his lover Vincent Warren. However, it is not just a case that O'Hara was a fan of Stein but that the two share certain modes of exploration. Both writers had strong relationships with art and artists, which ultimately influenced their writing praxis. Stein drew on aspects of Cubism in her writing, while O'Hara was affected by the spontaneous and gestural nature of abstract expressionism (Glavey 2015). Perhaps even more significant is that both poets sit at the centre of wide-ranging and dynamic social groups, comprised of other writers and artists. The two were both generous with their time, galvanizing those around them to write or paint better. While Stein achieved this more patriarchally, inviting people to the Rue de Fleures so that she could talk to the men while their wives went on to the kitchen, O'Hara moved through social gatherings and cultural institutions, fulfilling a more institutional curator role at the Museum of Modern Art (MoMA).

Eileen Myles, arguably, has descended from both O'Hara and Stein, though they only name the latter as an influential literary precursor in their statement 'The Lesbian Poet'. There, Myles claims Stein as one of their poetic mothers before also commenting on the poet's butchness. They argue it is significant that the most important poet of all time was both a woman and butch, ultimately defying our expectations of how gender and sex might be realized through a body. Myles' focus suggests that Stein is revered as a matriarch not purely of Modernism but also for the relationships she created between the text and sexuality, which can be mobilized by following generations of queer writers. Myles moved to New York in order to become a poet, something they deemed necessary to achieve before they were able to become a lesbian. They quickly became part of the St Mark's Poetry community, developing friendships with other poets such as Ted Berrigan, Alice Notley and Berndatte Mayer. Significantly, O'Hara and Myles did not overlap within New York City, and so the latter felt the former's presence mostly through the people who surrounded them. They were able to recognize O'Hara's New York–orientated 'I do this, I do that' style in the work of Ted Berrigan, as well as coming to know the first generation of New York School poets through caring for Jimmy Schuyler towards the end of his life. Thus, Myles occupies an interesting position in that they were socialized in similar circles to that of O'Hara, but experienced a very different version of the city – one that was less institutional and more impoverished. In *Women, The New York School, and Other True Abstractions*, Nelson teases out an interesting lineage through Stein, to O'Hara, to Myles, recognizing how the different embodied experiences of each inevitably affected how their poetics took form. Importantly, Nelson creates links through a 'not caring' posture that originated with O'Hara and took on slightly different significances with Myles. Myles' femaleness, their explicit lesbianism, results in a form of 'not caring' that is highly concerned with gender and gendered labour; it does not have quite the same freedom as O'Hara's version. As such, Myles can be seen as a poetic descendent of O'Hara, but also as someone who walked New York City with different kinds of fitful enthusiasms.

While Myles moved to New York in order to become a poet, Nelson moved to New York to study poetry directly under Myles. This has ultimately resulted in a close friendship between the two poets, with Nelson serving as the executor of Myles' literary estate. In a 2016 interview with *The New York Times*, Myles says, 'I've known Maggie Nelson for 20 years. That's totally what the poetry world is, is those kind of relationships' (Correal 2016). This seems to suggest that the poetry world of Nelson and Myles is not that dissimilar to the groups of artists and writers with whom Stein and O'Hara interacted. As my previous paragraph demonstrates, Nelson has critical investments in the New York School that range beyond her creative practice. Investigating the poetics, style and postures of the New York School, Nelson traces influence as far back as Stein, before turning to O'Hara, ultimately considering Mayer, Notley and Myles. She tracks a lineage of 'not caring' through the poets, thinking about how it can be enacted by female poets, some of whom are mothers, others of whom are of indeterminate gender. Nelson argues that in spite of their indebtedness to O'Hara's camp dismissal, the poets she considers are not able to practice the same kind of levity in their own 'not caring'. Given the poetic and critical ways that both Myles and Nelson approach Stein and O'Hara, it is possible to say that there is a certain familiarity at work, even a queer intimacy. In their analysis of and references to the deceased united or grouped through specific kinds of poetics, their usage of flippancy throws aspects of their unique queer culture into relief. The first chapter of this book addresses the poetics of flippancy and how irreverence and lightness are constructed through creative works. It considers, initially, ideas of shame in relation to lyric writing and how this affect is particularly mirrored through queer identities. Considering how this relates to Narcissus and Echo, I think about how the use of the lyric and the sameness of queerness can be used to create a first-person troublemaker realized across the work of all four writers. This chapter also addresses flippancy as both difficult and elusive to pin down. Initially, I place it in dialogue with ideas of performance and performativity, thinking about how the performance of levity might in some ways problematize both gender and sex essentialism. Then, I consider flippancy in relation to affect and affectation. While flippancy is not an affect, it comes into existence among and in-between circulating affects that are far more serious and weighty. Affectation resonates with performance, suggesting aspects of 'trying it on' in order to elicit specific forms of response. Finally, I turn to ideas of aesthetic categories and ugly feelings to address how flippancy might use its very unseriousness to call both genre and gender into question. Ultimately, these ideas relate to both becoming and unbecoming, in which each writer engages in orientations that allow them to reject normativity while still developing their first-person identity.

The chapter on Stein makes a case for the coexistence of camp and butch within the poet's work, both of which are brought together through a flippant approach to the contingency of identity. Considering how Stein as a figure conveys both campness and butchness through her writing, it is clear that the force of her personality still animates the work long after her death. The camp levity, positioning things as-what-they-are-not, relishing playfulness and the non-serious, is apparent in both *Lifting Belly* and *The Autobiography of Alice B. Toklas*. While the former plays with proper nouns, gendered pronouns, repetition and sexual suggestion, the latter enacts a form of drag, in which the butch Stein dons the identity and appearance of her femme lover. There is a swaggering aspect to Stein that is recognizably butch, a status only reified by the relationality written into both texts I examine; the butchness exists because it is offset by the 'you' or 'her' of Alice. By contrast, the chapter on O'Hara thinks how the poet draws on elements of camp in order to traverse urban and artistic landscapes. Given that the poet was writing in a pre-Stonewall context, addressing O'Hara's irreverence is necessary for considering how a queer identity is configured through the poems. Using the poet's manifesto to extrapolate a poetics of flippancy, I trace the nimble tongue and lightness of foot through literary precursors, canonical references, conversations with friends and the telephone. O'Hara's manifesto also demonstrates a wilful unseriousness. In spite of his genre of choice, the poet continually deflates both the manifesto and the poems it aims to describe. He suggests that statements of poetics should be replaced with poems, which in turn should be replaced with the telephone or movies. O'Hara does not hope for adherents or a following, but rather develops his own distinctive step, which moves with such rapidity it far outstrips the cumbersome following of his readership. This approach to the manifesto enables me to think through the lyric 'I' figure present within a significant proportion of O'Hara's work. While the 'I' is not always consistent, in the same way that the poet's style did not remain uniform through the body of his collected works, there are moments in which a clear figure emerges. Focusing on lightness and irreverence, I consider how O'Hara suggests a form of queer politics and poetics. His emphasis on sex in both his poetic writing and manifesto foregrounds a queer relationship with the text of the poem itself, while his continual references to others also ensure an outward facing and contingent way of writing. This is accompanied by a resistance to commit, continually demonstrated in the way that O'Hara addressed collectives as well as the genres of choice. This studied distance and irreverence create a tension of flippancy, in which the poet establishes a form of mobility that is both inherently sociable and inherently self-protective.

Myles allows for a further facet of queerness to be explored through their writing, which encompasses statements of poetics, essays, art writing, poetry, memoir and novel. Notably, unlike Stein and O'Hara, Myles is alive at the time of writing, which allows for a more dynamic and immediate engagement with their work. Myles has not just produced multiple written outputs but is also very active on social media, particularly Instagram and Facebook. They were a vocal supporter of Hillary Clinton, having run their own presidential campaign against George Bush as a piece of performance art in the early 1990s. These particular public-facing modes of engagement ensure that Myles, as a figure, is understood with vitality and wilfulness. Their social media is highly politicized, while the presidential campaign material shares a number of stylistic aspects with their essays and poetry. As a result, a significant part of my argument is thinking about Myles as an embodied presence in relation to their work. I begin with an analysis of the promotional video for *Inferno (A Poet's Novel)* in which Myles' appears, answering questions and reading extracts from the text itself. The promotional video, while obviously created with a particular purpose in mind, gives an insight into how Myles reconciles their embodiment with their proper name, using the latter as a means by which to destabilize selfhood. Myles recognizes that their name operates as a passport to the world, as sheer extimacy, but does not necessarily reveal anything of the poet that is personal or intimate. Considering their essay 'The Lesbian Poet', I think about how Myles toys with gender in a way that is not dissimilar to Stein. While claiming a female destiny for themselves, Myles also creates a space to 'become man', which is only possible in moments of intensively felt freedom. These aspects of gender play are also realized in the way that Myles writes about sex, focusing on pornography particularly. Porn allows the writer to unpack their own poetics while considering how we are cultured to approach specific bodies in specific ways. Throughout their work, Myles carries a constant irreverence, with their speed of movement and lightness of phrase implementing a poetics of flippancy. This is, however, problematized through their overt political engagement, in which the emotional and physical labours of femaleness and lesbianism muddy the uncomplicated levity we might associate with flippancy.

Nelson's work reflects on trans identity, in addition to queerness as a political, social and cultural movement. While Myles has refuted the female pronoun, celebrating the freedom of being without gender, Nelson specifically addresses these ideas within *The Argonauts*. As I have established, Nelson sits at the end of this particular queer lineage and synthesizes the work of Stein into a consideration of O'Hara, before using the poetics of both to consider the work of a female second-generation New York School. While, therefore, Myles is butch and gender shifting, Nelson is queer and emphasizes trans experience, explicitly addressing the way in which labels and gender categories are mobilized such as to oppress those who inhabit them. Unlike her precursors, Nelson's queerness is explicitly tied to both social movements and theory. She does draw on not just the material of life, narrating the highly personal story of her falling in love and having a child, but the theory that circulates around such a life. For Nelson, this academic approach bleeds necessarily into the everyday, and so *The Argonauts* creates a synthesis that actively undoes any hierarchies that might be applied to lived experience versus academic writing. I read Nelson's flippancy in conjunction with the critical work that she has done on the New York School, in which she makes important distinctions about the types of levity that can be performed by different types of poets. This allows me to approach concepts of 'not caring', which differ radically depending on gender, sex and experiences of motherhood. Considering Nelson's unique position and experiences as outlined through *The Argonauts*, I make a case for the book creating juxtapositions of great seriousness and lightness in a form of flippant whiplash. The movement of the text itself facilitates these leaps between gravitas and levity, with Nelson practising a consistent irreverence throughout. Sceptical of groupings, in a way that is similar to O'Hara, Nelson calls radical queer culture into question, suggesting that we need to aspire to greater openness as opposed to further radicalism. Her text most explicitly considers queer politics, using writing as a means by which to create a messy, transgressive and digressive space, in which sex and gender can come apart and together. *The Argonauts* mobilizes the irreverence of flippancy, but does so in such a way that it becomes a critique of both queer culture and the self's positioning within such political and public discourses.

As I will establish in each of my chapters, the intersection of a poetics of flippancy and queer theory within the work of the writers under discussion opens up spaces of possibility, which is inherently political. The relationship between flippancy and queerness seems a natural one. Queer focuses on the digressive, tangential, the irreverent and unbecoming, as I will establish in the following chapter. As such, the aspects of queerness on which I aim to focus are reflected fully in a poetics of flippancy. It is my belief that flippancy is inherently linked to language. It is impossible to have a flippant environment, affect or scene, but it is possible for individual subjects to communicate flippancy through their language choices. As such, flippancy is a linguistic strategy, one that is made evident through the juxtapositions of lightness and seriousness. It is for these reasons that I aim to trace a poetics of flippancy through writers who pay particular attention to the ways in which queerness can enter both the content and form of the text. I want to suggest that each poet under discussion here reflects different aspects of queer identity, all of which are slightly at odds with or uncomfortable within their wider culture. In spite of the progress claimed by more optimistic queer movements, there is still an unease associated with Nelson marrying Dodge in the time of Prop 8. While dissimilar to what Stein and Toklas may well have experienced, Nelson is still not easily able to enter marriage with a partner in the twenty-first century. Thus, while there are clear differences in their representation of queerness, in addition to differences within wider social contexts, each poet explores cultures and experiences that are unwelcome within wider society. Flippancy mediates this, allowing for the queerness to thrive and develop, while jarring against the wider and more serious social contexts. I believe that the poetics of flippancy and its queer resonances are realized not purely through language and language choices but through the movement of language, irreverence in terms of context and the juxtapositions of seriousness and unbecoming lightness. What seems most important, and what I will reflect on in my conclusion, is that these factors open up spaces of possibility within the text, suggesting spaces of possibility for existence, which are necessary for the existence of queerness and queer subjects.

1

The Poetics of Flippancy

In discussing the poetics of flippancy, I want to consider first the queer and shameful lyric 'I', primarily as a means by which to approach the self-reflexive and identity-driven writing of Stein, O'Hara, Myles and Nelson. Although many of the works I address move away from the genre of lyric poetry, they each draw on aspects of the lyric which are then transmuted and transformed in relation to specific context. The lyric's relationship with avant-garde and experimental writing is a fraught one, with various encampments emerging in relation to the use of first person and its bearing on the interiority of the writer themself. In *Lyric Shame: The 'Lyric' Subject of Contemporary American Poetry*, Gillian White argues that 'given that "expressive lyric" is the chief abjection of a powerful and increasingly canonical avant-garde antilyricism now forty years in the making, it is an identification that opens these poet's work to shame' (2014: 2). Identifying the Language poets as the key advocates of an anti-lyric movement, White goes on to track a contemporary lineage of genre shame. This shame is read in dialogue with the avant-garde creating a binary from the experimental and feeling, in which the formally innovative is not able to coexist with the personal expressions of an 'I'.

This problematic of the 'expressive' lyric is perhaps best exemplified by an argument between critic Marjorie Perloff and the poet Eileen Myles. In her article 'Reinventing the Lyric', published in *Boston Review*, Perloff critiqued mainstream poetry writing, suggesting that lyrics focus on regular syntax and 'the expression of a profound thought or small epiphany' (Perloff 2012). Looking to create some kind of metaphysical identification with the reader, the seemingly personal becomes formulaic and contrived, relying heavily on easily accessed feeling as opposed to language and form. Perloff even went so far as to write that these poems positioned the 'lyric speaker as a particularly sensitive person who really *feels* the pain' (Perloff 2012). Such an emphasis seems to suggest that claims to pain and feeling allow the speaker to assume a position of martyred authority which might not be substantiated through the verse itself. She goes on to claim, therefore, that Language poetry usefully posed 'a serious challenge to the delicate lyric of self-expression and direct speech: it demanded an end to transparency and straightforward reference in favour of ellipsis, indirection, and intellectual-political engagement' (Perloff 2012). Also championing Conceptual Poetry as an antidote to the anaemic feeling of mainstream poetry, Perloff celebrates the negation of 'the essence of lyric poetry' (2012) with the feeling speaker usurped by formally experimental writing practices.

Myles took great exception to this understanding of the lyric, writing a response 'Painted Clear, Painted Black' for *The Volta*, critiquing Perloff for eliding feeling poetry with femininity, while praising more masculine modes of writing. Myles wrote that Perloff's article 'seems so macho and destructive. In Perloff's universe one needs to access feeling ... in an *avant-garde way*' (Myles 2013). Indeed, Perloff's article does not denounce feeling entirely but seems to suggest that there are superior forms of incorporating the personal into writing. She cites both Susan Howe and Charles Bernstein as strong examples of using personal trauma to create formally innovative pieces, drawing on appropriated material and experimental practice in order to express loss. Myles responded by writing that 'feeling (how about we try substituting "being female" for feeling just as a stunt) is always a problem (a good one) in literature' (Myles 2013). Myles genders the lyric, and criticism of it, to highlight the way in which Perloff's writing serves to silence and marginalize those who might be drawing on personal experience in the 'wrong way' as a foundation for the lyric speaker. They write that Perloff's call for the end of transparency means 'the refusal of the direct and indirect speech that women and people of colour and queers and other assorted weaklings of the underclass have always employed' (Myles 2013). While Perloff makes a case for poetic form as being ideological, her rejection of the lyric and general emotional transparency is also a political position, one that, Myles argues, is derived from privilege. This is even reflected in the very style in which the two writers present their arguments, with Perloff's tone and lack of first person lending the piece an authoritative but distant sense of academia. Myles, by contrast, relies heavily on the 'I', making reference to their own gang rape, placing the self as an integral aspect of the argument.

It is these scholarly arguments, represented neatly by Myles and Perloff, that adhere shame to the use of lyric writing. Long predating the poetry wars initiated by the Language poets, there was a still a problematic gendering associated with lyric writing. White writes that the lyric was initially associated with 'overabundant affect (read feminine)' and was necessarily rehabilitated in the twentieth century 'as the authentic site of homosocial, hypermasculine self-actualization' (White 2014: 253). This clear gendering of the lyric's history leads White to ask 'what person (of what gender) should be associated with "the lyric I" or its shame?' (White 2014: 253). The shame identified by both Myles and White is ostensibly feminine and female; it is affect-driven and feeling-orientated. However, this particular strain of misogyny is not purely directed towards women-identified speakers and writers but any manifestation of femininity. It, therefore, could apply to the overly camp speaker, one who stands distinct from the hypermasculine self-actualization of the early twentieth century. This particular form of shame also seems to assume that a feminine expression of feeling is one entirely devoid of formal or structural innovation. Instead of experimentation, there is a sincerity at work that assures the reader of the poet's capacity to 'really *feel* pain'.

In *Self and Sensibility in Contemporary American Poetry*, Charles Altieri writes that the lyric, in fact, exists within a tension of sincerity and artifice:

> The desire for sincerity or naturalness, for poetry as communication, seems continually in tension with the highly artificial means required to produce the desired effects at a level of intensity adequate for lyric poetry. The effort to create the image contradicts the image, and we find it hard not to become suspicious about the values claimed for the ethos of naturalness. If we prove so easy to move, or if we are so willing to ignore the artificial means required to produce the desired effects at a level of intensity adequate for lyric poetry, it becomes difficult to trust any of the emotions produced by claims for direct expression. Yet the obvious alternative, the extreme forms of reflexivity exemplified by the post-modern novel, seems a dead end for the lyric.
> (Altieri 1984: 15)

The lyric is never a pure instance of feeling being communicated to the reader. Rather than offering forth an uncomplicated representation, the lyric is a tension of the natural, or sincere, and totally artificial. Feeling, then, is complicated through the very nature of constructing poetry, which strays from the genuine into a far more performative and formal approach to emotion. Altieri goes on to claim that 'the "sincere" self, then, is one poets are tempted to posit as always beyond language' (1984: 22). The artifice of poetry is such that the sincere self cannot exist within it and any claims to *really feel* are rendered impossible by the form of communication. Language, through removing the possibility of a sincere self, creates a lyric poetry that is aligned with insincerity and high artifice, as well as a sense of shame.

This speaks usefully to queer identities, which historically have a complicated relationship with both artifice and shame. In *Gay Shame*, editors David M. Halperin and Valerie Traub write: 'Gay pride has never been able to separate itself entirely from shame, or to transcend shame. Gay pride does not even make sense without some reference to the shame of being gay' (2010: 3). The very history of LGBTQ identity leads Halperin and Traub to believe that even the positive and publicly realized aspects of queerness are nonetheless encumbered with shame. This sense of shame is not solely realized through a binary with pride but can also be understood as an important affect that mediates and moves the internal into the external. In 'Shame, Theatricality, and Queer Performativity: Henry James's *The Art of the Novel*', Eve Kosofsky Sedgwick writes that 'shame effaces itself; shame points and projects; shame turns itself skin side out; shame and pride, shame and dignity, shame and self-display, shame and exhibitionism are different interlinings of the same glove' (2003b: 38). Much like lyric writing and the use of a personal pronoun, shame allows for demonstration and projection, as well as a form of self-revelation that is analogous to being turned skin side out. The self-display and exhibitionism of shame also resonate strongly with the posturing and self-presentation that inevitably haunts usage of the lyric 'I'. As Sedgwick further suggests, 'shame is the affect that mantles the threshold between introversion and extroversion, between absorption and theatricality, between performativity and – performativity' (2003b: 38), all concepts to which I shall return in my specific discussion of flippancy. What is perhaps most important about this relationship between queerness and shame is recognizing that the negative affect seems intrinsically linked to the identity. The emphasis on 'pride' as a public celebration of queerness is always haunted by its opposite, shame. Rather than perceiving this as entirely negative, Halperin and Traub ask 'are there important, nonhomophobic values related to the experience of shame that gay pride does not or cannot offer us?' (2010: 3). It is perhaps the case that the exhibitionism and self-display of shame, in conjunction with the high artifice of the lyric, might in fact offer up possibilities for the speaking subject. Instead of conforming to success narratives of pride, or attempting to communicate the 'real feeling' so derided by Perloff, the combination of queer shame and lyric shame can forge new and divergent paths.

This allows for the concept of the queer lyric to emerge. Fundamentally different to the normative lyric, one for whom heterosexuality is assumed, the queer 'I' is required to find different formations of poetic expression. In *Queer Lyrics (Difficulty and Closure in American Poetry)*, John Emil Vincent suggests that 'queer lyrics do not simply record lives lived and feelings felt. At their best, they offer performances, or demonstrations of living and feeling' (2002: xiiv). This description of the queer lyric seems to resonate with the ways in which experimental writing, as understood by Perloff, have challenged the simple epiphanic model of lyric writing. Rather than the poem appearing as an expression of feeling or moment of realization, albeit expressed through artificial means, the experimental or queer lyric performs and demonstrates. The pretence of naturalness, therefore, falls away in favour of a recognition of the inherently staged aspects of poetry writing itself, as well as the demonstrative and performative aspects of identity and feeling. Vincent further suggests that in exploring 'nonheterosexuality', queer poetry strains against category definitions, calling both sexuality and the lyric into question. That said, he recognizes that 'much of the most exciting modern and contemporary poetry hovers at this edge, its lexical and affective power arising from the unmappable, but somehow accessible journeys out of and back into the known' (Vincent 2002: 1). To me, this question of accessibility resonates with the argument between Myles and Perloff regarding the 'transparency' of poetry. Where 'accessible' might seem negative for an experimental poet, in this particular context it seems to relate to allowing the reader access, a necessary measure for them to orientate the difficult space of the poem. This begs the question, however, of the ways in which a queer poetics differs from other forms of experimental or innovative writing. Vincent, having drawn parallels, makes a useful distinction, writing 'homosexual and heterosexual desire and bonds, given their different cultural valuation, have entirely different available narratives, legality, forms of expression, as well as different available relations to abstraction, specification, self-definition, community, ritual, temporality and spatiality' (2002: 30). In spite of the overlaps between contemporary writing and the queer lyric, queerness is dictated to by the forms of expression and cultural contexts in which the identity manifests itself. The social difference between homosexuality and heterosexuality inevitably results in different relationships with language, narrative, legality, as well as concepts such as self-definition and community.

    The queer lyric's relationship to performance and demonstration as well as cultural manifestations, narrative, expression, abstraction, specification and self-definition all have an important place in relation to making trouble. Stein's *Lifting Belly*, for example, uses repetition and iteration to create a same-sex interaction between an 'I' and 'you' that seems endless. Euphemistically describing the female orgasm as cows coming out, and relating pleasure to sound, the text offers a temporality for the lesbian sex act that is both continuous and present, exceeding and stretching the heteronormative sexual encounter.

The Autobiography of Alice B. Toklas, by contrast, uses both performance and demonstration to allow for Stein's own self-definition. Masquerading as her lover, Stein performs an inter-couple drag act, in which taking on the role of Toklas allows for the poet to write herself into a community and identity. The queerness of displaced selfhood bends and worries identity stability and interchangeability among the two female figures. O'Hara, by contrast, uses his 'Personism: A Manifesto' to claim true abstraction for the first time in literary history. While his text moves with a confident slipperiness, offering too many referents for the reader to orientate fully, the work does not border on abstraction in spite of its claims. Instead the manifesto and the poems explore community as a form of self-definition, turning sex into a lens for approaching creative production. Myles manages similar performances of self, with a speed of movement that is analogous to O'Hara's. Their promotional video serves as a useful lens through which to understand this rapidity, as well as approach their posturing dykehood. Myles demonstrates an uncertainty of selfhood, all the while confidently occupying a prominent position within all of their work. Maggie Nelson, perhaps more theoretically reflective on her status as a queer writer, uses *The Argonauts* to discuss her relationship with language, recognizing its failure to express coherently and fully, as well as its failure to best represent the self.

The queer lyric, therefore, is an important term for all four writers, even while they might deviate from the 'I' driven poems of self-identity and feeling. They all exhibit qualities of queer lyric writing, if that is to be understood as the jarring against boundaries of feeling, performing and gesturing identity, all the while questioning and challenging their chosen forms of expression. The works I study directly address the artifice and 'act' of writing but make space in which 'nonheterosexuality' can be explored, all through the foregrounding and presence of a self. They do not experiment with a fragmented or disrupted selfhood, but rather play with a more consolidated, performative self who is consistently deployed across a range of genres. For me, the queer lyric as an area of exploration is therefore vital in spite of Stein's playful third-person address, O'Hara's manifesto, Myles' self-interrogatory prose and Nelson's memoirs. Stein's work *The Autobiography of Alice B. Toklas* foregrounds artificiality and posture, undermining any ideas of the authentic self while still attempting some form of self-definition. Indeed, Stein's elliptical work and her novel do not match the form of lyric writing at all, but simply mobilize some of the poetics of the queer lyric as understood by Vincent. O'Hara's manifesto, Myles' promotional video and poet's novels and Nelson's critically inflected memoirs do not constitute lyric writing in the true sense of the form, even while their poetry does. Thus, while the queer lyric seems troublesome to the genre as a whole, these four writers further trouble the place of the 'I' within poetry, mobilizing aspects of queer lyricism to facilitate expression within other genres. As such, they map onto understandings of the queer lyric, even while they deviate from it, further challenging the simplicity of categorization that occurs between genre. Both the poem and prose are a space for performance, one that always thwarts an easy clarity of self-expression. It is possible that in their move beyond poetry, all four writers are enacting a sense of failure; the genre is too concise, uncertain, elliptical to express everything.

Narcissism and echoes

These problems of selfhood and representation move me away from the lyric into a reckoning with Narcissus. Initially, I want to think about the mythological figure in relation to queerness and self-recognition, and then probe it further as a strategy of ironic expression that might allow for a poetics of flippancy to emerge. In Ovid's myth, Narcissus was a young, handsome man, who fell in love with his own reflection. Continually surrounded by admirers, Narcissus was incapable of reciprocation, only feeling a pull of desire when he first beheld himself in the surface of water. In some ways, this seems analogous to the loneliness of the lyric 'I' and reflective of the writer's attempt to express their uncertainty within the surface of a text. Locked within a self-referential form, the lyric is at once the identity of the speaker and their mirrored reflection. The uncertainty of the lyric, thus, can usefully be considered as a form of flawed, reflective surface. What is especially interesting about Narcissus is that his self-knowledge led to his demise; if he had been kept from his true nature, or true reflection, then tragedy would not have befallen him.

Due to the nature of Narcissus loving his own reflection, the figure can be, and is, aligned with same-sex relationships, where attraction emerges in relation to sameness as opposed to difference. In *Reflecting Narcissus: A Queer Aesthetic*, Steven Bruhm writers that this association 'conflates homosexuality with egoism and selfishness and with self-delusion and excessive introspection' (2001: 2). Egoism can easily be affixed to lyric writing, manifesto and memoir, with the intense focus on the self constituting a form of excessive introspection. Bruhm's writing thus offers an important rehabilitation of Narcissus, in which he is positioned as a productive queer figure, one I interpret as useful for considering the queer troublemaker. Rather than same-sex lyrics purely expressing what

Perloff dismisses as 'real feeling' and a lack of poetic complexity, the queer Narcissus engages in the expression of selfhood with greater dynamism and experiment. Bruhm writes that 'queer Narcissus refuses knowledge and re-fuses it, as much plagued by the fleeting chimera of self-knowledge as he is constituted by it' (2001: 16). In the work of Stein, O'Hara, Myles and Nelson there is a continued rejection of the established, dominant discourses, simultaneous to the creation of alternative orientations and forms of knowledge. The fleeting chimera of self-knowledge, which is represented through both memoir and the use of the lyric 'I', is as much an attempt to know the self as a celebration of the self's uncertainties. It is this very relationship with knowledge and the self that constitutes a queer Narcissus, as well as a troubling of the assumptions that could be made for queer self-expression within the form of lyric (and various other manifestations of 'I'). Queer troublemaking, thus, is realized in the use of an imperfect 'I' and the flickering nature of knowledge, rejection and constitution.

The relationship with knowledge exhibited by Narcissus is evident in the four queer troublemakers of this book. Stein's posturing as Toklas to explore her own identity creates a series of mirrorings that simultaneously generate and reject knowledge. The façade of Toklas is analogous to the water in the Narcissus myth, creating a reflective surface through which the subject of the writing, Stein, is able to see herself better. Myles establishes similar relationships with selfhood, relying on the moniker Eileen Myles, as well as the lyric 'I', while refuting any true knowledge of their own identity. Myles' work is heavily dependent on consistency of voice, in conjunction with a continual denial of fully constituted selfhood. In this way, both writers resonate with the Narcissus of Bruhm's writing, in that the self is 'the centralizing, unifying trope whose presence only bespeaks his absence, whose self-identification can only engender the slippages of desire' (Bruhm 2001: 18). This concept of presence and absence speaks to O'Hara's lyric writing, in which the continual movement and lightness of the central figure constitutes a tension of there and not-there. Indeed, Myles describes O'Hara's writing as 'queenie' and 'slippery' on account of the way that both desire and selfhood were constituted through continual mobility. Nelson's fixation on the failure of language to express experience is also a form of presence and absence. *The Argonauts*, for all of its words and theorizing, is ultimately lamenting the absence of true, easily expressible, meaning. While these writers, then, might all constitute a centralizing and unifying trope, where the work acknowledges the self as the centre of creation, the reflections and slips allow for a selfhood that is more mutable and changeable. Even though the writers all seem to present a consistent self, one uniformly identifiable across their bodies of work, there is also a consistent probing of the self which is always positioned as part performance and part uncertainty.

While Narcissus represents interesting possibilities for queer self-expression, it also forms the basis of Denise Riley's exploration of irony in her work *The Words of Selves: Identification, Solidarity and Irony*. Using the figure of Narcissus to formulate a model for successful ironic utterance, Riley stands as an important precursor to the development of flippancy, which while inherently different to irony could stand as its inheritor. Instead of focusing on Narcissus himself, Riley expands her critical view to include Echo. Moving away from the presence and absence, materiality and reflection, sign and embodiment of the male figure, Echo is condemned to existing as voice incarnate. Interestingly, in *Reflecting Narcissus*, Bruhm describes Echo as effecting

> a queerly disruptive paradigm in which Narcissus' love for another man is replicated in the desire of a woman doomed to the same doubling imperative, a replication that is dazzling and confusing in the way it both conflates and separates desiring subjects, desiring objects, objects and subjects of desire.
>
> (Bruhm 2001: 13)

Where Narcissus falls in love with his own reflection, Echo is condemned to repeat language back to the original speaker, totally incapable of voicing her own unique speech. Having been cursed to repetition, Echo falls in love with Narcissus and unable to articulate original thought, the nymph is compelled to watch the man she loves die through his own self-regard. The figure of Echo then could in some ways be positioned as passive and non-interventionist, with repetition her only capacity for expression. This doubling imperative, while interesting for Bruhm in its relationship with sex and desire, is mobilized by Riley to think about how irony can operate as a politically effective strategy. In her rewriting of the Narcissus and Echo myth, Riley humorously outlines the detrimental nature of this reflective and re-reflective relationship as such:

> So exiled I fell for Narcissus. I had no voice to plead so I'd pursue.
>
> He called 'I'd die before I'd give myself to you!' I shrilled 'I'd give myself to you!' ran nearer.
>
> If he'd cried 'I'd die before I'd fuck you', at least I could have echoed back that 'Fuck you'.
>
> Sorry – I have to bounce back each last phrase. Half-petrified, I voice dead gorges.
>
> (Riley 2000: 161)

While Echo might lament her inability to tell Narcissus to fuck himself without the necessary spoken precursor, this extract illustrates Riley's claim that irony 'queries that whole concept of the model plus its copy' (2000: 158). Irony, then, can interrogate the pre-existing; it is used to challenge our understanding of the established while also encouraging focus on what it means to reproduce such hegemonic models and utterances. Through repetition, the original is reframed and recontextualized, creating a critical mutability for dominant or prevailing modes of existence.

Riley writes that 'if verbal irony states the opposite of what its speaker or writer means, the listener or reader must "get it" – must already have grasped enough of something to realise that something does need to be got' (2000: 147). When the listener or reader do 'get it', irony can expose 'a personal category's historicity and fragility by isolating it as both real enough yet also as an artefact, eminently questionable' (Riley 2000: 163). Irony, therefore, has great potential power in regard to troubling authority. It calls upon the established but subverts its status, creating instead a context in which the hegemonic can be called into question. Furthermore, Riley claims, 'to be able to deploy a category ironically frees you to recognise its historical formation and consequently its potential to alter and disintegrate' (2000: 166). Recognition is central to a historical appreciation that ultimately allows for alteration, questioning and disintegration. However, this also serves to foreground irony's potentially dangerous contingency. The act of reframing needs to be obvious; if recontextualization is not evident, then irony purely becomes repetition. In the worst cases, this repetition seems to adhere to and support the original, as opposed to critiquing and interrogating. If the audience do not understand the ironic utterance, then irony itself is entirely lost.

Riley's formulation of irony also recognizes the strategy's dependence upon the continued intactness of categories. While 'disintegration' might be the final outcome of the strategy when it is used effectively, irony needs the existence of these stable categories in order to operate at all. Through the reproduction of the original, irony invests in the original remaining stable enough that disintegration becomes apparent. Once the irony has been appreciated, the original category and new ironic iteration still have to coexist, even if one of them does so as an artefact. It is inevitable, then, that in spite of the powers of critique that call the historically formulated into question, irony is bound up with hegemonic stable categories even while it attempts to work against them. In this sense, irony works along the same binaries that it could be used to critique: the original–the copy, the stable–the disintegrating. Even the necessity of an understanding audience establishes an us–them binary, in which the 'us' is ever-enlightened and the 'them' remains fixed as proponents of hegemonic and historical order.

While Riley does not focus on flippancy in her consideration of irony, she does write that 'if you can put irony on or off at will, it looks congenitally unserious and flippant' (2000: 152). Irony is not a form of flippancy nor does it ever degenerate into flippancy. However, the way that irony is done, or performed, if not sustained or committed enough, can be considered as flippant. Riley's use of 'will' suggests that those who make use of irony in a casual way, trying it on and taking it off, might be wilful. In her book *Willfull Subjects*, Sara Ahmed argues that will, and being perceived as wilful, is essential to both a feminist and queer politics. She describes queer feminism as 'a history of willful parts, parts that *in willing* are *not* willing to reproduce the whole' (Ahmed 2014: 121). This wilful form of reproduction seems to counter irony directly, using a resistance of parts (not the whole) as a means by which to ensure that dominant narratives are not simply replicated. Riley's irony does require the reproduction of the whole; the original utterance needs to be realized as it was first deployed. By contrast, the wilful subject demonstrates a lack of willingness to capitulate to the pre-existing models, even if such an engagement is motivated by critique. Ahmed writes that as a result of this, 'willfullness could be thought of as political art, a practical craft that is acquired through involvement in political struggle, whether that struggle is a struggle to exist or to transform an existence' (2014: 133). Both Narcissus and Echo are caught in struggles that result in a form of stasis; they are repetitious and therefore predicated on sameness, even if that sameness can be wielded as critique. He is tied to the water that reflects him, while she is caught in the continual repetition of someone else's language. Were Echo enabled to drop her curse of repetition, it would be possible for both existence and transformation of existence. In spite of the congenital unseriousness associated with flippancy by Riley, it creates a space in which postures and performances can be taken on and off at will by the wilful subject who carefully responds to their immediate environment and culture.

Flippancy, then, could be considered as a 'failure' of more serious political linguistic strategy. Among other possibilities, which I will explore within the next section, to be flippant is to fail in sustaining anything. In Riley's case, it is specifically to fail at consistent irony. It is also to fail in serious communication, with the subject made to appear both non-committal and too wilful for the concerted effort of rigorous political action. However, this failure has a possibility of being recuperated politically, much like the capriciousness of 'will' can actually be understood as a form of resistance. In *The Queer Art of*

Failure, Jack Halberstam writes that failure is a way 'of refusing to acquiesce to dominant logics of power and discipline as a form of critique. As a practice, failure recognizes that alternatives are embedded already in the dominant' (2011: 88). Rather than reproducing the dominant, as in the case of irony, a failure of commitment is a means by which to recognize alternatives to, and escape routes from, the dominant. As Halberstam writes, 'under certain circumstances, failing, losing, forgetting, unmaking, undoing, unbecoming, not knowing may in fact offer more creative, more cooperative, more surprising ways of being in the world' (2011: 2). Flippancy, too, as a particular form of failure, allows for a subject to unmake and undo, critiquing the dominant logics of power without reliance on reproduction, thus finding new and more surprising ways of being in the world.

What is flippancy?

As this chapter is demonstrating, flippancy might be easier to define based on what it is not, as opposed to what it is. My focus on the lyric 'I' and Narcissus, both of which offer a possibility for writing, reflects the way in which the queer troublemakers elude certainty and stability in favour of openness. In *The Art of Failure*, Halberstam writes that such forms of non-proscription, of failing, can allow for work and writing to 'make a mess, to fuck shit up, to be loud, unruly, impolite, to breed resentment, to bash back, to speak up and out, to disrupt, assassinate shock and annihilate' (2011: 11). While failure has both anarchic and violent potential, flippancy will also fall short of fulfilling the strength of some of these gestures. Given the wilfulness with which it rejects seriousness, it seems that a poetics of flippancy is at best a form of disruption that is impolite, mostly achieved through writing that constitutes a form of speaking up and out. While that might breed resentment, it lacks the shocking and annihilating capacities attributed to truly radical failure. While I elide flippancy and its poetics with a form of failure, therefore, it is also useful to return to the authority of the dictionary to glean some understanding of the term itself. Flippancy is defined as a 'disposition to trifle', while 'flippant' is more expansively a nimble tongue, a playful subject or a person who displays unbecoming levity in the consideration of serious subjects (*OED* 2014). What is significant is that both flippancy and flippant are linked to a subject; they are not an atmosphere, affect or public feeling. Instead, flippancy is an embodied performance, requiring the quick-moving tongue, play and an unbecoming lightness of approach.

It is flippancy's association with the subject that makes the poetics of flippancy so inherently linked to the four troublemakers: Stein, O'Hara, Myles and Nelson. While all four of the poets engage with aspects of the poetics of flippancy I shall outline here, each one allows for different manifestations, depending on their own unique usage of the nimble tongue and preferred forms of play. Uniformly, however, the flippant tongue makes speech central to the poetics, suggesting a fast-paced style that moves with deftness for language and subject matter. It is easy to see the links between this particular way of speaking and the queer lyric, which focuses on performance and demonstration as opposed to a faithful expression of true feeling. The state of play that is associated with flippancy is both deliberate and wilful, intentionally chosen to highlight the discrepancies between the lightness of approach and the heaviness of the context. In this way, flippancy is almost entirely an 'unbecoming levity', an unbearable lightness of flippancy, that suggests a surface engagement while one might look for depth, a lack of appropriateness in the face of a topic that actually demands respect and reverence. Unlike irony, flippancy does not operate through binary systems, in spite of the oppositions I have drawn here. The nimble tongue and the state of play as well as a disposition towards lightness all create a sense of mobility that ensures the speaking subject is not locked into a position directly opposed to that of their context. This ultimately allows for a critique of monoliths, with dominant power structures being called into question through the subject's interaction with them.

Having elaborated on the dictionary definition, it is perhaps useful to turn to how flippancy intersects with poetics. As the rest of this section will demonstrate, flippancy situates itself at a number of difficult intersections, always linked to a subject, but often performative instead of natural, affected instead of truly felt. This raises numerous questions about what flippancy actually is: Is it a style or a tone? Could it be considered a form of posturing that foregrounds the artifice of poetry? Might it be best described as a performance that makes light of more serious contexts? Is it one of these possibilities or all of them working in conjunction with one another? Whether combined or separate, these aspects of flippancy are understood in relation to the subject, as well as their context. The context could be wider societal and cultural factors gestured to by the writing, or alternatively the writing itself, which might have specific genre and stylistic associations. The relationships and contingencies of flippancy can also be developed in relation to the act of writing, with specific attention to how the poetics are a form of becoming and 'unbecoming' as suggested by the dictionary definition. It is also important to consider how the flippant subject can draw on uncertain and amorphous affects of their particular context in order to facilitate their affectations and performances. In order to address these aspects of flippancy, I want to think about the relationship between affect and affectation, and performance and performativity, as well as the utility of ugly feelings and aesthetic categories in regard to developing a poetics.

In order to consider the unbecoming aspects of flippancy, I want first to address concepts of becoming, which seem integral to the realization of a self within writing. Giles Deleuze in *Essays Critical and Clinical* describes becoming as 'an objective zone of indistinction or indiscernibility that always exists between two multiplicities, a zone that immediately precedes their natural differentiation' (1998: xxx). Unlike the binary created through irony, becoming allows for multiple states to be entertained simultaneously. A subject, as a result, enters a state of in-betweenness where they are neither one thing nor the other, but orientated and determined by both. Deleuze goes on to elucidate that 'one term does not become another; rather, each term encounters the other; and the becoming is something between the two, outside the two' (1998: xxx). Becoming, then, is a liminality that thrives on the uncertain positions that occur both between and outside. For Deleuze, this is also highly pertinent to the process of writing, which he describes as 'a question of becoming, always incomplete, always in the midst of being formed ... it is a process, that is, a passage of life that traverses both the livable and lived' (1998: 3). While this is a useful definition of writing, it is in no way unique to either queerness or flippancy. In fact, all writing, regardless of how normative, could be considered to conform to the process of becoming as outlined by Deleuze, where the texts themselves are situated between the livable and the lived, writer and reader. Nonetheless, this 'in-between' creates space and flexibility in which a writer can explore aspects of uncertainty in such a way as to challenge heteronormativity. Indeed, Riley writes in *Words of Selves* that 'my awkward navigations to *become*, coupled with my constitutional failure to fully *be*, are what actually enable political thinking and language' (2000: 5). Becoming is central to the writing process, but is also vital for political thinking, language choices and identity. This uncertainty produces a productive form of failure, enabling a subject or speaker to develop a relationship with their contexts, one that will forever be in flux.

So, if this 'becoming' is uniformly felt by writers and political subjects alike, then it is its pairing with 'unbecoming' that is particularly applicable to the queer troublemakers and their poetics of flippancy. Given that flippancy is defined as an 'unbecoming levity', then its poetics will be set within a tension of both becoming and unbecoming. In the *Queer Art of Failure*, Halberstam writes when applied to gender politics, failure can be 'an unbecoming, not from being or becoming woman but from a refusal to be or become woman as she has been defined or imagined' (2011: 136). Speaking to the same context of political thinking, identity and language choices as Riley, Halberstam is offering an opposite mode of engagement; rather than a more holistic form of becoming, there is the deliberate and highly resistant unbecoming. Flippancy in political and poetic contexts, in being what is not expected or imagined, creates space in which the speaking subject does not occupy a subject position fitting of traditional gravitas. As such, flippancy is a form of refusal that creates new ways of being in the world not predicated on traditional or normative modes of operating. Unbecoming, for the most part, is used within an adjectival sense, rarely mobilized within a verb incarnation. The former describes something unsuitable or improper, much like flippancy emerging within a context of seriousness. However, when Halberstam uses 'unbecoming' as a verb, the word signifies a process of becoming unsuitable: the doing of being improper. If this is the case, then becoming a troublemaker – inappropriate and improper – is a necessary political strategy that rejects staid and acceptable modes of being. This becoming unbecoming does not have a single trajectory or mode of operation and as such creates space for participation in unexpected and novel ways. Halberstam claims that 'if taken seriously, unbecoming may have its political equivalent in the anarchic refusal of coherence and proscriptive form of agencies' (2011: 136). Flippancy, characterized by its lack of seriousness, refuses the coherence associated with gravitas and instead offers a politically inflected light-heartedness that is simultaneously a becoming and unbecoming.

The becoming unbecoming of a flippant troublemaker can be highly linked to the affective environments from which they emerge. In fact, Deleuze and Guattari state that 'affects are becomings' (1987: 256) often associated with strong feeling but impossible to define with total clarity. They transport a feeling subject between multiplicities, creating a sense of motion that is carried through force and intensity as opposed to specific emotion. A similar concept is foregrounded by Melissa Gregg and Gregory J. Seigworthy in their *The Affect Reader*, where the two define affect as arising:

> in the midst of *in-betweeness*: in the capacities to act and be acted upon. Affect is an impingement or extrusion of a momentary or sometimes more sustained state of relation *as well as* the passage (and the duration of passage) of forces or intensity.
>
> (2010: 1)

This in-between is much like the becoming that allows for political thinking to develop. It creates spaces of engagement in which the parameters cannot clearly be defined, in the same way that participation and feeling cannot be specifically elucidated. As a result, a passage can emerge in which acting and acting upon simultaneously contribute to the affectivity of a specific moment, or historical context, or literary text. However, as I have already stated, flippancy itself is not an affect; it lacks the force and intensity that is necessary to move subjects from one state to another. The flippant subject, then, could be understood as what Ahmed describes as an 'affect alien'. Exploring this concept, Ahmed writes about the feminist killjoy, stating that 'the feminist is an affect alien: she might even kill joy because she refuses to share an orientation toward certain things as being good because she does not find the objects that promise happiness to be quite so promising' (Ahmed 2010b: 39). The affect aliens refuse to line up with the predominant feelings suggested by communities and objects they encounter. If flippancy itself is not an affect, it is a resistance to the overwhelming affective pull of the context in which it exists. Predicated on inappropriateness where inappropriateness is unwelcome, rendered unbecoming through the levity it practices, flippancy always places the subject as slightly alien to the affects with which they are surrounded. If affects are becomings, then, flippancy is the recognition and refusal of this very process. As such, a poetics of flippancy is an unbecoming, wherein the subject relishes the space of in-betweenness to explore inappropriate levity.

The concepts of 'acting' and 'being acted upon' as suggested by Gregg and Seigworthy can therefore be usefully extended into the 'acting out' of flippant response. In *The Words of Selves: Identity, Solidarity, Irony*, Riley outlines a mutable approach to identity politics, in which various signifiers can be constructed as opposed to essentialized. She writes that 'self-descriptions, including those of "identity politics," are indeed costumes, whether avant-garde or hopelessly outmoded. To wear one means first trying it on – and sometimes in both senses' (Riley 2000: 151). Trying it on allows for the putting on and taking off of various identity signifiers and their associated behaviours. Much like an act, this mutable approach to a politicized selfhood allows for a subject to try something on to see whether it suits both them and their position within a wider context. Riley elides this with 'trying it on' in a different sense, one that is associated with challenge. Here, the subject pushes the identity to an uncomfortable limit, perhaps getting away with something unexpectedly. This wilful dressing in and shedding of identity speak to the way in which Riley argues that irony can become flippancy; if taken on or off at will, then the seriousness of the gesture fails. Both trying it on and taking something off at will, to me, are a form of acting out. Not just purely putting on an act, the flippant subject is also acting in a way that distinguishes them from their environment. The 'out' associated with the act also implies that the flippant subject is determining ways in which they can be differentiated from the behaviours that are associated with their affective environments. Instead of simply acting and being acted upon, the flippant subject refrains from total and uncomplicated involvement, instead choosing to act out.

It could be, then, that flippancy works within and alongside affect but is primarily a form of affectation. While this is a concept I will explore further in my Frank O'Hara chapter, it seems important to outline the differences and possible resonances here. Affectation, unlike the seemingly uncontrollable aspects of affect, is performative, deliberate and embodied. In this way, it can be a form of trying it on or acting out, in that it intentionally leads the subject to push back against the context with which they are engaging. While affectation itself might seem contrived, the acting out is a necessary aspect of a troublemaking flippancy. Thus, while affect encourages a subject to act, having been acted upon by feeling contexts or external forces, affectation is the deliberate cultivation of a front or attitude that allows for a subject to act out. Acting out is understood as a form of making trouble, where the outwardness of the gesture is a wilful interruption or disruption of the status quo. To affect airs, to act out, demonstrates a resistance to the models of feeling that establish exclusionary norms for anyone who exists on the margins. This affectation and outwardness resonate with Ahmed's definition of the troublemaker as 'one who violates the fragile conditions of peace' (2010a: 60–61). Ahmed argues that peace can be maintained when those who do not traditionally align ultimately conform to prevailing moods or feelings. So, for example, a feminist might laugh along with a sexist joke such that she is not positioned as other. Alternatively, a queer-identified person might remain closeted in the face of homophobic culture. The conditions of peace, while they might seem strong and established to those who uphold them, are actually a fragility that is predicated on the silence and capitulation of a few. To act out within these contexts is to challenge the assumptions of peace, creating instead turmoil and conflict that ultimately is more open and egalitarian.

For these reasons, I see the relationship between affect and affectation as mapping well onto concepts of performance and performativity. In *Gender Trouble*, Judith Butler defines performativity as 'not a singular act, but a repetition and a ritual, which achieves its effects through its naturalization in the context of a body, understood in part, as culturally sustained temporal duration' (2006: xv). The duration and the subconscious way in which performativity works on the body is not dissimilar to the operations of affect. However, the two differ fundamentally in that performativity is reiterative action that compels the body to become an established sex or gender upheld by cultural values as opposed to any biological predestination. Gender, thus, is realized through the ways a subject engages in the ritual of the culture's naturalization of their body. Through exploring performativity, Butler's text aims to 'show that what we take to be an internal essence of gender is manufactured through a sustained set of acts, posited through the gendered stylization of the body' (2006: xv). Here, Butler is suggesting that what we assume to be innate or natural to sex and gender are actually a direct result of 'acts', performances that are not inherent to us as either male or female but socially determined. Eschewing essentialism in regard to both sex and gender, Butler believes that gender is established and identity constructed through a complicity in gendering acts. The queerness of her text, and especially a focus on the multivalent gender trouble of drag queens, calls this performativity into question, finding spaces in which a complex intersection of sex, gender and sexuality means that the culturally constructed acts begin to fail. Potentially rupturing the subject's easy participation within the reiterative acts of heteronormative gender, queerness introduces a different form of temporal duration, one that is perhaps focused on a more conscious engagement with the gendered stylization of the body.

An awareness of performativity, as Butler outlines, allows for a focus on the possibility of performance in a way that frees the subject from socially constructed gender constraints. Much like the drag queens Butler invokes, turning aspects of performativity, which is often considered innate and involuntary, into a full performance exposes the fragility of our gender constructions as well as offering alternative modes of being. Once gender, sex and sexuality become realized or resisted through performance, the space is opened such that other possibilities emerge. In what ways, then, can a lyric subject subvert her own time's gender performativity through foregrounding artifice and performance? Through demonstrating an awareness of the ways gender is conditioned, and the way in which society and culture can demand that certain behaviours are concretized through repetitive action, can a subject escape or at least exhibit a knowingness in relation to gender identity? And how might flippancy facilitate both a knowingness and a resistance?

Finally, I want to turn to ideas on aesthetic categories and ugly feelings in order to think about how flippancy might allow for feeling and failure to coalesce. In her introduction to *Ugly Feelings*, Sianne Ngai considers her book's scope, writing that the work is 'a bestiary of affects, in other words, it is one filled with rats and possums rather than lions, its categories of feeling generally being, well, weaker and nastier' (2007: 7). Ngai's enterprise seems especially important to my viewing of flippancy, which does not have the strength and solidarity of gay pride nor the abjection of queer shame. It is also without the biting strength of a community predicated irony, and for the most part, simply manifests as a failure to commit all the while insisting on talking nonetheless. Ngai believes that minor affects 'are far less intentional or object-directed, and thus more likely to produce political and aesthetic ambiguities, than the passions in the philosophical canon' (2007: 20). Flippancy, I have argued, is not an affect, but instead arises in response to particular affective contexts or relationships. It is situated far more appropriately within affectation and performance than the strength of unbidden feeling; flippancy must be deliberately cultivated and in that way is lacking the involuntary and transportative nature of other affects. That said, much like Ngai's ugly feelings, flippancy is not object-directed, one is not flippant towards, but perhaps flippant away from. If flippancy reads as a general rejection, or an uncommitted response, then it cannot be orientated through object attachment. Thus, it too thrives in the spaces of ambiguity, in regard to both aesthetics and politics.

In Ngai's *Our Aesthetic Categories: Zany, Cute, Interesting*, she makes a case once more for focusing on categories and affects that occupy positions of triviality. Much like flippancy's unbecoming levity, the ugly feelings and seemingly insignificant aesthetics situate themselves beyond powerful or forceful movement. Indeed, Ngai writes that 'these images of indifference, insignificance, and ineffectuality all point to a deficit of power' (2015: 18), all of which arguably fuel a flippant subject as well as characterizing her. However, in prioritizing these especially weak aesthetic categories, Ngai is able to explore the diverse and digressive, as opposed to object-orientated and powerful. Most importantly for the particular categories of focus is that they 'strangely dramatize their own frivolity or ineffectuality' (2015: 22). Existing within power structures that reiterate their own unimportance, the zany, cute and interesting draw on the performance and affectation I have outlined for flippancy. While unable to refuse their categorization as weak or ineffectual, they are able to practice a form of resistance through knowingly embracing their status among other aesthetics. This form of knowing acknowledgement, which seems fundamental to flippancy, rejects traditional forms of power and instead practises a form of self-exploration that refuses and re-fuses. Each of the poets I explore within this book works with aesthetics in a different way, some embracing the camp and the beautiful, while others are configured through the brutal and violent. For this reason, flippancy cannot be explored as a simple aesthetic category nor as an ugly feeling that sits insignificantly in relation to powerful affects. Instead, flippancy can be understood as operating in similar ways in regard to wider contexts of power and dominance. It is not object-orientated and could be considered weak in relation to the more critical irony suggested by Riley, for example, but nonetheless, has a penchant for the dramatic within a context that would otherwise deny its drama.

Conclusion

A poetics of flippancy is inherently troubling, in the first instance because it does not take poetry or poetics seriously. Following the lightness with which it engages with genre, flippancy is also wilful, in that it is deliberate and intentional; failing, on account of its refusal to commit or remain; potentially ugly in its lack of gravitas alongside other more powerful and involuntary feelings; and finally, an affectation, in that it encourages the putting on of attitudes and airs. As Riley suggests with identity politics, a poetics of flippancy is a case of trying it on, in both senses. It is developing a way of speaking and writing that best accommodates a nimble tongue while allowing for content that is light in the face of serious subjects. All of these concepts have negative connotations. As opposed to representing power, strength and political or poetic commitment, flippancy is a willing subversion, destruction and irreverence. Stein, O'Hara, Myles and Nelson, through their aesthetics, feelings, narcissism of self-expression (lyric or otherwise), refusals to stay still and to stay quiet, as well as their rejection of dogma, manifest a poetics of flippancy that is both multiple and contingent.

Much like the irony outlined by Riley, the poetics of flippancy is a purely linguistic strategy that emerges in relation to specific contexts. The unbecoming lightness cannot be appreciated unless the environment and subject matter are appreciated as serious. Similarly, the nimble tongue needs to be understood through the shape and movement of the poem itself. While this parallels with irony, flippancy also deviates in that it does not follow the same rigid model proposed by Riley, even while the poetics might offer up similar forms of critique of dominant discourses. Eschewing Echo's limitations and the problematic of reinforcing prevailing opinion, flippancy takes the established and rejects it through a lack of serious engagement. While Riley says that at worst, irony can become flippant, I think that the non-committal performative aspects of flippancy allow for more freedom and mobility on the part of the poetic speaker.

On account of the negative associations with flippancy, it is necessary for the flippant speaker to demonstrate a certain amount of wilfulness. Without the seriousness of irony and the power of other affects, flippancy is difficult to sustain as a series of postures and posturings. The flippant subject must also be willing to bring lightness to situations that otherwise demand gravitas and to continue a certain freeing mobility even while a particular topic demands attention and fidelity. In her work *Willful Subjects*, Ahmed describes the difficulty of being both wilful and wordy, writing: 'You become mouthy. Perhaps we are called mouthy when we say what others do not want to hear; to become mouthy is to become mouth, reduced to the speaking part as reduced to the wrong part' (2014: 154). In spite of the negativity of being reduced to the mouth, this is fundamental to all poetry, which ultimately is a genre of mouthiness.

Flippancy also mitigates some of the difficulties that could be associated with the politicized and righteous avant-garde. Ahmed writes:

> Avant-garde life worlds are populated by subjects who think of themselves as willful, as disobedient, as opposing norms, as giving up on conventions that hold others in place. But the self-perception of freedom from norms can quickly translate into the freedom to exploit others, to engage in behaviours that are almost exact approximations of the norms that subjects think of themselves as opposing.
>
> (2014: 172)

Flippancy, in failing to commit and falling down on seriousness, does not seem to resonate with the avant-garde world that goes on to replicate the normative structures it has rebelled against. A poetics of flippancy will not lead and will not incite the revolution, and while disobeying the normative, it does not align with a sanctimonious and righteous avant-garde. What it does practice is a lack of seriousness within all contexts, where calling the self out, and calling contexts out, is an integral part of revealing the power structures and discourses at work. Unlike the stronger feelings outlined by Ngai, and the difficulty of the rebellious avant-garde as extolled by Ahmed, flippancy is too light to wield the power it has rejected.

Throughout this chapter, I have positioned flippancy as a form of failure. Although certainly not present within Stein's confident work, failure operates as a theme through the work of O'Hara, Myles and Nelson. Failing does not render the three speakers miserable or unhappy, falling down against the standards upheld by a heteronormative world but instead offer spaces of alternative connection. Failure allows for a critique of the standards of success, which more often than not are associated with certain identities. Flippancy's failure to commit, and failure to communicate seriousness, is thus necessary for encountering and questioning the dominant while allowing for orientations away from the goals society outlines for acceptable subjects or citizens. A poetics of flippancy enacts a similar way of engaging and working, where the poem itself might fail in regard to resolution and narrative or the memoir might foreground the experiences of a speaker deemed marginal or unimportant. It is also the case with the work of Nelson and Myles that the self-aware experimental memoirs seem to reject the usual confessional aspects of the genre, in the same way that O'Hara's attempt at a manifesto fails in the genre's usual gravitas and explicit political engagements. To fail within genre is to treat it with lightness that allows for its sensitivities and dominant patterns to be probed.

The work of all four poets draws extensively on performance and affectation, all of which seem necessary counters to performativity and affect. The latter can bind the subject into passionate engagement, transporting them along socially accepted lines through reiterative practices, or alternatively, moving them through widely shared and powerful feeling. Emphasizing the performance of identity, and the affectation of lightness in the face of serious subjects, the four poets recognize the potential intensities of their feeling contexts, but also call them to account. Performance and affectation, then, become a self-aware refusal to participate or capitulate. As such, while flippancy is inherently unseriousness, it is also inherently troubling. It refuses to offer up concerted commitment when such a commitment is called for; avoids aligning with both predominant and counterculture trends; it embraces failure as a means by which to allow for alternatives. The unbecoming levity and nimble tongue are both central to the writing of Stein, O'Hara, Myles and Nelson, and ultimately create works of queer troublemaking, in which a poetics of flippancy manifests as resistance to prevailing discourses of seriousness and commitment.

2

'He Cannot Understand Women. I Can': Gertrude Stein and the Camp Butch

One of the difficulties of writing about Gertrude Stein is that she is a multiply reinterpreted and reimagined icon. Not only has Stein imbued her writing with her force of personality, but she has also created a strong legacy of high Modernism, lesbian histories and women's writing. In this way, Stein can be appropriated across a spectrum of writing and theory, while the compelling details of her personal life form a fascinating basis for biography. Whether realized in the monochrome colourful intersections of Andy Warhol's *Ten Portraits of Jews*, or through O'Hara's romantic meditation on the light hair of a lover's torso, or even in the mass-printed now famous photograph of Stein and Alice B. Toklas walking their giant poodle Basket, Stein's legacy is one of multiple ownership. She seems to transcend the boundaries of mass-culture, high culture, experimental poetics, queer culture, feminist histories and voyeuristic interest in the domestic lives of others. It is perhaps for these reasons that Stein has been claimed by feminists as the central figure of Modernism, creating a coterie culture in which her home was central, and by lesbians for her practically-a-marriage to Toklas before same-sex unions were even possible. It is perhaps also because of the fascination with Stein as a figure that she has been rejected by both feminists and lesbians, perceived as a patriarch who celebrated male genius while relegating her female partner to the kitchen. Even Stein's war heroism, which she describes extensively within her writing, is thrown under question by her unlikely collaboration with the Vichy government. It becomes, then, impossible to place Stein who eludes the simple categorization of Cubist, Modernist, feminist, lesbian, innovator and patron. At times she is all of these descriptors, and at other times, scrupulously evades the fixity associated with each one. It is for these reasons, and perhaps on account of the shifting legacies of Stein, that the writer could be considered a queer troublemaker. Her work against easy taxonomies and definitions allows for a new form of orientation for both the written text and the reader, with the movement and evasions creating spaces of possibility that are both troubling and generative.

In spite of Stein's refusal to inhabit stable categories, there are two predominant methods for reading her work that dominate scholarship surrounding the writer. In his essay 'On Reading Stein', Michael Davidson writes that these modes of interpretation are as follows:

> One proposes that all her writing is play, that it derives strictly out of her early researches with William James and motor automism and was later invigorated by Cubist formalism. The other proposes that Stein is a kind of hermetic Symbolist who encodes her sexual and biographical information in complex verbal machines which contextualise their own environments ... one wants her to mean nothing and the other wants her to mean intrinsically.
>
> (1984: 196)

In this sense, Stein is approached as either wholly inscrutable or in need of decoding. Emphasis on play and autonomism suggests that the work is purely concerned with the material of language and its aesthetic possibilities – Stein's writing is introspective, an inward-facing set of experiments in structure, form and materiality. Symbolism, by contrast, suggests that Stein needs to be decoded in order for the reader to understand embedded autobiographical information, all of which enhances understanding of the texts. This is especially problematic because it posits that Stein's work is primarily read for its bearing on her personal life and that the writer made use of code because she was trying to shield aspects of her identity, notably her queerness. A reader of Stein, therefore, is forced to navigate these two assumptions of her writing, either accepting the mutual exclusivity of play and symbol or traversing the difficulties of meaning and non-meaning.

This binary is not the only problematic approach that has emerged from Stein's studies. In his essay 'The Impossible', John Ashbery makes a case for dividing Stein's work into the worthy and then silly, meaningless chatter. Mounting a defence of *Stanzas in Meditation* as a significant improvement on Stein's earlier, facile work he writes:

> It [*Stanzas in Meditation*] will probably please readers who are satisfied only by literary extremes, but who have not previously taken to Miss Stein because of a kind of lack of seriousness in her work, characterized by lapses into dull, facile rhyme; by the over-employment of rhythms suggesting a child's incantation against grownups; by monotony.
>
> (Ashbery 1957: 250)

Ashbery does not elucidate what he means by 'literary extremes', but it is possible that this refers to avant-garde and experimental writing. However, in my reading, this extremity could also be applied to critical approaches to Stein as either autobiographical symbolism or the introspective meaningless language games. Ashbery suggests that readers subscribing to such literary extremity would not have appreciated Stein's previous work, in some senses because of the monotony it provokes. Later in the essay he states that *Stanzas in Meditation* communicates a monotony of 'the fertile kind, which generates excitement' (Ashbery 1957: 250). This taxonomy of monotony sets up an interesting proposition for Stein's work, in which some aspects of dullness are generative for the reader, while other forms of boredom are less satisfying. In fact, the less satisfying form of monotony could be understood as relating to the lack of seriousness, dull and facile rhyme, and the overuse of rhythm, qualities Ashbery attributes to Stein's earlier work. Ashbery, thus, is not dividing Stein's writing around the typical binary of play or symbolism but instead binaries of early and late, as well as bad boredom–good boredom.

Elements of Ashbery's criticisms are shared by Bob Perelman in his article for *The L=A=N=G=U=A=G=E Book*. In his discussion of 'Roast Beef' from the Food section of *Tender Buttons*, Perelman writes:

> I wonder if she hears/sees/thinks the word just before or as she writes – or only after. Does she 'mean it,' or is it just *prattle* (singsong, babyish joy in denotation [standards, streamers, curtains, bed linen], grammar becoming a 'weak voice')
>
> But "it is so easy to exchange meaning, it is so easy to see the difference" and on through the rest of the excerpt is definitely not babe talk, is exemplary in its variety of use, surface and suggestion.
>
> (Perelman 1984: 200)

Here, Perelman interrogates the intentionality of the writer, wondering whether Stein 'means' the work or whether she is allowing herself an automatic form of prattle. Of course Stein does not 'mean' within the traditional sense at least, in which a clear message expressed in transparent language can be assimilated by the reader. Significantly, Perelman is not asking whether the work itself 'means' anything, in this way eschewing a symbolic approach to the text, but rather whether Stein herself can be attributed with any kind of creative motive through a reading of the work. This seems to support a similar approach to that of Ashbery in dividing the work into the insipid and the experimentally meaningful. Perelman suggests that prattle is a form of 'babe talk', which of course could relate to the baby invoked earlier in his analysis but could also be understood as linking to Stein's very femaleness. This is perhaps further supported by the fact that Perelman's examples of weaker Stein writing very much relate to the domestic sphere (curtains, bed linen). It is also significant that the babe talk disappears when the work becomes more characteristic of surface and suggestion; the former must submit to the latter, they cannot be synonymous, nor can they coexist.

Both Ashbery and Perelman seem united in their dismissal of specific aspects of Stein's work. Ashbery recognizes that the lack of seriousness in the early writing is off-putting, while Perelman believes that the surface and suggestion cannot work simultaneous to the prattle and babe talk. I want to consider briefly both critics' writing on the role of the 'baby' in relation to the lack of seriousness in Stein's work. While the rest of my chapter will make a case for balancing the autobiographical symbolism with the structural playfulness of language and repetition, in this instance it seems important to recognize that 'Baby' was a nickname that both Stein and Toklas used for one another (Shields 2018). Although it might be simplistic to understand all of Stein's work as simple obfuscated autobiography, it is impossible to avoid that particular texts and even signifiers are associated with the woman herself and her queer identity. It becomes the case, then, that the lack of seriousness and intentionality outlined by both writers seems related to the aspects of Stein's writing that most express sex, intimacy and lesbianism. This problematic of autobiography also jars against the personality that Stein expresses through her writing, where the latter might be assumed as a function or result of the former. Indeed, In 'From "Impossible" Writing to a Poetics of Intimacy: John Ashbery's Reading of Gertrude Stein', Emily Setina writes that Stein was concerned that 'her success was only an effect of her personality, that without personality her work had no meaning because it was written in a private language that would be undecipherable and unpalatable without Stein's strong personality to sell it' (Setina 2012: 160). Significantly, even though Setina suggests Stein did write in a private language, she implies that language would be impossible for a generalized audience to decode. As such, the intimacy and inexplicability of Stein's work would not engage or even receive an audience were it not for the tangibility of personality running through. This personality, which is still evident in the texts now, can be untethered from the woman herself; it is not embodied but rather a tone that resides throughout all of the works. Setina goes on to elucidate that 'in Ashbery's account of *Stanzas*, the poem refers to its author; it bears a determined relation to Gertrude Stein and allows, despite the poem's abstractions, a sense of closeness to her' (2012: 160). This closeness does not come through the decoding of and identifying specific material aspects of Stein's life, but rather through recognizing the vivacity and forcefulness of the voice, which communicates an intimacy with the material while creating an intimacy with the reader.

What Davidson, Ashbery, Perelman and Setina allow me to do is configure Stein as a difficult and elusive writer, as well as character. Davidson neatly outlines problematics of approaching the work, in which it is easy to feed into a binary understanding of Stein's particular writing methodologies. Throughout this chapter, I intend to fluctuate between both approaches, recognizing that Stein may have drawn on some codes that I am able to interpret and some codes that will be far beyond my identifying. However, I also want to consider the play of the language itself and the way in which the structures and repetitions allow for a poetics of flippancy to emerge in a more formal sense. To my mind, Ashbery and Perelman both demonstrate the ways in which Stein's earlier and later work could be dismissed on account of its lack of seriousness. Here, I have explicitly linked this lack of seriousness with a femininity and lesbianism evident throughout the texts, where intimacy and the domestic are considered disinteresting in contrast with formal innovation. What I want to suggest, by contrast, is that the lightness, in part created through rhythm and rhyme, and the babe talk that might seem without clear intentionality, is all part of the surface and suggestion of a poetics of flippancy. In fact, these aspects of Stein's work can be rehabilitated in both *Lifting Belly* and *The Autobiography of Alice B. Toklas* in such a way as to suggest a particular poetics. Setina, usefully, outlines a difficulty that haunts this book as whole: personality. All of the writers I discuss foreground their selfhood, playing with the compelling and distinctive personalities that they carry through their individual writing. This is inherently different from autobiography, but nonetheless contributes to the ways in which I am reading flippancy throughout every text under discussion.

'We know how to differ': Problematizing flippancy

One of the difficulties apparent in working on flippancy within Stein is that the poet is often positioned and understood as a paragon of seriousness. As such, I want to give some consideration to how Stein might be rehabilitated for a poetics of flippancy, with a particular focus on the camp aspects of her writing. Although both Ashbery and Perelman are problematic in their relation to Stein's lesbian feminism, as well as her less serious writing, I want to mobilize aspects of their critical writing in order to approach a poetics of flippancy. If Ashbery is to be believed that the force of Stein's personality creates a complex relationship with the reader, then the writer's presence within the texts needs to be defined. Similarly, if Perelman is concerned by whether Stein really 'mean[s] it', then the poet needs to be considered alongside intentionality and deliberateness. I am reluctant to attempt establishing Stein as a flippant woman herself, though I am sure there is a case to be made for a lightness that might coexist uneasily with her self-assured genius. I will also not be tracing Stein's structures and definitions back to a particular and easily identifiable intentionality. Rather, I want to suggest that Stein's prattle, babe talk, surface and lightness are communicated through the writing in such a way that the reader is orientated differently. Avoiding the mutual exclusives that seem to determine the critical reception of Stein's work, is it possible to recognize the personality of the writer as manifested through a work that is still unbecoming, light in relation to the heavy, and consistently surface when there is space for depth? Although Setina makes a strong case for the forceful nature of Stein's personality propelling and generating interest within her texts, this particular voice is difficult to interpret as light and irreverent. Stein's legacy is one of seriousness; she positioned herself as a genius, fully invested in the experimental brilliance with which she approached writing. She was also a patron, high Modernist and socially influential, all of which imbue the writer with a sense of gravitas as opposed to levity. However, when considering Stein's use of both camp and butch, the seriousness with which she is associated opens up to allow for a poetics of flippancy.

While her 'Notes on Camp' are much celebrated, Susan Sontag revised her stance on the topic in the afterword to *Against Interpretation*. There, she considers the repercussions of championing camp against a wider culture of diminished seriousness. Sontag notes 'what I didn't understand ... was that seriousness itself was in the early stages of losing credibility in the culture at large' (Sontag 2009b: 312). It seems that rather than celebrating camp, Sontag lamented the lack of seriousness that she perceived making its way through culture. While Sontag might see this as the case for culture more generally, there are still a number of serious and dangerous aspects of queer experience, many of which ensure that lightness is thrown into stark relief, as opposed to the predominant sense. Sontag's original 'Notes on Camp' focused on homosexuality and gay cultures, describing camp as a cult that is a variant of sophistication. She makes reference to both Oscar Wilde and Christopher Isherwood, gently suggesting that there is an identifiable lineage for the sensibility. Slightly removed from 'camp', Sontag deems herself capable of writing critically on the topic because she does not wholeheartedly share in it. This enables her to make a distinction between two varieties of camp, a differentiation that does not necessarily stand up to the way in which she outlines and approaches the sensibility within the rest of her 'Notes'. She writes that there exists a 'pure camp', which is tied to seriousness, and then 'intentional camp', which is performative. In pure camp 'the essential element is seriousness, a seriousness that fails. Of course, not all seriousness that fails can be redeemed as Camp' (2009a: 312). In spite of lamenting the disappearance of seriousness, then, Sontag once saw it as integral to a particular form of camp. When seriousness is attempted, but fails, it is rehabilitated as pure camp. It could be that some readings of Stein emphasize this aspect of the writing, with the reader perceiving a failure of seriousness where the writer herself has attempted gravitas. However, I believe that Stein's camp is more of the cultivated and performative variety. In this way, when the writing demonstrates campness, it is because Stein wills it to be so, as opposed to because her text has failed in its conveyance of the serious. Sontag herself seems to problematize the pure camp when she writes that 'the whole point of Camp is to dethrone the serious. Camp is playful, anti-serious' (2009a: 288). Pure camp obviously lacks the intentionality and autonomy necessary for acts of play and dethroning. It may well be the case, then, that pure camp lies in perception, where the failure of seriousness is recognized by an audience, whereas intentional camp is communicated through performance.

In his 'Introduction' to *Camp: Queer Aesthetics and the Performing Subject: A Reader*, Fabio Cleto clarifies the pure and the intentional further, reframing the terms in a particular consideration of performance. He claims that in naïve camp 'all that one needs is the *perception* ... of artificiality, especially in things that try to seem natural: in short one needs to perceive a *failed seriousness*' (Cleto 1999: 24). So, it is not so much that naïve camp originates from the subject or object itself but rather emerges through perception. As I have stated, this can extend to the way in which Ashbery and Perelman view Stein, but it could also be the case that her texts are perceived as highly artificial. The repetition, rhyme, continual movement and part code do convey a sense of the contrived, entirely separated from what might be considered natural speech or language use. By contrast, deliberate camp is 'the very act of performance, intentionality, and paradoxically so, producing a failure of seriousness, acknowledging its "essence" in the unnatural, in the *inessential* and the contingent' (Cleto 1999: 24). This intentionality draws on the same kind of failure, but it is one that is clearly and identifiably produced. It also recognizes and foregrounds the unnatural and contingent, which it could be argued is key to Stein's way of writing. When considering camp in Stein, then, it is possible to see it as both naïve and deliberate. The two, in conjunction with one another, are tied to failure, performance, the inessential and the contingent, as well as configured through the perception of the reader. While some of the camp in Stein arises from my own reading, both *Autobiography* and *Lifting Belly* are deliberately performative, making unnatural use of language in such a way as to highlight artificiality and contingency.

It is these qualities that I intend to examine in relation to a poetics of flippancy. Although Stein might seem to represent a tension between seriousness and lightness, the latter creates a clear space within the work such that the texts themselves are able to explore, experiment and deviate. In *The Queer Art of Failure*, Halberstam writes that 'the desire to be taken seriously is precisely what compels people to follow the tried and true paths of knowledge production' (2011: 6). Stein's innovative writing certainly deviates from the tried and true paths of knowledge production. Through a highly performative camp and butching of the text, Stein is able to innovate the space of the poem, and autobiography, while still communicating queer investments. Although her work often strays from disciplinary correctness, in repetitions, structure, playfulness, rhythm and rhyme, Stein's incorporation of specifically queer and same-sex references also demonstrates how the work deliberately deviates from the tried paths of heteronormativity. In her resistance, Stein creates texts that thrive on deviation, establishing a queer poetics that requires new forms of orientation on the part of both writer and reader. While my focus thus far has been on defining camp in such a way as to approach *Lifting Belly* and *Autobiography of Alice B. Toklas*, in order to establish a flippant reading methodology for engaging with Stein's work, I want to turn to the idea of butch as figure, symbol and style. It is not purely that Stein creates works of both naïve and deliberate camp but that this is combined with aspects and elements of butchness, which is developed through both texts under discussion. Both butch and camp are facets of queer culture that in conjunction within Stein's work illuminate how the poetics of flippancy can move throughout the writing.

Butching camp and camping butch

In order to consider the combinations of the butch and camp, I want to consider female masculinity. Halberstam argues that not all signifiers of masculinity are derivative of purely male culture but could instead arise from women, which is foundational to understanding the development of butch identities. Butches are not attempting to impersonate or appropriate the masculinity of men but are in fact developing a relationship with masculinity that is not necessarily at odds with their gender. As such, butches can be identified and read through the complex relationship between performance, affectation, gender presentation and sex. Halberstam writes that the butch 'tends to see herself as something other than woman-identified-woman' (1998: 120). The butch's identification, therefore, is more self-determined, concerned with surface and performance, as opposed to an essentialist relationship between sex and gender. By this I mean that the butch defines herself through particular self-presentation, a self-presentation that allows for the sex and gender to become mutable. In considering Stein as a butch, Karen Allison Hammer writes that 'in queer and lesbian circles, *butch* is curiously both a clearly recognisable and abstract identification, sometimes simply defined as "you know one when you see one"' (2015: 30). This kind of physical identification seems to preclude the text, suggesting that butchness is best realized in an embodied sense. However, it may well be the case with Stein that this recognizable and abstract identification is embedded within the writing, such that the text communicates a sense of the butch. Less embodied and more textual, in this instance it is the case that 'you know one when you read one'.

Hammer finds that '*butch* is theoretically powerful precisely because it does not demand a true gender identity. The term can describe a woman who has embraced a masculine style' (2015: 31). Butchness, thus, allows for a flexibility between sex and gender, in which identification becomes both more performative and autonomous. It does not associate itself with forms of essentialism, preferring the contingent constructions of masculinity that can emerge from a female body. Hammer recognizes that the term 'butch' only came into public circulation after Stein's death and in fact was not a word used to describe lesbians within her lifetime. As such, while it is impossible to determine whether Stein would have identified as a butch, Hammer claims that Stein 'was not interested in definition or explication, but instead in the *play* of opposing terms. She found enjoyment in the zone of undecidability, and may have found literary and sexual fulfilment because of the interplay and incongruity of female embodiment and masculine style' (2015: 32). Certainly, neither of the texts I intend to discuss here shy away from female embodiment nor do they attempt to tone down confidence that Hammer describes as 'butch audacity'. Stein's writing demonstrates certainty and flare in its performance of language and selfhood in *Autobiography*, drawing on undecidability and interplay in order to convey both Stein's genius and her relationship with Toklas.

Both *Autobiography* and lesbian readings of *Lifting Belly* would suggest it is necessary to address the relationship between the butch and the femme. In the autobiography, Stein takes on the voice of her femme partner in order to narrate her own experiences, while the poetry is a continuously shifting text orientated through 'you' and 'I' that sometimes refers to domesticity, sometimes sex. The femininity of the femme offsets the masculinity of the butch, allowing for the latter to become legible in a matrix of gender and sexed relations. It is my contention that this legibility does not need to be confined to the real-life relationship of Stein and Toklas but can also be understood through the voice of the text and the reader. If, as Ashbery suggests, Stein's work establishes a form of intimacy through the forcefulness of personality, then it is possible that the reader becomes the 'other' through which the writer's voice takes on the characteristics of butchness. By this I mean that Stein's writing, in its forceful swagger, makes a femme of its readership. Although *Autobiography* and *Lifting Belly* have their relation to a loved one, or sexual partner, inherently written into the text, they also reach outward to the reader as one who might 'read' the dynamics, recognizing and thus endorsing the butch characteristics that emerge. In *Queer Phenomenology*, Ahmed discusses the butch and femme relationship refuting the assumption that such a pairing is based off a model of heterosexuality. She writes that 'butch-femme is not a copy of the real thing that resides elsewhere, but rather is a serious space for erotic play and performance' (Ahmed 2006: 99). Once more, the serious seems to collide with aspects of identity, namely play and performance, that necessitate greater levity. Ahmed claims that the roles of the butch and femme demonstrate that there is no original model for gender, sex or sexuality to follow. Instead of attempting a form of heterosexuality, one characterized by lack, the butch-femme are actually empowered through their own performance and play. She elucidates, 'I suggest that butch and femme are for lesbians erotic possibilities that can generate new lines of desire only when they are just that: possibilities rather than requirements' (Ahmed 2006: 99). The butch is neither imitative of straight males nor is it a necessary role throughout lesbianism. Rather, in conjunction with the femme, it offers up a space of play and performance, in which possibilities are multiple. Instead of serving as a fixed identity, one that is grounded in an original and thus more authoritative model, the butch is engaged in a series of unbecomings that have their own openness and lightness. In *Gender Trouble*, Butler writes that 'one might wonder what use "opening up possibilities" finally is, but no one who has understood what it is to live in the social world as what is "impossible," illegible, unrealizable, unreal and illegitimate is likely to pose that question' (2006: x). Opening up possibility, then, is not only playful, performative, contingent and mobile but a highly political act for identities which might otherwise be read illegibly and considered unreal.

That butch relies on the figure of the femme immediately makes it distinct from 'camp', which is contingently formulated through perception and failure, as opposed to a dialogic recognition. Indeed, there are a number of ostensible differences between butch and camp; butch is associated with lesbian cultures, while camp is often located within cisgender, homosexual male contexts. In considering the concept of lesbian camp, Halberstam turns to female drag artists, writing:

> Although I do not think that camp is unavailable to lesbian performers, I do think that because camp is predicated on exploiting the theatricality of gender, it tends to be the genre for an outrageous performance of femininity (by men or women) rather than outrageous performances of masculinity.
>
> (1998: 237)

Her supposition is that male performances of femininity are camp, while female performances of masculinity cannot be categorized as such. If we are to extend this into the butch, the demonstration of masculinity would not necessarily be considered as camp. It is not an outrageous performance, even while it is still performative, and it does not send up femininity as the key characteristic of fun or parody. Camp is most effective in male bodies performing aspects of femininity because the clear disjuncture between biology and self-presentation is very apparent. Halberstam clarifies that 'only lesbian performances of femininity can be inflected with camp because camp is always about femininity' (1998: 238). For camp to exist within a lesbian culture, there has to be an intentional performance in which the performance is clearly distinct from the identity of the performer. For example, it would be easier for a butch to pull off a camp performance of femininity than it would be for a femme.

However, if we are to take Halberstam's definition of the butch as something other than a woman-identified woman, then the butch does not differ too significantly from Sontag's formulation of camp as 'things-being-what-they-are-not' (2009a: 79). Camp shares the denial of essentialism that the butch foregrounds. It does not necessarily demand a set gender identity but expects a specific form of recognizable performance. Similar to understanding butch as 'I know it when I see it', camp needs to engage with strategies of recognition such that it is legible as an intentional and autonomous way of behaving. Sontag also defines camp as 'to understand Being-as-Playing-a-Role' (Sontag 2009a: 280) which once more foregrounds the performative nature of existing, which can be realized through the playfulness of performance. It is not inconceivable, therefore, that butch and camp could coexist with one another, particularly given that Stein relished the zone of undecidability and the play of oppositional terms.

While I have tried, in some ways, to outline the confluences of butchness and camp here, I want to emphasize the incongruity of both that they may only be brought into existence or indeed 'seen', when they are recognized or perceived by the reader. As such, the butch camp situates itself somewhere between the text itself and the reader's response. It is part predicated on recognition, where the butch is witnessed and the camp is legible, where together they bring a certain lightness and playful performativity to female masculinity. The overlaps of the two also recognize the affected nature of butchness within the text, where the camp quality of being as playing a role is manifest within the clear masculine-orientated identity of the text. Finally, the camp butch recognizes a deviation from the normative and then a further deviation from what might be expected of the non-normative. It brings lightness to the ways in which we recognize the butch, and it foregrounds gender performativity when we approach the camp. Thus, in Stein's work especially, it encourages the reader towards the levity associated with gender slippages, all of which are entirely deliberate, and our recognition of them.

Ultimately, the butch camp allows for flippancy to emerge, where the unique performativity and affectation of both facets of queer culture oscillate to create space for such a poetics. Similarly to some aspects of camp being realized through perception, the flippant poetics of Stein have been extrapolated from two very particular texts, with two particular queer performances working in conjunction with one another. I am orientated through the writing by the suggestions of the butch camp, in the same way that the texts call for the reader to orientate themselves differently, recognizing performance, uncertainty and things appearing as other than what they are. The sex acts of *Lifting Belly* immediately emphasize the performative nature of the 'act', while the sleight of identity in *Autobiography* is a sustained performance of otherness, in which femininity is placed in dialogue with the more masculine energies of Stein's writing. Both works when considered through a framework of butch camp suggest a range of textual possibilities, in which the unserious is thrown into relief by the seriousness in a process of unbecoming levity. Affectation and performance come to the fore in such a way that the nimble tongue, sense of play, and lightness of approach of the poetics of flippancy are apparent. In both *Autobiography* and *Lifting Belly*, Stein's work maintains a taut surface of movement and play, in which the reader is denied depth of content through the style of the language itself. The mobility evident in the narrative deviations of *Autobiography* and the ever-changing sometimes-sex-sometimes-not of *Lifting Belly* allow for the speaking subject to maintain levity and style. It is these qualities that enable the two texts under discussion to suggest forms of becoming and unbecoming, in which Stein becomes Alice to become Stein again; in which the sex act is constituted and reconstituted, made everyday and banal, and then exceptional once more. Both texts reject the coherence suggested by gravitas, harnessing aspects of the butch camp to create spaces for performance, affectation, lightness and mobility, all of which are consistent with a poetics of flippancy.

'Poetry is doing nothing': Stein's structures

Lifting Belly is understood to have been written between 1915 and 1917 but was published posthumously, while *The Autobiography of Alice B. Toklas* was published much later in 1933 and propelled Stein into a position of unexpected celebrity. While both texts exhibit clear relationships with both butchness and campness, Stein's desire for celebrity has been interpreted as specifically butch. She declared, quite clearly, that she wrote *Autobiography* with a desire to be famous, exhibiting an audacity and desire for respect that is associated with the butch identity (Hammer 2015: 34). Given the time in which *Lifting Belly* was written, and the temporal scope of *Autobiography*, both texts directly address the First World War. In this instance, I will not be focusing on the representation of war through two texts not because the seriousness of the conflict is antithetical to my flippant purposes but rather because the flippancy of the texts themselves is achieved through the dialogue of form and content in relation to gender identity and performativity. The backdrop of war does create a juxtaposition in which the other considerations could be positioned as unbearably light, even unbecoming in their levity, but my focus will be on the deviations, movements, performances and affectations of both the style and the figures presented within both texts. *Lifting Belly* is a sixty-page epic poem, heavily lineated and written in the continuous present, a temporality that Stein developed to describe her particular style of writing, while *Autobiography* is written in prose and aims to communicate the day-to-day aspects of Stein and Toklas' life together. The latter is the most normative of Stein's texts, which might explain its initial popularity, as well its resistance to the categories of writing established by both Ashbery and Perelman.

The poetics of flippancy within Stein's work is facilitated by her structures of writing. Whether poetry or prose, Stein's sentences and phrases have a specific style, one that seems to deviate and to err, experimenting with the nouns, verbs and adjectives, undoing and unmaking them through unexpected parallels and descriptions. Stein had very clear ideas about the difference between poetry and prose, in addition to the emotion that might be held within the space of a sentence or a paragraph. In 'Poetry and Grammar' she wrote:

> Prose is the balance the emotional balance that makes the reality of paragraphs and the unemotional balance that makes the reality of sentences and having realized completely realized that sentences are not emotional while paragraphs are, prose can be the essential balance that is made inside something that combines the sentence and the paragraph.
>
> (Stein 2004a: 135)

This seems to suggest that prose can temper both the paragraph and the sentence, bringing emotional possibilities to the former and realizing the unemotional nature of the latter. Furthermore, it mediates the differences between the paragraph and sentence; as the commonality shared by both, prose is able to balance the changing of feeling between the two structures. In 'What Is English Literature', Stein elucidates further, stating that 'paragraphs are emotional not because they express an emotion but because they register or limit an emotion. Compare paragraphs with sentences and you will see what I mean' (2004b: 53). It is not, therefore, that the paragraph structure is inherently emotional, but that it creates space in which emotion becomes recognizable to a reader, either through the way in which it has been limited or registered. Stein does not specify how the paragraph might offer the reader such emotional insight, but it is clear that she considers prose to be the genre that allows for the carrying of emotion between structures that register, limit or deny its presence. It is not necessarily the case that Stein is considering these structures in relation to content, by which I mean she is not considering how these particular components work in relation with the unfolding of a tragic story. Rather, she is considering the constructions themselves as establishing particular relationships with emotion and mediation through their structure. The balancing, therefore, is located within the form itself, as opposed to how the form engages with the content. It is important to note that Stein does not name the 'something' in which the prose resides. She also does not suggest a means by which to bridge the sentence and paragraph, purely acknowledging that prose's existence within both facilitates such a combination. The openness of 'something' suggests that this unidentified quality might be applicable to the construction of poetry too.

By contrast, Stein defines poetry as 'essentially a vocabulary just as prose is essentially not' (Stein 2004a: 136). Stein is not saying that poetry *is* vocabulary, but a vocabulary, wherein the space of the poem and relationship between words creates a new lexical field to be interpreted. The reader is expected to orientate themselves through the content and form so as to understand the unique usage of selected words. 'Vocabulary' suggests that the poem consists of a body of words, with specific purposes, all of which can be comprehended through both a definition and usage. It also brings the relationships between the words into question. A vocabulary can be a list of words with definitions or alternatively the range of words available to the person speaking. This does not suggest coherence and cohesion in the form of sentences and lines but rather an exploration of a communicative tool as unique to the space of the poem. Stein goes on to discuss this concept more extensively when she writes:

> Poetry is concerned with using with abusing, with losing with wanting, with denying with avoiding with adoring with replacing the noun. It is doing that always doing that, doing that and doing nothing but that. Poetry is doing nothing but using losing refusing and pleasing and betraying and caressing nouns.
>
> (2004a: 136)

Here, Stein addresses the processes of poetry, which are always in motion, teasing and testing the nouns under consideration. If poetry itself is a vocabulary, then it is comprised of nouns that are both used and abused. The meaning and integrity of the words might get lost, or be left wanting, be denied their traditional position among others. Stein focuses specifically on the noun, claiming that poetry is concerned with subjecting the noun to a series of destructive, as well as tender, unbecomings. It seems that poetry is especially concerned with the noun because the genre is a means by which to mobilize and enliven the words. Stein writes that in contrast with the noun, 'verbs and adverbs and articles and conjunctions and prepositions are lively because they all do something and as long as anything does something it keeps alive' (2004a: 126). As such, Stein calls for a poetry that teases the noun and enacts violence on it, allowing for a loss and refusal that in turn is also a caress and adoration. As opposed to following a straight and narrow relationship between signifier and signified, poetry becomes a new space of vocabulary, in which the noun itself can be called into question, lost, refused, betrayed and abused.

Given her focus on emotion within the sentence and paragraph, it is interesting that *Autobiography* is a text almost entirely without affect. *Lifting Belly*, by contrast, has an affective pull, with the brevity of the lines, mobility and momentum carrying the reader through permutations of lightness and relationality. In addition to poetry as a vocabulary, Stein describes the genre as 'movement in space' (2004a: 144). If poetry is movement in space, it becomes a force of in-betweenness, moving the reader from their original position to liminality. The reader reflects this, engaging in a perpetual orientation, forever mobile within the space created through the works. In *The Practice of Everyday Life*, Michel de Certeau defines space as 'composed of intersections of mobile elements. It is in a sense actuated by the ensemble of movements deployed within it' (1984: 117). Through her investment in components of language as alive and doing something, as well as Stein's multiple treatment of nouns, the poetry calls for the reader to become mobile themselves, contributing to the ensemble of movements contained within the space of the writing. It is also for these reasons of structure, genre, movement and mobility that camp and butch are so appropriate in approaching Stein. Cleto writes that camp 'works as all parts of speech, and has no static grammatical functioning, for it is at once an adjective, a noun and a verb' (1999: 12). This is not dissimilar to the functioning of butch, which is also adjectival, verbal and a noun. It describes a butch, who is a masculine presenting woman; it can be used adjectively to describe how the woman presents; it can be active in the deliberate making-masculine of the woman, who may well be 'butching' it up. Rather than just relegated to nouns or adjectives, the butch camp is active and mobile, a vocabulary that comes together in an unusual conjunction.

The affective and affectless nature of both *Lifting Belly* and *Autobiography* makes them useful texts for the discussion of a poetics of flippancy. They both share aspects of mobility, in addition to affectation, with gender performance being both done and undone throughout the texts. Whether concerned with the 'sex act' of lifting belly or the 'drag act' of being Alice, both works intentionally unsettle identity so as to question the categories of selfhood and gender relation that might otherwise be imposed. As such, they also resonate with the camp and butch, offering the reader something other than what initially appears, teasing out a deliberate indeterminacy, a quality which is reinforced through Stein's unique approach to genre and structure. Hammer writes that 'a lack of conclusion is part of the butch style ... The internal contradictions at play in butch means that we never quite close the door on questions of sex, gender, or text' (2015: 41). Both Stein's style and the way she approaches aspects of sex, as well as a consistent love object (Alice), allow for both elements of camp and butch to come to the fore, which when combined create a mobile, affected, performative poetics of flippancy. The love object of *Autobiography* is and is not Toklas, and is and is not Stein. Through the title and the assumption of Toklas as narrator, Stein places her lover as the central object of the text, an objectification that is confirmed through the identity shift in the final paragraph of the book. Similarly, Stein appears to be the central object of the text, beheld and described by the character of Alice. In *Lifting Belly*, while there is a 'you' and 'I' of the text, which suggests a coherent-speaking subject and addressee, there is a proliferation of unattributed pronouns, as well as multiple names invoked without context. As such the 'I' is seen as unstable and performative as the historical characters and indefinite as the anonymous pronouns that enter the poem. This mobility reflects Stein's understanding of poetry as movement in space. It is these contingencies and relations that allow for a poetics of flippancy to emerge, concerned with identity and identity evasions, all of which are realized through a sense of play and category refusal.

'They delighted in telling tales to each other': Sociable mobilities

One of the key aspects of flippancy is the nimble tongue, which facilitates levity in the face of serious subjects. The quick moving tongue is not only a fast-paced response but a continued movement of speech and language, which allows for the internal contrasts of unbecoming and levity in both *Autobiography of Alice B. Toklas* and *Lifting Belly*. Both texts are fundamentally different in tone; they are written in different genres and are both associated with different objectives for the writer–reader relationship. *Autobiography*'s dense prose and description, conveyed to the reader through the Alice narrator, is all ultimately proven to be a ruse. Whatever investment we have had in Alice herself, the scenes she describes, or the characters conveyed, we are made to realize at the end of the novel that all of these perceptions have been contrived by Stein herself. This final trick of the text offers retrospective lightness to the writing, in which details and discussions are injected with the levity of play-acting. *Lifting Belly*, by contrast, moves through very short lines and shifting attentions with an immediate and apparent levity, as well as a range of uncertain pronouns and references to seemingly irrelevant figures. In spite of the immediate flippancy of *Lifting Belly*, and the more considered ruse of *Autobiography*, there are aspects to both texts that foreground a specific levity throughout.

In *Autobiography*, Alice is not quite an 'unreliable' narrator, but she is an inconsistent one, unable to complete a chain of narrative without erring or deviating. This methodology for telling stories is encapsulated best in the second chapter, 'My Arrival in Paris'. There, Alice states 'there are a great many things to tell of what was happening then and what had happened before, which led up to then, but now I must describe what I saw when I came' (Stein 2001: 10).

The tenses within the sentence, as well as the specific temporalities invoked, suggest that the writer will not be constrained by chronology or chronological order. The 'now' of the statement makes the reader very conscious of the act of writing itself – that Alice is willing herself to description within that particular moment of creation. The past continuous of 'happening' gives an indeterminate length to the time Alice is describing, whereas the past perfect of 'what had happened before' seems very much elapsed and concluded. The use of both 'before' and 'then' gives the past a non-specific quality, in which the reader is aware of a timeline of events, but unable to map them precisely onto the wider timeline of the book itself. Having established this confusing relationship to the past, which is apparently replete with stories, Alice refocuses the reader on the writing itself and what she saw when she initially came to Paris. What Alice has seen, and intends to discuss here, is the myriad of interesting art work in Paris at the time of her arrival. Four pages after this slightly confusing approach to the temporality of both arrival and narration, Alice has deviated significantly again, only to reassure both herself and the reader 'but this time I am really going to tell about the pictures' (Stein 2001: 14). This is the third time in the chapter in which she has directly addressed her deviation, guaranteeing a return to the original topic under discussion. It is difficult, therefore, in spite of the clear chapter titles, all of which offer a specific timeframe, to follow the chronology of the novel. While the first two chapters address 'Before I came to Paris' and 'My Arrival in Paris', respectively, this logical order is reversed when it comes to Gertrude Stein, so that the next two chapters are 'Gertrude Stein in Paris, 1903–1907' and then 'Gertrude Stein before she came to Paris'. The freedom of movement created by Alice's fluctuations, both within the structure of the book and the narrative itself, allows for the work to deviate through anecdote and history. The reader treats the history of Alice and 'Gertrude Stein' lightly because their stories are combined with anecdote, gossip, irrelevancies, promises to stay on track and an antinormative chronological narrative structure.

Throughout the novel, Gertrude Stein remains at the centre of the text and Paris itself, in spite of the digressions and tangents that Alice leads the reader through. Not only does her presence cohere the erring and deviations of the narrative, but it also coheres the range of celebrity writers and artists. The mass proliferation of names and stories makes the book appear to be work of high-Modernist gossip, which is fitting with the fact that Stein is a self-confessed gossip. Alice offers an example of this when she writes on Matisse and Stein discussing his recently established art school, delighting in the exploits of the students: 'Matisse was a good gossip and so was she [Gertrude Stein] and at this time they delighted in telling tales to each other' (Stein 2001: 75). Not only are Matisse and Stein trading stories in this instance, but they are discussing a particular student who had swindled a fee waiver while still able to afford a small Picasso, Seurat and Matisse. The two indulge in the exchange of tales, but relish in the minor scandal, passing on information that presents the subject very unfavourably. This kind of treatment continues throughout the book, in which Alice reports Stein's pithy comments on a few artists she encountered and clearly did not warm too in spite of their achievements. After attending a Futurist exhibition, Stein and Toklas had the misfortune of meeting the artists themselves. Alice reports 'in any case everybody found the Futurists very dull' (Stein 2001: 137). Even while these words are not attributed directly to Gertrude Stein, the reader is aware that this is consistent with the opinions of Stein the author. Similarly, when discussing a meeting with Ezra Pound, Alice writes that 'Gertrude Stein liked him but did not find him amusing. She said he was a village explainer, excellent if you were a village, but if you were not, not' (Stein 2001: 127). While it seems flippant to judge great Modernists on whether they are amusing conversationalists, Stein's unique form of dismissal is particularly so. A village-explainer sounds both parochial and earnest, someone who takes on a role of self-importance within an insignificant community, conveying points and messages to people who may well already have heard or understood. The fact that Alice relays Gertrude Stein making a distinction between herself and a village only serves to heighten the lightness of the comment. These moments continue throughout the text, whether stated as fact by Alice, and therefore originating from the mind of Stein herself, or directly attributed to the figure of Gertrude Stein. This all works to create a real sense of mobility in the text, where Alice moves towards figures and then away from them, relishing moments of digression in relation to the wider narrative that she is purporting to create. This kind of gossip is anti-serious and highly camp, dethroning figures and events that might otherwise be interpreted as having gravitas. When this form of judgement is mediated by the voice of Alice, the opinions also take on a butch authority; they are seen as audacious and swaggering at the same time that they are light and irreverent.

This treatment of artists and enjoyment of gossip are not the only instances of unbecoming levity in the face of serious subjects – or at least, subjects who would like to be taken seriously. Gertrude Stein is also particularly dismissive of the sufferings of others, rendering their negative experience as material for art or as unwelcome conversation topics. In a description of a visit to Picasso in his home, Alice describes the following: 'Not long before a young fellow had committed suicide, Picasso painted one of the most wonderful of his early pictures of friends gathered round the coffin, we passed all this to a larger door where Gertrude Stein knocked' (Stein 2001: 27). Suicide comes unexpectedly into the narrative and is just as quickly dismissed, becoming inconsequential to the anecdote being relayed. The suicide is removed to the past, once through Picasso having painted the coffin, and then even further, through Gertrude Stein knocking on the door. The suicide is subordinated to the art it produced, which in turn is subordinated to the focus of the tale, which is Gertrude Stein's visit to Picasso. Where the death of a young man might warrant some gravitas, the focus is entirely upon the art and the social visit. There is no time for reflection and the death comes to seem incidental to the true story, which is just a visit to a friend. This flip dismissal of the death serves to demonstrate the mobility of the speaker, who restlessly ploughs through historical detours, only to continue on the story of Gertrude Stein. Similarly, when the Van Vechtens separate, Gertrude Stein finds herself on the end of an unwelcome conversation. Alice reports that 'Mrs Van Vechten told the story of the tragedy of her married life but Gertrude Stein was not particularly interested' (Stein 2001: 148). Entirely without empathy or emotional identification, Stein is positioned as indifferent to suffering. She also appears motivated by that which is of 'interest'; the pain and suffering of others may well exist, but it is neither dynamic nor engaging. This dismissal of particularly heavy emotion means that Gertrude Stein continues lightly through the text, juxtaposing her particular agenda with the quickly forgotten incidents around her. Once more, this reiterates a sense of mobility, where neither Gertrude Stein nor Alice as narrator want to get mired in the emotional difficulty of others. While light gossip is fine and even enjoyable, the earnest or miserable stories of others are wholly unwelcome.

Lifting Belly is also concerned with temporality and the way in which plays with tenses can create a sort of indefinite continuity that facilitates movement and rapidity. The text is written in the present continuous, which Stein defined as 'one thing and beginning again and again is another thing. These are both things. And then there is using everything' (2004c: 25). As opposed to locating this particular temporality in relation to the other tenses, Stein defines it as multiple beginnings and agains. This suggests both repetition and newness, where a thing might take on different forms through multiple iterations. The using everything suggests that the present continuous is expansive and arbitrary; the material of it can be anything, but the anything will be used productively through the process of beginning and again. Certainly, within *Lifting Belly*, the title term features in almost every line, finding new iterations in the repetition and beginnings, creating a vocabulary of sameness and difference. The present continuous allows for the term to become multiple, realized in different ways, different places, even seeming different in its usage. The 'using everything' associated with the present continuous seems particularly important for the text, where the poem expands such that it has capacity for significant tangents, deviations and differences. The tangents cannot be understood in the same way as *Autobiography*, because there is no clear narrative nor intention for the text. Rather, these deviations and reorientations exist between the lines themselves, which sometimes appear in strange juxtaposition or contrast. Importantly, *Lifting Belly* has been read as a lesbian love poem, fixated on the act of sex between two women, particularly Toklas and Stein herself (Mark 1995). The text, including much of its unique vocabulary related to making cows come out, and Ceasar, is decoded as detailing orgasms and the pleasure that can be derived from pleasuring someone else. This interpretation of the text very much supports the butch and femme binary I have discussed previously, in which the masculinity of the former is understood through its relation with the latter. The ability to please and pleasure, as well as the dexterity with which the text moves, suggests the nimble tongue of flippancy in both a textual and sexual way.

However, the term *lifting belly* itself is incorporated into a multiplicity of phrases, many of which do not directly correlate to a secret amorous code devised by Toklas and Stein. The term is buried alongside numerous names, seemingly condensed anecdotes and unexpected or incompatible phrases, none of which can be easily reduced to sexual innuendo. On account of the beginnings, agains and everythings of the writing, *Lifting Belly* seems both indefinite and continuous, maintaining the same mobility throughout until the poem comes to an end. There is no moderation and no sense of pause, in spite of the divided sections, but rather a rapidity that comes with the renewal and repetition. *Lifting Belly* does not become turgid but creates a range of reimaginings and reconfigurations, all of which contribute to the flippant mobility of the writing. Similar to *Autobiography*, *Lifting Belly* includes a host of characters but they are configured in an entirely different way, incorporated into the text without elucidation or anecdote. Instead, they sit as unknown signifiers, contributing almost purely to the movement of the text. In Section II of the book, Stein writes:

Lifting belly.
Lifting belly. Splendid.
Jack Johnson Henry.
Henry is his name sir.

> Jack Johnson Henry is an especially eloquent curtain.
> We see a splendid force in mirrors.
>
> (Stein 1995: 18)

Jack Johnson Henry intrudes on the text for three lines before he disappears as suddenly as he entered. There seems to be no relationship between the 'Splendid' that precedes his arrival, which is separated with both a full stop and a line break. Within the third line of his presence, Jack Johnson Henry becomes subordinate to a curtain, where the proper name is replaced by the especial eloquence of the drapes. The relationship between the name and the domestic item is unclear; it is impossible to know whether this is a form of code or a play with the domestic items and acts of naming. It is possible it could be both, or simply, a quick movement of observation that leads from one concept into another. The use of 'sir' within the fourth line suggests a dialogue, in which the identity of Jack Johnson Henry is a discussion point between a sir and unknown speaker. That said, the lack of capitalization places the sir as less important than the name invoked, as well as less formal. Stein shifts from Jack Johnson Henry to mirrors. This could relate to domestic Henry and the curtain, or in fact it could relate to the following line, which reads 'Angry we are not angry' (Stein 1995: 18). Once more, however, the emphasis of the full stop and line break suggests an individuality to the single line, which is not united with its precedent, nor follower. In similar use of the full name, Stein writes later in the text:

> Think of it.
> Lifting belly in the mind.
> The Honorable Graham Murray.
> My honorable Graham Murray.
> What can I say.
>
> (Stein 1995: 38)

Once more, the name exists within the text without elucidation or purpose. Rather it comprises part of the mobility of the writing, in which the repetition of the proper noun allows for a sense of play and reimagining to come to the fore. It is also significant that the proper nouns deviate from the process of 'lifting belly'. The proper nouns are not linked to the key term of the text as a whole, and as such, they stylistically seem like deviations from the focus of the writing. Nonetheless, they experience the same treatment as the title term, both abused and caressed by Stein such that they become part of the play, repetitions and beginnings.

The use of proper nouns is not dissimilar to the way that pronouns operate throughout the poem. There is a consistent use of 'I' and 'you', which suggests either a second-person addressee or the use of the second person as the object of discussion. However, there is also a continued use of gendered pronouns, none of which are made legible as a specific person. They are instead floating signifiers, unlocated and unspecified within the text as a whole. For example, Stein writes:

> No in respect to the woman.
> Can you say we meant to send her away.
> Lifting belly is so orderly.
> She makes no mistake.
> She does not indeed.
> Lifting belly heroically.
> Can you think of that.
> Can you guess what I mean.
>
> (Stein 1995: 36)

In spite of the structure, including full stops and line breaks, it would be possible to read this fragment of the text as coherently relating to one particular woman. The first line invokes 'the woman', which is a non-specific signifier as compared to the use of the proper names. As the text progresses, this single female identity is queered through the reintroduction of the term 'lifting belly'. While the first two lines introduce the woman, then attempt her dismissal, 'Lifting belly' seems to reorientate the reader back to the key aspect of the text; the act concerned with both newness and repetition. The writing then returns to an indeterminate 'she', but it is possible that this is a different 'she'. Is she the one lifting belly in an orderly fashion or is it the speaker referring to herself in third person? These questions raise some difficulties for the poem. It could be that lifting belly is an act accessible and open to everyone, just as it could be the case that every second- and third-person reference throughout the poem is an example of the speaker referring to herself. It is these very tensions that lend the text an openness and instability. After the two lines referring to the indeterminate 'she', the text invokes a heroic 'Lifting belly', before returning to an 'I' and 'you' which have been rendered unstable.

There are also moments within the text in which this invocation of the male pronoun seems to resonate especially with a butch posturing, or butch audacity, as Hammer phrased it. Stein writes:

> He cannot understand women. I can.
> Believe me in this way.
> I can understand the woman.
> Lifting belly carelessly. I do not lift baby carelessly.
> Lifting belly because there is no mistake. I planned to flourish. Of course you do.
> Lifting belly is exacting. You mean exact. I mean exacting. Lifting belly is exacting.
> Can you say see me.
>
> (Stein 1995: 41)

This section opens with an unknown gendered pronoun that could be specific or stand in for a generalized and unspecific male figure. The speaker demonstrates a dominant and confident knowledge of women. The first line differs slightly from the previous sections I have analysed, in that Stein uses two sentences in order to make a direct link between the content, a link that would be rendered more uncertain and disconnected through lineation. The man does not understand women, but the 'I' does. While the lyric speaker cannot be wholly conflated with Stein, it is significant that a lesbian author who included some of her code words for sex into the poem is making a statement of superior understanding for the 'I' over the male-gendered pronoun. 'Women' is not repeated, but 'woman' does occur later within the section, where the speaker suggests a personal and in-knowledge relationship. What follows is a return to 'lifting belly', which at once disrupts the assertion of superior and specific knowledge and moves the speaker into a moment of insinuation. The use of 'baby' here is significant in both that it is a Toklas and Stein code word and that it leads Stein into the repetitions, playful singsong, babe talk that both Ashbery and Perelman critiqued. The section finally moves from women (category), to woman (specific), to baby (potential code), to 'you' and 'I'. It is unclear whether the second-person address is being used to reify the lyric speaker, by which I mean the speaker seems to be referring to themselves as both 'I' and 'you'. Alternatively, it could be a dialogue with an other, a distinction that is ultimately confused and tested further by 'Can you say see me'. This way of writing creates a poem in which the many-gendered pronouns make their way in, disrupting the potentially self-referential or dialogic nature of the second person, breaking down the categories of a set lyric mode.

Caesar also works throughout the text as a continual reference point. It has been claimed that Stein herself was called Caesar on account of her resemblance to a Roman emperor, and so the repetition of the proper noun has been understood as a metonym for the writer herself (Mark 1995). While eliding herself with an emperor of Rome is just another example of the butch swagger, the multiplicity created through the term is also reminiscent of the camp tenet that things should be rendered what-they-are-not. Ceasar is not always authoritative but a continued shifting presence, in which the autobiographical investments of the reader are challenged and reconfigured throughout. Stein's use of Caesar moves between the singular and the plural, which undoes the concept that in each usage it might be a stand-in for the writer herself. In Part II of the poem, for example, Stein writes 'Lifting Belly is so round./Big Caesars./Two Caesars./Little seize her' (Stein 1995: 24). The plurality of the Caesars suggests that this does not refer directly to a person or character, and the homonym 'seize her' seems to conflate the proper noun with the action itself, such that the terms are not quite interchangeable but certainly related. Later in the poem, Stein writes:

> I wish a seat and Caesar.
> Caesar is plural.
> I can think.
> And so can I.
> And argue.
> Oh yes you see.
> What I see.
> You see me.
>
> (Stein 1995: 28)

In spite of the consistency of structure, including line breaks and full stops, this section uses repeated vocabulary in order to create links and connections. The use of the conjunction 'And' also forges relationality where the structure and punctuation might suggest otherwise. Here, the 'I' even appears to become multiple, where in one iteration it can think and in another iteration it too can think. This is extended through into the 'you', which could be the speaker referring to herself in second person, or alternatively invoking an unknown second person, or even extending the content of the poem out to the reader. The continued use of the second person throughout this text could be read as both introspective and consciously opening the space of the poem for the reader; it sits within the tensions outlined in the opening paragraphs of this chapter about the spaces for access within Stein's writing. Caesars, too, opens up possibilities through its different iterations: 'Lifting belly is my joy./What did I tell Caesars./That I recognised them' and 'Lifting belly permanently./What did the Caesars./What did they all say' (Stein 1995: 29). This movement and play ensures that Caesar cannot be encoded as one thing, whether it is associated with thoughts and processes of seeing, or recognition and joy, or speech acts. These contrasts between the signifier, and its context demonstrates how the term cannot be reduced to one single concept nor can it be considered to denote a coherent identity. While it might be self-referential on occasion, there are other moments where it has no clear relationship with the author of the text itself.

In her introduction to The Naiad Press' edition of *Lifting Belly*, Rebecca Mark writes that 'Alice made delicious Caesar salads. Gertrude ate them', then goes on to elucidate further:

> Think of Caesar not only as a general, as Gertrude, as a salad, as cease her, seize her, sees her, and finally as seizure, a tremor during sex, an orgasm. If Caesar is all of these, then it is all at once, burning and heating, the death and the renewal, the ceasing and the seizure, the pleasure.
>
> (Mark 1995: xxxii)

It is important to note that the multiplicity arising from Mark's interpretation of the text is derived from the word play and rhyme, both aspects of Stein's writing dismissed by Ashbery and Perelman as childish or too feminine. Mark makes it evident that the Caesar can contain multiples that are at once sex, visibility, action, militarism, self-referentiality and slightly more obscurely salads. It is my contention that this particular reading draws attention to the problematic binary approaches to Stein's writing, as well as the possible benefits of the conjunction of butch and camp. In attempting to attribute Stein with a sophisticated and queer code, Mark suggests to her reader that the text might hinge, among other things, on the salad that Stein liked Toklas to make. Although this is suited to my purposes of flippancy, in which a salad and an emperor of the same name receive equal treatment, it does suggest a need to read too much into Stein's own life in order to decipher an obscure text. However, in rejecting this reading entirely, the reader would not move through the compelling and sometimes breathless allusions to sex and desire; it is interesting to become dizzy among the self-conscious, singular and multiple 'I' in a series of moves we could also attribute to the author's presence within the text itself. The Caesar aspect of the text, as well as Mark's reading, also typifies the combination of the butch camp within Stein's writing. There is a tonal butch swagger throughout, in which the force of personality propels the reader through the text that sometimes needs to be decoded and at other times does not. While it is impossible to tell which sections warrant or are intended to be decoded, the reader can appreciate the pure style of the work, found in the babyish appreciation and quick movement of sounds. This pure style is camp, in which the butch tonality and confident mobility of the writing create a lightness of foot that can be read as a pure enjoyment of the nouns. It is in this way that Stein's poems become a vocabulary, with the reader fluctuating between trying to create autobiographical links and then purely appreciating the caressing of the nouns within the text of the poem itself.

'Husband obey your wife': Performances and performativity

As with the camp and butch dynamic, both texts have a complicated relationship with both performativity and performance. It could be argued that Stein's writing is inherently performative, conveying a series of plays in which her treatment of the noun is very deliberate. Given her writing on prose and poetry, Stein had clear ideas surrounding the genres, both of which are realized through sentences, paragraphs, lines and stanzas. *Lifting Belly* and *Autobiography* are performative not purely in the textual sense but also in regard to gender and sexuality. It is these aspects of identity that are fundamental to my queer poetics of flippancy, in which unbecoming levity is a means of emancipation and deconstruction. In 'Poetry and Grammar', Stein writes that 'a noun is a name of anything, why after a thing is named write about it. A name is adequate or it is not. If it is adequate then why go on calling it, if it is not then calling it by its name does no good' (Stein 2004a: 123). If something has been named, then it is no longer necessary to write about it. In spite of Stein's call for nouns to be treated in a very mobile, playful and sometimes violent way, here, 'a name is adequate or it is not'. If the name suffices, then there is no reason to repeat it, and if it is not adequate then the proper noun should not be repeated; the failure can be realized in a simple iteration, as opposed to through multiple engagements. This statement seems directly to counter the methodology in both *Lifting Belly* and *Autobiography*. In the former, the term 'lifting belly' dominates the text; it is named, and named again, as if the whole work is reliant on its presence, disappearance and return. The term Stein has coined is clearly inadequate, but Stein continues to write the name, even though it would seem to do no good. The same could be said of the way in which 'Gertrude Stein' is repeated in its totality within *Autobiography*. In 'I Am Not Who "I" Pretend to Be: *The Autobiography of Alice B. Toklas* and Its Photographic Frontispiece', Corrine Andersen writes that 'Toklas' incessant repetition of the name "Getrude Stein" places such an emphasis on the exterior that it teeters on the edge of farce' (2005: 32). That said, in 'Poetry and Grammar', Stein writes that 'actual given names of people are more lively than nouns ... there is at least the element of choice even the element of change' (2004a: 127).

Imbuing the proper name with greater possibility than the simple noun, she considers the possibility of autonomy and change, both of which could be realized through the performative repetition. It is possible, then, that the repetition of *The Autobiography of Alice B. Toklas* is recognizing both the inadequacy of the name and the more positive possibilities for change and development. Thus, repetition of the name foregrounds Stein, heightening her importance, it also enacts the inadequacy of the name when it comes to capturing the subject. In 'Lifting Bellies, Filling Petunias, and Making Meanings through Trans-Poetic Authors', Susan Holbrook writes:

> Amidst Stein's subjection of naming to the troubling effects of indirect treatment, error, and proliferating definitions, we find the recurrent thematization of the trouble with names. The complexity of the poet's stance can be attributed to the fact that the declaration and the obfuscation of names can contribute to both liberatory and regulatory ideals.
>
> (1999: 762)

While Stein clearly outlines an approach to the use of nouns in 'Poetry and Grammar', *Lifting Belly* and *Autobiography* play with the trouble that accompanies the processes of naming while celebrating the possibilities contained within obfuscation and declaration.

As I have stated previously, *Lifting Belly* has been interpreted as a sex poem, in which lesbian eroticism is celebrated. The idea of sex immediately invokes questions around performance and the act, which are enhanced by the figure of Caesar being presented as multiple. The use of random gendered pronouns, and proper names, as well as tangents and deviations, none of which seem to relate to sex, conveys a performative deviance, in which the juxtapositions are extremely pronounced through the line breaks and full stops. These sudden and dizzying shifts in focus, as well as the approach to gender throughout the text, engages problematically with the concepts of gender performativity as outlined by Butler. The clear separation and delineation of the 'he' and 'she' demonstrates that Stein is not attempting to undo any understanding that we might have of the separate sexes and genders. Although the pronouns are not necessarily accompanied with descriptions that elucidate and clarify, their separateness does little to blur the clear categories of sex. That said, however, Stein does challenge gender and sex in different ways within the text itself, destabilizing the associations of masculinity, and even maleness, with a male-identified body. Through introducing concepts of the husband and wife, Stein is able to posit same-sex relationality that engages with our heterosexist assumption, while also undermining it. She writes:

> Do believe me when I incline.
> You mean obey.
> I mean obey.
> Obey me.
> Husband obey your wife.
> Lifting belly is so dear to me.
>
> (Stein 1995: 53)

The repetition of 'obey' creates a relationship between four of the lines. Again, the interplay between the 'I' and 'you' is difficult to define. It could be a first person addressing a second person or the speaker switching between the 'I' and the 'you' as modes of self-reference. That the 'I' echoes 'you' with exactly the same statement creates a sense of sameness between the two; sharing the language almost makes them interchangeable with one another. The imperative nature of 'obey me' could clarify the first- and second-person position further, wherein the 'I' takes ultimate dominance over the 'you' in spite of their shared vocabulary. Alternatively, 'obey me' could work as the confluence of the 'I' and 'you', so that as opposed to separable entities, they are united through this self-referential single imperative. This is extended into 'Husband obey your wife'. While we might assume that the 'I' of the text, if it is sometimes Stein and sometimes not, would identify with the more masculine role, here it seems almost elided with the role of the wife. If 'obey me' and 'husband obey your wife' are to be understood as constructed in the same way, then it could be assumed that the me is demanding that their husband obey them. Thus, the 'I' within this instance is assuming a more female role. However, the interplay and interchangeability of the 'you' and 'I', in conjunction with the genderless 'me', suggest that the relationship with husband and wife might be more complex. In fact, the marital relationship might not operate through a heterosexual binary. The movement between the first and second person, as well as the mirroring dialogic nature of the text, suggests that the gendered roles have become untethered from a clearly male or female body. Instead, they are tied to an ever shifting and reorientating 'you' and 'I', both of which remain indeterminate throughout the text.

> Stein returns to the theme of husbands two pages later, writing:
> Lifting belly is so good.
> Little husband would.
> Be as good.
> If he could.
> This was said.

> We know how to differ.
> From that.
> Certainly.
> Now we say.
> Little hubbie is good.

(Stein 1995: 55–56)

The diminutive use of 'little' in relation to the husband could be read in a number of ways. It could feminize the 'husband' to suggest a non-male husband; it could be used as a means by which to reduce the male figure, but it could also be a form of intimacy, with 'little' reading as endearment. In the phrases above, the rhyme ensures a sense of continuity, with the rhyming good, would and could suggesting a range of conditionals and possibilities. Again, it is difficult not to read this section of the work as a questioning of heterosexuality, where structure and content coalesce to critique a husband who wishes he was as good as two women. Similarly, if within the poem as the whole, this husband figure is read as non-male, this extract could be interpreted as a dismantling of gendered and sex understandings. The line 'we know how to differ', embedded among the repetitions of husband and good, seems to open the space of the poem and the definition of gendered roles. Having invoked this difference, Stein returns to the husband who has been resolved, in this instance as a 'good' 'hubbie'. Here, the figure becomes rehabilitated within an intimate endearment, finding resolution through the difference posited by the speaker of the poem. The togetherness of this section allows for the husband to become different and better, with the figure being deconstructed through inadequacy, sustained through difference and restored by the 'we'.

In *Lifting Belly*, the 'I' is mutable, with the first person dissolving into the second on some occasions and on others being echoed by the you. At times the addressor and the addressee seem to collapse together, through either switching positions or invoking the first-personal plural, which is capacious enough to hold both the 'I' and 'you', as well as the unidentified 'he' and 'she's' of the poem. This movement of the subject through first, second and third person is echoed in the speaker's approach to gender categories. Heternormativity is called into question throughout by the shifting and arbitrary nature of gender within the work. The pronouns seem to have little relation to the proper names and are never elucidated such that they become symbolic of femaleness or maleness. This is clearly extended through Stein's use of the husband and wife, roles which are determined through a particular socially constructed ceremony, as opposed to any essentialist kind of identity. By offering a version of husband that seems to shift beyond its binary with wife, as well as its gendering as male, Stein untethers the figure from male biology, emphasizing instead the relationality and contingency of the term. As such, the husband can obey the wife without a crisis of power reversal, in the same way that the you and I can echo one another in their stating of 'obey' without bringing the poem to a tension of authority. That the good little Hubbie finally emerges after difference has been acknowledged seems to demonstrate that the role can be opened beyond its category affiliations. While the category of husband in many ways remains intact, those who are able to inhabit it become more diverse and divergent. This broadens and widens the understanding of the roles within a relationship, suggesting that husband does not need to be a male and dominant force within a marriage, but rather one who recognizes their relationality with a declared (not necessarily legal) wife, where both might be of the same sex and gender.

A number of these performative tensions also play out in *Autobiography* where Stein takes on the position of her lover in order to narrate her own life. As Carolyn A. Barros writes, 'Alice is not "standing in" for Gertrude; Gertrude is making Alice perform Gertrude' (1999: 180). This positions the text as working at two levels of performance, in which Alice the narrator is performing Gertrude's life for the sake of the reader at the same time that Stein the author is performing as Alice the narrator. The whole book is written from the perspective of Alice until the final pages, in which the narrator reveals: 'About six weeks ago Gertrude Stein said, it does not look to me as if you were ever going to write that autobiography. You know what I am going to do. I am going to write it for you. I am going to write it as simply as Defoe did the autobiography of Robinson Crusoe. And she has and this is it' (2001: 272). The big reveal at the end of the text allows Stein to claim her rightful position as author of the autobiography, which instead of focusing on the life of Alice, as we might expect, is actually concerned with the performance of Gertrude Stein. The 'autobiography' of the person in the title has been written by someone else and therefore is disqualified from the genre. It is not the case, however, that Stein has written a biography of Toklas through the guise of autobiography, but rather has written an autobiography of herself through the performance of Alice writing an autobiography, which actually reads more like a biography of Gertrude Stein. As Barbara Will writes, 'hyperbolic, excessive, and queer, *The Autobiography of Alice B. Toklas* is in the end nothing if not a performance, an enactment of authority and all its privileges which in its excessive, theatricalization is also a subversive undoing of both authority and identity' (2000: 139). The focus on Gertrude Stein throughout the text undermines our general understanding of the genre, in which Alice is neither the central figure nor the author, even while she might be the narrator. She is not even the primary voice, but rather a mouthpiece for a domestic life in which Stein's brilliance dominates. It is also problematic that Stein's big reveal elides her own text with a work of fiction. In drawing parallels with Defoe's writing, Stein undoes the genre category of autobiography even further; not only is our subject of the book out of focus, the narrator different to the author, but the writing itself finds the greatest parallel in a fictional account of a shipwrecked man. Stein, then, is also performing the concept of autobiography to us, all the while ensuring that the audience is well aware of the framework for performance. The act is only successful because the reader can recognize it has been done well.

Riley suggests that flippancy is an inability to commit, or indeed, the inability to sustain commitment to a particular set of actions or modes of behaviour. Even while she encourages 'trying it on', she argues that to put irony on or off at will might appear to be flippant and wilful. Here, Stein is trying it on in two senses; she is donning Alice as an identity to perform herself, and she is testing the reader to see how far she is able to sustain the ruse. However, at the end of the text, the author is no longer able to sustain the façade of Alice, choosing ultimately to reveal herself. Interestingly, there is no shift in register and voice, but rather the reveal is delivered as if Alice is still the narrator. As such, the flippancy of the shift, the 'taking it off', is highlighted further. Stein desires to continue the performance, even though she wants to draw the reader's attention to the ruse that has allowed such a performance to take place. It is important to recognize that this ruse of identity is already very apparent to the contemporary reader. In the first edition of the text, Stein went to great lengths to conceal her identity as true author. She insisted that her name be absent from the front cover, spine and title page. The cover image, while predominantly of Stein, had Alice standing hesitantly in the doorway and was captioned 'Alice B. Toklas at the door, photography by Man Ray' (Andersen 2005: 26). The first readers of *Autobiography*, then, would be surprised by the reveal at the end. However, once Stein's book became increasingly famous, with reviews and a planned book tour of America, it was clear to the potential readership who the true author was. As such, only a select number of first readers would encounter the text without the knowledge of Stein's authorship. Other readers, both those in the know and those reading more contemporary editions with Stein's name on the cover, are asked to delight in the act from the very first page.

Significantly then, whether determining the difference between narrator and author at the end or beginning of the text, the reader is asked to recognize that Stein is performing an almost drag act of Alice B. Toklas. Understanding the work through a lens of drag undoes how the reader might understand the relationship between gender and sex, even within same-sex relationships, and makes a case for the combination of butch and camp. If, as Halberstam claims, camp is to some extent always linked to the performance of femininity, then Stein dons a façade of femininity that would not usually be associated with her as a writer or woman. The very fact of the performance, particularly the performance of Alice's femininity, makes Stein's comparative butchness even more pronounced. However, Stein also addresses the butch as something other than woman-identified-woman when she broaches the subject of wives and geniuses. In 'My Arrival in Paris', Alice claims:

> Before I decided to write this book my twenty-five years with Gertrude Stein, I have often said that I would write, The wives of geniuses I have sat with. I have sat with so many. I have sat with wives who were not wives, of geniuses who were real geniuses. I have sat with real wives of geniuses, who were not real geniuses. I have sat with real wives of geniuses, or near geniuses, of would be geniuses, in short I have sat very often and very long with many wives and wives of many geniuses.
>
> (Stein 2001: 18)

The category of genius is established early within *Autobiography*, with Alice claiming that she has only met three in her life, one of whom is Gertrude Stein. This more expansive passage, however, serves to outline the kinds of relationships she maintained with the geniuses and the women who accompanied them. Throughout the text, it is Alice and not Gertrude Stein who demarcates this particular category for the readership, seeming to decide who is able to reside within it. The category is made possible by not only those who occupy it but those who sit beyond it, principally, the wives who sit with Alice. In spite of this quite clear binary of wives and their geniuses, the way in which Alice describes the multiple couples she has encountered undoes the clarity of differentiation. Most important is that geniuses and their wives create an alternative to the gender binary – it is not husbands and wives, thus undermining the heteronormative union. Much as *Lifting Belly* complicates the role of the husband, placing it alongside difference made recognizable through two women, *Autobiography* positions Gertrude Stein and Alice as a genius and a wife. Although Alice herself is not, and cannot be, a wife, she inhabits the same space as the wives, which by extension makes her appear to occupy the same category. More important is that Alice has sat with wives who are not wives and wives who are real wives, who in spite of their differences are all understood through the same names and terms. In this way, the category of wife is exploded, such that it incorporates the 'real wives' and the 'not wives', flippantly approaching an identity that is realized through a union as opposed to essentiality. The category of wife is both itself, and its negation, and Alice.

This kind of explosion also operates in exactly the same way for Gertrude Stein. While the wives are assumed to be female, the geniuses cannot be assumed as male by virtue of her existing within the category. Groupings of men are disbanded in favour of a new demarcation of genius, which transcends gender boundaries, and also undoes the relationality of husband and wife, allowing for same-sex pairings. The interplay here teases out concepts of masculinity, genius, maleness, partnerships and the instability of the categories that contain such descriptors. Arguably, Stein's butchness is part of her access to the category of genius, while Alice's femme role allows her to sit with the wives. However, both the wives and geniuses are established as what they are not, which not only makes light of the very terms themselves but resonates with both definitions for camp and butch. The butch is known when it is seen, and the camp delights in things appearing as they are not. The geniuses Alice describes are real, not real, near and would be, but all still fall under the particular genius taxonomy. This kind of definition and pairing makes space for failure, in which the failure to be a wife and the failure to be a genius can nonetheless coalesce under categories of wife and genius. This also demonstrates that there are perhaps no better words for what Stein is attempting to articulate through Alice, and as such, the names themselves, while deployed, must be recognized as insufficient. Will writes that 'if the position of "genius" (like that of "wife") can be theatricalized, camped up, parodied, then it is no longer essential, natural or fixed in a hierarchy of dominancy and exclusion'(Will 2000: 146). Here, the performance, the theatre and the camping Stein effects through the drag-act perceptions of Alice question natural assumptions, working against any essentialism that might be associated with men and women. She also undoes the rigidity of socially constructed categories, such as the male and female, so that genius and wife become the alternative. As well as the alternative, they are also categories of failure, encompassing the many, a number of which do not belong.

Conclusion

In this chapter, I have made a case for Stein's two texts *Lifting Belly* and *The Autobiography of Alice B. Toklas* foregrounding the butch camp. Stein allows for Alice B. Toklas to enter both texts, realized at times in the 'you' of *Lifting Belly* and as the central narrator of *Autobiography*. Through bringing in this feminine presence, Stein allows for the femme positioning of Alice to consolidate herself as butch. In both texts, she creates a robust masculinity, one that resonates more with Halberstam's understanding of the relationship between sex and gender presentation. Stein's masculinity is of her own making, not reliant on male precursors but rather configured through the way in which she relates to Alice and the way in which she experiments with writing. Stein also conflates herself with male historical figures of great authority, such as Caesar, creating a role of dominance and leadership for herself that can be tried on at will, but also changed, resituated and made multiple. Similarly, in *The Autobiography of Alice B. Toklas*, Stein creates a category of genius for her to inhabit. This separates her out from the wives, and by extension female counterparts, offering up space in which she as a woman can become something other. This other is not purely freeing in relation to gender identity but also freeing in terms of her capacity of brilliance, introducing a sense of self-confidence that is associated with the butch swagger. Stein's work combines this butchness with a certain amount of camp, which might explain why camp figures such as O'Hara and Warhol were so drawn to her as both an icon and a writer. While Stein's camp could sometimes be seen as naïve, my focus here has been on the ways in which the two texts intentionally perform camp. In their fast movement, with their focus on styles, and the play with things-as-what-they-are-not, both the long poem and autobiography are playful in the way that Sontag and Cleto outline. Through focusing on a deliberate dethroning of the serious, I have attributed Stein's camp with the same level of autonomy as her butchness. Both are selected and combined such that they emerge deliberately throughout the texts.

The butch and camp feed into the way in which personality drives the texts. As Setina suggested, Stein had some anxiety that her personality ensured the success of her work. As such, the writing cannot stand divorced from Stein the writer if they are to have full impact. While I have not analysed this in relation to Stein's whole body of work, both *Lifting Belly* and *Autobiography* have a problematic relationship with Stein as a woman, given that both are reliant on aspects of her life and knowledge of her. However, this is not to suggest that the texts are any less experimental as a result of this. Rather, they shift our focus somewhat such that we are able to explore the instability Stein brings to identity and sex through her emphasis on selfhood and the lyric 'I'. Thus, while Stein's forceful personality could be read in the mobility of the writing, the tone and the certainty, such a reading does not undo that the texts themselves are playful and experimental. For this reason it is impossible to adopt one position in the binary reading of Stein's work, as all play and symbol or all embedded code. Both *Lifting Belly* and *Autobiography* shift between these two modes of writing to create a continual sense of movement. This also ensures that selfhood, personhood and identity are also able to shift, such that there is a fluidity among categories that would not otherwise be facilitated.

While the juxtapositions of the butch and camp speak to the poetics of flippancy, they are also realized in numerous ways through both texts. The nimble tongue and quick movement are particularly relevant to Stein's very mobile writing. *Autobiography* is characterized by gossip and digression, bringing an unexpected lightness to Modernist Paris. Alice, as a narrator, also revels in digression, doubling back on herself and following tangential stories that do not contribute to the lines she purports to be following. This supports the sense of movement within the text, where the narrator seems to move restlessly among numerous ideas, even while her central focus remains Gertrude Stein. The same poetics are easily traced through *Lifting Belly*, where the I and you shift and change throughout a text that makes unclear references to proper names while also drawing on third-person pronouns. The proper nouns bring a sense of dismissal and instability to the text, where they enter and exit easily, among the continual return to the act of lifting belly. The small lines and regular breaks, as well as the syntax of the poem, continues a sense of mobility, with the present continuous creating a rapid movement that could be understood as the speedy workings of the nimble tongue. The poetics of flippancy and butch camp are all best realized through the approach to wives and husbands in *Autobiography* and *Lifting Belly*. Stein takes a playful approach to the two terms, undoing their typical association with the union of marriage. The fact that she chooses to focus on the husband and wife also usefully counters any essentialism that might be associated with gender and sex. That husband and wife might apply to her and Alice demonstrates that each role is not necessarily tied to a heteronormative and state-sanctioned union nor the expected man and woman. Through focusing on these particular roles, Stein moves our expectations from the gendered into the way in which a couple might relate to one another. This approach to the union is flippant, in that it treats marriage lightly, opening it up to those who might not otherwise have access to such positions. This is extended through a flippancy in regard to identity. Stein uses husband and wife to denote wide and varying categories, categories which are often not inhabited by either husbands or wives. The lightness with which Stein approaches the relationship of the people around her, as well as her own relationship, is campy, allowing for people to be-what-they-are-not, while exploding typically gendered categories. This same campness is married perfectly with butchness in *Lifting Belly*, when the husband appears to learn lessons from two women, while simultaneously being untethered from typical expectations of masculinity through the use of 'little'.

3

'There's Nothing Metaphysical about It': Frank O'Hara's Flippant Manifesto and the Poetry of Tight Trousers

At Frank O'Hara's funeral, Larry Rivers stormed to the front of the collected crowd to speak. He had anticipated that O'Hara would be the first among their friendship group to die; the poet did 'too much living, which would drain away his energy and his will to live' (Gooch 1993: 9). Rivers went on to describe O'Hara as a friend who 'never let me off the hook. He never allowed me to be lazy. His talk, his interests, his poetry, his life was a theatre in which I saw what human beings are *really* like. He was a dream of contradictions' (Gooch 1993: 10). The intensity with which Rivers eulogized his dead friend foregrounds some of the issues at the heart of O'Hara's scholarship; how is it possible to comment or offer any kind of sustained critique without becoming derailed by the poet's compelling, personal style? Throughout the expansive body of the poet's work, there is a clear indebtedness to the social, with poems and essays emerging directly out of conversation and encounter. This formed a poetics at once animate and lively, and in the rare moments where solitude is allowed in, introspective and circumspect. The temptation for anecdote can sometimes usurp the seriousness with which O'Hara's poetry took shape. This particular problematic is especially pronounced in scholarship that prioritizes and celebrates O'Hara's levity and lightness; such emphasis could easily be sidetracked into a digressive relaying of the poet's life, focusing on the moments that have become almost legendary following his death.

In *Frank O'Hara Now*, Robert Hampson and Will Montgomery warn that writing on the poet can often fail to 'free itself from anecdote and reminiscence, as if the chatty, witty voice that speaks in many of O'Hara's best-known poems defined the writings' intellectual horizons' (2010: 2). While Hampson and Montgomery outline a necessary recuperation for the serious O'Hara, their work raises a difficulty for queer troublemaking and the poetics of flippancy. Given that the poet himself was prone to conflate his life with the poems, commenting in a 'Statement for Paterson Society' that 'it's a pretty depressing day, you must admit, when you feel you relate more importantly to poetry than to life' (1975: 114), it seems that the text and the world beyond it were often treated as interchangeable, even sometimes in a conflicted dialogue with one another, in which the beauty and immediacy of both are in competition. Given that O'Hara invested in poetry to this extent, it seems necessary to approach his writing with an eye to the anecdotal and digressive, while focusing above all on the texts themselves. This was well demonstrated at the fifty-year anniversary event for O'Hara's death, hosted at the ICA gallery in the UK, aptly titled 'O'Hara and Friends'. There, the panel papers were academically rigorous, considering the different critical facets of O'Hara's work, while the breaks and evening poetry reading were characterized by fond reminiscences, all from people who had never met the poet himself. It is the immediacy of O'Hara's work and the aliveness of anecdotes about the poet that bestow a feeling of intimacy, even upon a readership within a totally different century and country.

How, then, to walk that tender and troubling line between friendship, eulogizing, loving and writing critically? And how, if at all possible, can it be done with the poet's own distinctive walk, on the balls of the feet, with the poise of a dancer? Montgomery and Hampson write that 'O'Hara's cheerfulness is the cheerfulness of one who has encountered and embraced suffering. The ready wit often conceals doubt and uncertainty' (2010: 4). In this particular work, it is not my aim to efface suffering or in fact to propose that the cheerfulness is one-dimensional in its realization. Instead, it is necessary to recognize the complex relationship between levity and flippancy and the seriousness that might motivate such a political strategy. 'What if the writing is, in other words, rather more strenuous in its ambition than O'Hara's cultivated flippancy sometimes suggests' (2010: 3) seems to be one of the key questions driving Hampson and Montgomery's work on *Frank O'Hara Now*. While I agree with both critics, this particular work will not tease out the seriousness from a cultivated flippancy. Rather, it will consider the way in which such a performance of lightness might in fact reveal a particular heavy politics, one which is tied to the poet's identity within a specific social and cultural context. Flippancy can itself be a strenuous ambition; maintaining a lightness is not natural but rather an intentional affected air that might ultimately emerge from doubt and uncertainty. That cheerfulness can coexist with suffering, and that flippancy might serve as a form of seriousness, creates a troubling affective approach to the poet's work. This challenging coexistence suggests that flippancy is a form of ambition, one that tests the sanctified space of the poem.

In order to address the relationship between the flippant readiness of wit and a greater seriousness underlying the poems themselves, I will approach O'Hara's writing through 'Personism: A Manifesto'. Originally written for Donald Allen's *New American Poetry*, 'Personism' was a tongue-in-cheek poetic statement that refuses to take the production of poetry seriously. The work rejected dogma and resisted mythologizing both poetry and the poet, resulting in a piece that practices a light and humorous resistance to the more bombastic and serious critical writing emerging from Olson and the Black Mountain School. The tone, movement, playfulness and levity of the piece serves to establish O'Hara's work as wholly distinct from a number of poetic groups writing within the same time frame; he seems to lack the genuine feeling of the confessionals, the academic seriousness of the Black Mountain School and the rampant masculinity of some of the Beat Poets. Analysing this chattering figure within 'Personism: A Manifesto', I will consider aspects of this identity and how they create a lighter and flippant poetics. Celebrating an irreverent poetics emerging from the manifesto, this chapter will focus on the insouciant and sociable O'Hara, in which what might seem like a camp form of style is actual queering, or troubling, of traditional social connections and poetry itself.

'Categorically the most difficult relationship': Subverting the manifesto

O'Hara tells his readers to expect everything of 'Personism', even though we won't get it: 'it's too new, too vital a movement to promise anything' (1995a: 499). It is not purely that the movement itself is too novel for adherents to be able to follow it properly but that Personism itself exudes an energy and vitality that ensures its restlessness. If 'Personism' as a category is still too vital to fulfil its promises, then the movement becomes one which is almost impossible to follow, something which is also true of the manifesto document itself. In 'Stepping Out with Frank O'Hara', David Herd writes that 'O'Hara has stolen the show and quite likely what you're experiencing already is yearning … To follow it [the manifesto], in the name of commentary, is to sound cumbersome. And yet, nonchalance is part of the allure, and anyway the thinking of "Personism" is too quick to let it go' (2010: 70). Here, Herd perfectly outlines the problematic of addressing O'Hara's manifesto within a critical sense. To unpack it neatly and chronologically is to introduce a cumbersome criticality to a piece that is characterized by its movement and elusiveness. Commentary, thus, becomes a form of yearning in which the original text far outstrips any academic companion, whose pace is rendered a comparatively slow walk. Instead of chasing O'Hara like the armed assailant he notes within the first few sentences of 'Personism: A Manifesto', I want to address the document as a space of possibility, in which tone, collectives, mobility and love become aspects of a flippant political strategy. In *The Promise of Happiness*, Ahmed writes that 'possibility is light in the sense that in possibility one is open to being blown this way or that, to being picked up by what happens, which can include being picked up in a good or bad way' (2010: 280–281). Mimicking the manifesto's own sense of possibility, then, I want this chapter to be open, blown this way and that among the references of O'Hara's work, picked up by the movement of the piece instead of walking in the poet's wake.

O'Hara ends his manifesto with the claim that 'in all modesty, I confess that it may be the death of literature as we all know it' (1995a: 499). In spite of moving the poem from the space of the page to between two people on the telephone, O'Hara's manifesto is far from the death of literature. Instead, his continual invocation of poets and writers throughout demonstrates a total indebtedness to canonical and innovative figures. The text is almost laden with names, although laden seems to suggest a heaviness that the work itself thoroughly refutes, continuing its movements and rapidity in spite of the proliferating writers within. The referents work purely to orientate the movements of the manifesto's speaker, as opposed to offering the reader a more comprehensive and considered approach to the field of literature. The manifesto is not only testament to the fact that O'Hara is well-read but almost demonstrates his willingness to deploy canonical writers and artists as if they are a throwaway comment. Even as O'Hara praises some, such as Hart Crane, William Carlos Williams and Walt Whitman, and seems to deride others, such as Antonin Artaud and Alain Robbe-Grillet, there is an egalitarianism at work in all of the names' cursory treatment. None warrant further attention than their initial use, instead they serve as a reference point from which the speaker can orientate on to a further and more interesting idea. O'Hara moves easily and fluidly between Allen Ginsberg, Vachel Lindsay, Whitman, Williams, Crane, Wallace Stevens, Pierre-Jean de Beranger, Artaud, Robbe-Grillet, Jean Debuffet and LeRoi Jones, with fleeting references to both Keats and Di Chirico. In mentioning these names, O'Hara defies expectation by refusing elucidation, creating a wide and expansive constellation for his own work that is so replete with figures it is almost laughable.

The laughable nature of his references is, in part, a necessary aspect of O'Hara rejecting the manifesto as a form. He opens the manifesto by stating that 'everything is in the poems' (1995a: 498). The manifesto will not, as a result, be a didactic document or even a statement of poetics; if the reader wants to find the latter, all they need to do is turn to the poems themselves. O'Hara reiterates this in his 'Statement for Paterson Society', in which he writes, 'I don't want to make up a lot of prose about something that is perfectly clear in the poems' (1975: 114). O'Hara's emphasis on both 'everything' and 'clarity' being found in the poems suggests that his prose is a deliberate and intentional rejection of both, which forces necessary attention back onto his chosen genre. These are also characteristics that O'Hara goes on to reject in his 'Statement for *New American Poetry*' in which he writes, 'I don't think my experiences are clarified or made beautiful for myself or anyone else, they are just there in whatever form I can find them. What is clear to me in my work is probably obscure to others, and vice versa' (1975: 113). This establishes a more complex relationship with all of O'Hara's writing, where the poems previously identified as clear are also posited as obscure and highly subjective in their beauty. Clarity and clarification are sacrificed in favour of form and style, which allows for a mobile figure to make literary figures, New York, friendship and sex, his animated space of traversal. The desire to evade clarity, as well as a reluctance to proffer a set poetics, is also clear in 'Statement for Paterson Society' where O'Hara writes:

> I ... wrote you about my convictions concerning form, measure, sound, yardage, placement and ear – well, if I went into that thoroughly enough nobody would ever want to read the poems I've already written, they would have been so thoroughly described, and I would have to do everything the opposite in the future to avoid my own boredom, and where would I be?
>
> (1975: 113–114)

Where art manifestos can work as a means of pointing, using prose to gesture to another genre, allowing for it to be explained, unpacked and elucidated, O'Hara rejects such a relationship. 'Personism' and his other statements of poetics resist stating poetics, instead focusing on the way in which his writing can trouble such a linear and basic relationship. By stating, openly, that everything is in the poems, O'Hara establishes an approach to the manifesto that wholly undermines the manifesto form: it might as well not exist. Instead of offering any form of clarification, or indeed any tenets that could be followed by adherents, O'Hara's manifesto is a light-hearted and uncommitted document that in no way tries to establish a literary movement. That O'Hara himself described the work as 'a little diary of my thoughts, after lunch with LeRoi walking back to work, about the poem I turned out to be just about to write' (1975: 114) indicates perhaps that the document has far more in common with O'Hara's own poems than it does a wider context of literary statements and manifestos.

This troubling relationship with the manifesto is further interrogated when O'Hara turns his attention to 'ideas'. He writes, 'I'm not saying that I don't have practically the most lofty ideas of anyone writing today, but what difference does that make?' (1995a: 498). In this sense, the manifesto is clearly outlined as a document that will not make a difference. Ultimately, it is the poetic writing of one individual, as opposed to a significant piece of work that is likely to effect great social change. Irrespective of how lofty his thoughts, O'Hara makes it clear that he does not view them as especially rewarding. Instead, they are an irrelevance to anything wider than his own writing. Through directing a readership to the poems, he is suggesting that a more dynamic relationship will emerge from attention to the writing itself. By contrast, the manifesto which is intended to outline great ideas and modes of thinking is lacking in its purpose and appeal. Through deflating the very fact of ideas, O'Hara ensures that the manifesto lacks a pompous authority that could be associated with the genre as a whole. This very act of undermining concept seems central to O'Hara's writing about readership. The manifesto states:

> But how can you care if anybody gets it, or gets what it means, or if it improves them. Improves them for what? For death? Why hurry them along? Too many poets act like middle-aged mothers trying to get kids to eat too much cooked meat, and potatoes with drippings (tears). I don't give a damn whether they eat or not. Forced feeding leads to excessive thinness.
>
> (1995a: 498)

What the poet is keen to avoid, then, in both introducing high concept and pointing to the elaborate way of thinking, is establishing the poet as unquestioned authority. Why should poetry be easy and in what way can it ever be useful? When the reader finally does get it, if they ever do, how are they meant to wield that information beyond the space of the poem or the space of language? Poetry should not be a work that promises self-improvement, that is its own form of death. Instead, the poem should be optional, a conversation that we can walk away from or a telephone that we put down. It should not be worthy or dense and certainly should not be crafted with any expectation of the reader or hopes for their self-improvement. Instead, works need to avoid the didacticism and intentional directedness of forced feeding, opting for lightness, mobility and an existence untempered by the possibilities of moral instruction.

This is reiterated through O'Hara turning to the cinema. Addressing the American public's relationship to poetry as a whole, he writes 'if they don't need poetry bully for them. I like the movies too' (1995a: 498). While O'Hara claims the inevitability of numerous adherents at the end of his manifesto, it is evident throughout the work that he is not deluded as to how many people are interested in poetry. In fact, the poet does not seem to need people to need poetry. In conflating 'need' with 'poetry', O'Hara seems to suggest that he is different in that he does experience such a need. This is softened somewhat by the fact that he claims to like movies too; he is not so dissimilar from the everyday man, who in not looking to poetry might go to the cinema instead. This is further reiterated when the poet writes that 'only Whitman and Crane and Williams of the American poets, are better than the movies' (1995a: 498). If the choice, then, for poetry reading that can rival the movies is so small, it is almost inevitable that the audience might seek out their gratification within the cinema. O'Hara, as presented within the manifesto, understands such an impulse, even empathizing through his own love of the movies. A number of O'Hara poems make direct reference to the movies, creating a relationship between genres that might otherwise seem at odds with one another.[1] What is interesting within the manifesto especially is that even while O'Hara is suggesting that the cinema might be more captivating for the wider public, placing it in dialogue with poetry creates an automatic relationship between the two. The movies are used not purely to denounce poetry, or set up a hierarchy of interest, but also to suggest that the latter might appeal with the same kind of immediacy and grandeur than the former does.

In addition to the movies usurping poetry, O'Hara also turns to the telephone as a means by which to negate the poem. Very similar to his argument that 'everything is in the poems', rendering the manifesto unnecessary, the poet ends his manifesto with 'if I wanted to I could use the telephone instead of writing the poem … the poem is at last between two persons instead of two pages' (1995a: 499). The poem is transported from the written word into something that can be spoken, spontaneously and easily. In the same way that the poem might be a gesture of dialogue, the telephone actually realizes dialogue, removing the work from the staid context of the page to the more alive and dynamic framing of a conversation. The complete lack of need for the page itself suggests that the poem should be realized in action; it can be lived and experienced, as well

---

[1] Some examples include 'In the Movies', 'To an Actor Who Died', 'For James Dean', 'Thinking of James Dean' and 'To the Film Industry in Crisis'.

as rendered in a more stable, written form. In this sense, the telephone is an aspirational reference point for the poem, in which the latter can participate in immediate forms of communication, intervening within the present moment as opposed to just documenting it.

However, there is also a sense that the telephone, and in fact the movies, are troubling to the poem's longevity. If reading can be replaced with going to the cinema, as writing could be substituted with picking up the phone, then is there any need for the poem at all? If this is the predicament of the genre, and O'Hara is resisting dogma and didacticism, then the manifesto offers up a series of possibilities for a poetry that can situate itself in dialogue with the thrill of the cinema and the immediate gratification of the dial tone. The poem can extend beyond itself into the living, creating conversation that seems animated enough to exist between two bodies. It can express need, desire, lust, momentary and transient thinking, as well as the more overblown and affectively overwhelming experience of the cinema-goer. The manifesto, then, while it troubles its own genre, ideas themselves and then poetry as a whole, seems focused on reconciliations between all three.

'The poem whose words become your mouth': Political possibility for tone

In order to consider the political possibilities of O'Hara's work, I want to elaborate on the image of picking up a telephone instead of writing a poem. This emphasizes two key concepts: the first is that the poem can be 'heard', and the second is that the act of writing is wholly analogous to the speech act. The phone itself is a unique form of communication in that it prioritizes the voice above all else. Untethered from bodies, as well as forms of physicality other than that of holding the phone, calls require that an inanimate object serves as the mediator for another voice across the wires. While the phone is pressed to an ear on one side, the dialogue, or meeting of voices, happens somewhere unidentifiable between the two. In *Sex, or the Unbearable*, Lauren Berlant writes that 'dialogue commits us to grappling with negativity, nonsovereignty, and social relation not only as abstract concepts but also as the substance and condition of our responses – and our responsibilities – to each other' (Berlant and Edelman 2014: xi). By placing the poem, ultimately, between two people, O'Hara is transforming the poem into a place of dialogue. In so doing, his work suddenly suggests response and responsibility; nothing is said that could not be placed in dialogue with an other, in the same way that by opening up the poem to possibilities of collaborative meaning making, the poet is demonstrating a responsibility to his readership. The work, thus, comes to grapple with ideas of sovereignty as well as relations in regard to the way that a poetic text might be produced. However, the telephone also creates a distance, in which the lack of the body and the space between two people might allow for further divulgences.

Tone is central to all of these concepts, as well as vital for a successful telephone call. If the tone of the speaker is misunderstood, then fundamental aspects of the dialogue become lost between the wires. Through equating the poem with the telephone, O'Hara seems to suggest that his readership needs to be able to appreciate not just what is being said but the way in which it is being said. In conjunction with actual references to mobility, O'Hara's manifesto is characterized by a lightness of tone, one that carries itself in such a way as to allow the assimilation of multiple different elements. In *Ugly Feelings*, Sianne Ngai articulates the problematic of tone when she writes that it is:

> reducible neither to the emotional response a text solicits from its reader nor to representations of feelings within the world of its story, and the slippery zone between fake and real feelings, or free-floating and subjectively anchored feelings.
>
> (Ngai 2007: 41)

O'Hara's poetry, of course, moves differently to a story. However, there is a sense that the reader must invest in the space that is being created, whether that is the poem staging a dialogue between an artist and poet or discussing the specificities of moving through New York City. While not a story, the poems allow for a world to take shape and form, with varying degrees of scope, from the deeply close and intimate to the vaster and more expansive. This movement is also echoed in the slippages between the fake and the real, in which day-to-day experience is used as the material for the poems, but the light posturing and affectation of the lyric speaker is perhaps closer to the free-floating and subjective. Ngai suggests that tone can be understood as follows: 'The formal aspect that enables these affective values to become significant with regard to how each critic understands the work as a totality within an equally holistic matrix of social relations' (2007: 43). For Ngai, then, the critic's position actually seems central to the understanding of tone, in the same way that the listener is central to the communication of meaning on the telephone. It also recognizes the way in which certain affects can be communicated through the written word, with an acknowledgement of the social relations and dynamics from which the original writing emerged. This is a holistic relationship, established through a number of contingencies, the most significant of which is not the writing itself. O'Hara's use of the telephone could be read as an endorsement of Ngai's statement that the understanding of tone ultimately lies within the domain of the critic. In the same way that the listener can quickly become the speaker in a telephone conversation, without physical or visual clues, O'Hara's open and fluid poems allow a space in which the reader can get caught up in the same mobility, going from staid and still to echoing the movements of the poet.

O'Hara's unique tonality situates itself between and among affect and affectation, through the lightness with which he moves, as well as the way he dismisses his genres of choice, and communicates flippancy to the reader. If this flippancy can be considered a style, or mode of deployment, then the tonal communication of the written page is vital. In contrast with 'affect', affectation is defined as the 'striving after, aiming at; desire to obtain', something that resonates perfectly with O'Hara's movement towards without ever arriving. Affectation can also be defined as 'artificial or non-natural assumption of behavior' (OED 2014), situating it as far more contrived and deliberate than affect. Rather than relying on reciprocity and organic development, in the way that affect emerges, affectation is the intentional cultivation of an outward attitude or appearance. As such, it operates as high artifice as opposed to public feeling, which can act and be acted upon. Affectation is not a series of actions that form relationships but just an act. For O'Hara, flippancy allows for a mediation of the act of feeling and putting on an act. Flippancy situates itself somewhere between affect and affectation, creating a political strategy of lightness in the face of heavy subjects, drawing on necessary high performance while being intrinsically tied to affective relationships.

The flippant tone of O'Hara's 'Personism: A Manifesto', which is light and irreverent in its mobility, resonates with the way that Sontag approaches 'camp'. In 'Notes on Camp', Sontag defines the term as 'a vision of the world in terms of style – but a particular kind of style. It is the love of the exaggerated, the "off," of things being-what-they-are-not' (2009a: 279). Though perhaps it seems too simple, or maybe even reductionist, to elide O'Hara with campness, it is the concept of 'off' ness that is especially useful for the manifesto. The poem is not a telephone call; the act of writing is not the same as the act of putting the receiver to your ear and dialling. The poem is also not an armed assailant chasing you, it is not dripping and potatoes and it is not the death of literature as we know it. The tone of O'Hara's 'Personism' continually undercuts the seriousness of the manifesto as a genre and poetic lineage as a whole. His work, thus, is a critique of earnest statements about poetry, shifting the expected polemical writing of the manifesto back on to poems themselves. The manifesto as a whole then becomes what-it-is-not. It is anti-polemical and evades offering a prescriptive poetics that can be followed. This defining poetry through what-it-is-not, with the objects that constitute the 'not' ness varying from the ridiculous to the banal, establishes a style where seriousness cannot be affixed to the act of writing poetry. With O'Hara's work, then, his specific form of flippancy could be seen as a tonal facet of a camp style.

This performance within the space of the poem speaks to affect's operations as 'in the midst of *in-between-ness*: in the capacities to act and be acted upon' (Gregg and Seigworthy 2010: 1). The artifice that is suggested by O'Hara's use of flippancy, and the middle ground between affect and affectation, seems well defined by 'in-between-ness'. While the affectation might be seen as counter to affect because it is too contrived and performative, the style and tone with which O'Hara deploys his manifesto does nonetheless have a feeling charge. It communicates force, enthusiasm and lightness, all of which serve to cohere the reader to the affective stickiness of the compelling piece. The way O'Hara deploys the performative is a form of Riley's 'trying it on – and sometimes in both senses' (Riley 2000: 151). This is very much reiterated by Ashbery's introduction to the collected works, in which he writes, 'one frequently feels the poet is trying on various pairs of brass knuckles until he finds the one which fits comfortably' (Ashbery 1995: viii). The trying it on, therefore, is a provocation to the wider readership and audience, attempting to reconcile the tone of the speaker with the gravitas that their genre choice usually implies. The affectation within the manifesto is a form of trying it on, affecting flippancy that works not only as performance but as a means by which to try out the reader and the subject matter. That is not to say that 'Personism' is devoid of feeling but that the 'off' ness of the tone – the congenital lack of seriousness – becomes a means of speaking down the telephone to wider poetic communities, American culture and ultimately, homosexual identity.

Returning specifically to the image of the phone once more, O'Hara is not just focusing the reader's attention on tone. He is also suggesting that all meaning resides within the mouth itself, in the noise that can be produced through the organ. The manifesto as a whole has a chattering, light tone. O'Hara seems to use the page in order to practice a light conversation, one that moves and flows naturally through a series of observations and thoughts. The colloquial nature of the work, in addition to the informality with which O'Hara approaches the canon, places the manifesto within the realm of conversational as opposed to didactic and authoritative. This tonal emphasis on light chatter, alongside the slightly affected light-heartedness given the genre of the work, creates a space in which the poet appears to be mouthing off. Much like Ahmed's wilful subject, the speaker 'become[s] mouthy … to become mouthy is to become mouth, reduced to the speaking part as being reduced to the wrong part' (Ahmed 2014: 154). In his manifesto, O'Hara willingly and wilfully reduces the poem to the mouth; if the telephone exists for the speaking voice to be realized, then there is no need for the poem. There is a significant difference here, then, in which it is not that the poet is being called mouthy because he is articulating unwelcome truths, but rather that he is self-describing as mouthy. The manifesto enacts this mouthiness with its continued stream of chatter. Through self-determining the manifesto, the poet and the poem as mouth, O'Hara is pointing to a tonally significant way of working, in which flippancy allows a freedom to contradict, resist and undermine.

'Make fecund my existence': Mobility and movement

'Personism: A Manifesto' also takes steps to elide poetics with the mobility of the speaking subject. In the opening of the piece, O'Hara describes running away from a knife-wielding attacker, writing 'you just go on your nerve. If someone's chasing you down the street with a knife you just run, you don't turn around and shout, "Give it up! I was a track star for Mineola Prep"' (1995a: 498). This analogy is suggestive of two forms of mobility: the first is that movement is central to the writing of poetry, and the second is that stasis can have violent consequences. The difference between mobility as central to poetry writing and moving as a necessity for survival is vast. Nonetheless, the two concepts come together in O'Hara's work in ways that I shall explore throughout this section. To approach this manifesto proposition in quite a literal sense, for now, O'Hara's work suggests that the idea for a poem is an armed assailant. When you think of something that could constitute the poem, you run with it. Here, the running that is traditionally seen as a liberating movement of synergy and development is actually equated with instinct and danger. That poetry, and the affected light-heartedness of O'Hara's tone, seem to deviate wildly from this violent context of creation only serves to heighten the ridiculousness of the analogy. The extremity of the image works in a flippant conjunction with the statement that 'you just go on your nerve', using the instantaneous as a methodology for writing. Importantly, this nerve-driven movement suggests that the poem can emerge in a way that is natural and organic, as opposed to dictated by clear structural decisions and determined end points. In *Queer Orientation*, Ahmed writes that 'to go directly is to follow a line without a detour, without meditation. Within the concept of directness is a concept of "straightness." To follow a line might be a way of becoming straight, by not deviating at any point' (Ahmed 2006: 16). By contrast, O'Hara's running away has no destination and no clearly pinpointed futurity. As such, his work can be all deviations and all absence of direction; it is a refusal to straighten up and an invitation to flail.

In 'Stepping Out with Frank O'Hara', David Herd writes:

> The step, I want to argue, is the measure of O'Hara's thinking, which is as much as to say that it is the prosody of his cognition. Of all poets it can be said of Frank O'Hara that there is something in his poetry, he gets to know. What he gets to know is his relation to his world, New York. And by the way he gets to know it – in the fullest possible sense of the term – is by stepping out.
>
> (2010: 72)

Movement, as a result, is not purely a poetics for O'Hara but a way of knowing. Creating the poem through running, going on the nerve, is a means by which to get at the surrounding world, translating its effervescence and energy to the space of the page. Thus, movement is not purely the instinctive response to the armed assailant but a form of relation and relating to the world beyond the poet. Herd writes that surrounded by a 1950s and 1960s capitalist-driven America, 'O'Hara places the step: light and graceful, poised and human; incremental, which means that nothing is taken for granted' (2010: 85). This is fundamental to the way in which I am approaching the O'Hara of the manifesto. Movement ensures that the poet takes nothing for granted; he celebrates contemporary and canon alike, paying close attention to friends and surroundings, drawing all aspects of life into lyrics that can reflect on love, companionship and art simultaneously. However, taking nothing for granted also relates to an identity politics that inevitably comes through O'Hara's writing. That the poet must always be ready to run from the armed assailant speaks to the fact that life itself, and the safety of the poet, must never be taken as given. In spite of the elegance that Herd suggests for the step, such lightness of foot and ease of movement also exists in a less pleasant dialogue with the American context in which homosexuality was still illegal.

What I find especially interesting is that Herd sees O'Hara's step as fundamental as Charles Olson's approach to breath. While 'Projective Verse' has a gravitas and seriousness entirely lacking in O'Hara's approach, Olson too was concerned with how best to introduce an embodied and individual form of measure to poetry. Imagining O'Hara running with the idea of the poem, and away from the knifed assailant, implies a breathlessness for the poet. Continual activity and movement ensure that the poems themselves cannot organize around a breath; indeed, there is no time for such structures to emerge from the poet who is either always moving or always talking. While the manifesto states that 'you' would not turn around to shout 'Give it up! I was a track star for Mineola Prep!', it seems that this is precisely what O'Hara would do in the situation. Still running, and still light of foot, it is hard to imagine the 'I' of O'Hara's poems not taking a moment to turn around and mouth off to the danger left in their wake. Once more, while the poet claims to be dictated by nerve and movement, part of this nerve should be located in the mouth, which even finds the right words within the inappropriate moments, or, perhaps more fittingly, the inappropriate words for the right moment.

The mobility of the manifesto is further realized when O'Hara refers to 'Personism' as a movement. This futurity is reiterated when O'Hara claims that the movement has not yet arrived, but 'like Africa, is on its way' (1995a: 499). The link to Africa ruptures the manifesto in an unexpected shift, entirely removing the work from its New York–centric step into a vaster and wider form of moving. The scope of the manifesto, which widens to include whole continents, maps onto the similar movement of 'The Day Lady Died' (1995b: 325). Narrating a walk through New York, the speaker stops to 'buy/an ugly NEW WORLD WRITING to see what the poets/in Ghana are going these days' (ll. 9–11). Before resolving the poem in Billie Holliday's death and a memory of listening to her sing in the 5-Spot, O'Hara shifts the scope of the poem, demonstrating how a speaker located within a New York mobility can widen their focus and thus the constellation of their practice. Taking shape among and in-between the myriad of reference points, much like the manifesto, the poet works as the mediator for everything. Much like the final stanza of 'Autobiographia Literaria' (1995c: 11), the speaker in the manifesto seems to say 'here I am, the/center of all beauty!/ Writing these poems!/Imagine!' (LL. 13–16). The changing locations of the manifesto also imply that the first-person position is navigating multiple spaces and places, creating a movement out of movement itself.

Whether the mobility of the 'I', the poet's hypothetical running or an actual poetic movement, O'Hara's work wholly rejects stillness. As Berlant writes, 'we can never be reminded often enough that the political program of happiness as regulatory norm is less a recipe for liberation than an inducement to entomb oneself in the stillness of an image' (Berlant and Edelman 2014: 18). Whether happy or sad, both of which O'Hara claim as necessary conditions for his writing in 'Statement for Paterson Society', the poet avoids becoming entombed within the image. Instead of following traditional scripts for happiness, which tend to realize themselves in stasis and stillness, O'Hara walks away from any such possible entombment. This resonates with Riley's belief that 'my awkward navigations to become, coupled with my constitutional failure to fully *be*, are what actually enable political thinking and language' (2000: 5). As Herd establishes, O'Hara's navigations are anything but awkward; they are graceful, light and deliberate in their movements. However, O'Hara still exists within a continual state of becoming, ever moving as opposed to arriving. In this state of in-between-ness, he refuses to *be* anything, using these processes as a means by which to reject the image of normativity that Berlant equates with stillness. The possibilities of this kind of movement are exemplified in 'Poem (Now it is the 27th)', where the speaker claims 'my force is in my mobility' (O'Hara 1995d: 345). The line breaks and brevity of the poem create a breathless pace, with the spatiality offering a constant sense of motion, all of which is perfectly expressed in the 'instability, suggestibility, sensibility' of the fifteenth line. O'Hara writes:

> my force is in mobility it's said
> I move
> towards you
> born in the sign which I should only like
> with love.
>
> (1995d: 345, ll.21–27)

The force of this poem is not associated with power; the mobility is a quick motion that belies lightness of foot and fragility. The speaker should only like, but instead, loves, while the line break between the 'I move' and 'towards you' speaks of a certain tentativeness. Instead, the force might be located in not the type of movement but the ability to move at all. The force emerges in the speaker's ability to keep going, with a lightness and finesse that ultimately replaces the need for a destination. What is important, perhaps, is that the 'I' only moves towards the you, as opposed to reaching them in a final clinch. What this suggests is a kind of restlessness for the speaker in which love is possible, but the freedom of mobility has not been negated by the loved one. O'Hara's works could be said to constitute a series of 'towards', in which the multiple objects and spaces under discussion are points of orientation that are never fully reached. This is clear from O'Hara's collected *Lunch Poems*, which for the most part document the poet's walks through the city – allegedly taken on his lunch breaks from work. 'A Step Away from Them' (1995e: 257) begins with the lines 'It's my lunch hour, so I go/for a walk among the hum-colored/cabs' (ll. 1–3). The poem ranges through labourers eating sandwiches, skirts flipping, Times Square, a number of resident New Yorkers, friends and then resolves in 'My heart is in my/pocket, it is Poems by Pierre Reverdy' (ll. 48–49). What initially appears to be an urban walk is exploded in the final stanza, turning to the heart before expanding it to address a long-distant French poet. 'Personal Poem' (O'Hara 1995f: 335) similarly begins with a walk: 'Now when I walk around at lunchtime/I have only two charms in my pocket' (ll.1–2) while 'Steps' starts with the intimacy of 'How funny you are today New York' (l.1), resolving in a stanza that seems to focus more personally, with O'Hara writing:

> oh god it's wonderful
> to get out of bed
> and drink too much coffee
> and smoke too many cigarettes
> and love you so much.
>
> (ll. 41–45)

While the 'you' gets the final line of the poem, it is the dynamism of the city, and the movement of its various components, as well as the speaker's excess of coffee and cigarettes that ultimately energize the final declaration of love. The poems as a whole reflects a constant chattering social walk, in which O'Hara's movement, his going towards but never quite arriving, can be regarded as a form of faithlessness that is analogous to flippancy.

The relationship between the faithless and flippant holds its own powerful force. This is particularly evident in 'Meditations in an Emergency' where O'Hara writes:

> My eyes are vague blue, like the sky, and change all the time; they are indiscriminate but fleeting, entirely specific and disloyal, so that no one trusts me. I am always looking away. Or again at something after it has given me up. It makes me restless and that makes me unhappy, but I cannot keep them still.
>
> (O'Hara 1995g: 197)

Here, the unhappy fleeting eyes are symptomatic of the necessary restlessness of the poem's speaker. While specificity and loyalty are absent, or at least called into question, the speaker is still incapable of remaining static. Movement is made possible through the sky, change and a lack of trust, all of which are identifiable with the O'Hara 'I' that moves continually toward, but can always change direction. In *The Promise of Happiness*, Ahmed writes that 'happiness scripts could be thought of as straightening devices, ways of aligning bodies with what is already lined up' (Ahmed 2010a: 91). The emphasis on happiness, and compulsion to be happy, actually effects homogeneity where emotion 'can be narrated as the hope or promise of becoming acceptable, where in *being* acceptable you must *become* acceptable to a world that has already decided what *is* acceptable' (Ahmed 2010a: 106). The speaker's fleeting blue eyes are their own form of unhappiness; through continual reorientation towards the 'something' that has given them up, or the generalized 'away', the speaker refuses to align or follow the lines created for them. In fact, the movements towards and away suggested by 'Meditations in an Emergency' and 'Poem (Now it is the 27th)' create a complex orientation of turns which are anything but neatly linear. As such, the body of the poem cannot align with what has already been lined up. Similarly, the works do not communicate a speaker who has attempted to become acceptable in a world which has already deemed them to be unacceptable. Instead, there is a resignation to the mobility inherent in refusing to align neatly. This resignation, however, when read in conjunction with the lightness of the voice and the movements of the works, seems almost celebratory and revolutionary, as opposed to a manifestation of deep unhappiness. The poems, in that sense, reject normativity, refuse a stable love object, queer traditional forms of orientation, and in so doing create a political position from what seems to be a highly self-reflexive and self-conscious work.

'Meditations in an Emergency' continues, invoking the past, as well as the present, allowing for temporalities to converge around the speaker's own restlessness. He expresses no interest in 'nostalgia for an innocent past' (l.11), finding such whimsical associations with better times long elapsed. The poem then moves through attractive blonds, religion, urbanity and the threat of impending heterosexuality, all of which are deployed and then dropped so quickly as to become flippant. The lyric 'I' has also tried love but rejected it: 'I am always springing forth from it like the lotus – the ecstasy of always bursting forth' (l.31). What was initially restless and potentially unhappy in the roving eyes becomes an ecstatic realization of freedom from constraint. The poem even resolves with the same happy imperative 'I've got to get out of here' (l.44), which could be the speaker staging their departure from the poem itself. The speaker then elucidates, 'I'll be back, I'll re-emerge, defeated from the valley; you don't want me to go where you go, so I won't go where you don't want me to' (ll.45–46). It is uncertain whether 'I'll be back' is addressed to the poem, the reader or the lover, but what is clear is that the speaker is invested in a glorious and slightly hyperbolic emergence. The tripping repetition of 'go' in the final sentence seems both convoluted and close to everyday speech, with the monosyllabic words contributing to the pace of the poem's final reflections on movement. The work communicates throughout that irrespective of the failure of love and possibilities of defeat, stasis is the worst state for the speaker, who must always be emerging in newness and vitality.

However, this O'Hara mobility is not without complexity. Framed positively within the previous two poems, the movement of the speaker is analogous to forms of refusal. It practices an anti-normative freedom, in which the 'I' can be orientated at will in any direction that deviates from the straightening lines of stability, heterosexuality or even love with longevity. However, this could also be a strategy for the expression of homosexuality within the poems, with a combination of revelation and elusiveness ensuring that the speaker's identity is one which allows flight. Movement, much like the manifesto suggests through the image of the armed assailant, can be construed as a necessity. The ability to run, and run fast, gestures to the material conditions of identity politics within a pre-Stonewall America (Nelson 2011b). It is for this reason that the city landscape expands to encompass lovers, other countries, literary references and reference points that are situated beyond the physical immediacy of New York. This constellated environment in which the speaker can move allows for the non-normative homosexual body to enhance its landscape through further possibilities of movement.

In 'Homosexuality' (1995h: 181) O'Hara writes 'so we are taking off our masks, are we, and keeping/our mouths shut' (ll.1-2) implying identity must not be articulated even if it can be seen. The poem then moves to 'and then we are off!/without reproach and without hope that our delicate feet/will touch the earth again' (ll.7-9). Here, the image of mobility is ambiguous, implying an exhilarating freedom for those moving, but one that is disassociated or removed from reality, the ground beneath their feet. In 'At the Old Place' (1995i: 223) homosexuality is similarly married to mobility, but in this case, the movement seems like a celebration of freedom. Joe and the lyric speaker 'skip like swallows' (l.5) through the streets, while 'Howard malingers. (Come on, Howard.) Ashes/malingers. (Come on, J.A) Dick/malingers./(Come on, Dick.) Alvin darts ahead. (Wait up,/Alvin.)' (ll.6-9). Even the description of the men's dances, once they arrive at the bar, demonstrates frenetic movement that constitutes shared experience. The poem ends, however, with three men who had defected earlier that evening entering The Old Place guiltily. O'Hara concludes the poem with '"I knew they were gay/the minute I laid eyes on them!" screams John./How ashamed they are of us! we hope' (ll.18-20).

In spite of the positive possibilities of these poems, the conflation of movement with homosexuality seems to gesture to a wider difficulty of openness and freedom. The use of the collective pronoun as well others' names creates a category or collective who are all subjected to the same experience, forced into a mobility that is far more analogous to fleeing the armed assailant than moving of one's own volition. In 'Shame, Theatricality, and Queer Performativity: Henry James's *The Art of the Novel*', Sedgwick writes that 'that's the double movement shame makes: toward painful individuation, toward uncontrollable relationality' (2003b: 37). In this instance, the affective nature of shame can powerfully act and be acted upon. It acts in making the characters of O'Hara's poem arrive late, and embarrassed to a gay bar, but it is also acted upon when the poet asks whether it is time to remove masks. There is both a loneliness and a relationality that emerges from this, where O'Hara is inextricably part of the group, but also removed enough to comment on their social situation. In 'Biotherm (for Bill Berkson)' (1995j: 436), O'Hara describes an encounter on the train, an act of interpellation, that consolidates him as a homosexual within a public space. He writes:

> Then too, the other day I was walking through a train
> with my suitcase and I overheard someone say 'speaking of faggots'
> now isn't life difficult enough without that
> and why am I always carrying something
> well it was a shitty looking person anyway
> better a faggot than a farthead

Interestingly, this instance of interpellation occurs when O'Hara is already in flight. However, his movement is enclosed within the space of the train, and his body is weighed down with the density of a suitcase. That O'Hara even comments on 'always carrying something' suggests that within this moment he had neither the levity nor lightness of foot to be able to flee or turn to face his verbal assailant. The denial of the run and the turn locks O'Hara in a position in which he is not able to 'go on his nerve'. In fact, the moment has to be resolved in the juvenile conclusion that it is better to be a faggot than a farthead. Caught in an individuation and uncontrollable relationality, in which one can be named or called by an unknown, O'Hara attempts to shift the shame into a nonchalant, shrugging insult. While the body cannot be flippant, the poem can.

'The darkness I inhabit in the midst of sterile millions': The person and collective

It might be for these reasons that O'Hara's work seems to practice a resistance towards being subsumed by collectives. Although the writing is inherently sociable, with proper names and references to friends occurring throughout, the poet rejects any formal affiliation, a model which 'Personism: A Manifesto' seems to follow. The work is wholly disinterested in converting followers, in spite of making great claims for numerous adherents. As Herd suggests, followers would inevitably slow O'Hara down; he is too fast, and we are left, quite simply, yearning in his wake. As such, the document embodies the need for an individuated 'I', in this particular case O'Hara himself. The manifesto seems to address the difficult ways the 'I' might retain their autonomy in spite of being constellated through a range of friends, lovers and writers. In *Women, The New York School and Other True Abstractions*, Maggie Nelson writes:

> O'Hara's insouciant, "not caring attitude" can also be read as a defensive stance – a kind of pre-emptive I-wouldn't-want-to-be-part-of-your-club-anyhow line, when you already know you aren't going to get in.
>
> (2011b: 68)

If this is true, then O'Hara's lightness and the flippancy with which he dismisses Personism's capacity to have any effect might gesture to a wider politics of collectives. Instead of just demonstrating a self-defence strategy, in which individualism is key, the interplay between community and the 'I' acknowledges that affiliation has complications. Nelson's analysis of O'Hara's attitude, or stance, seems to explain why the poet might have placed emphasis on the Person. She writes 'instead of venerating this "not caring", apolitical stance as desirable and timeless, we might consider it in the same context of being queer in the mid-fifties, where explicitly same-sex poems had to wait until after Stonewall to see the light of day' (Nelson 2011b: 69). In 'Personism: A Manifesto', the central figure is a necessary mediator of the range of spaces and references that exist around him. In that way, the document and poetics it describes would be impossible without a person to cohere the ideas. This said, that so much responsibility is placed on the individual figure, as opposed to their wider context, suggests that there is a need for the poet to evade fixed and stable groupings.

In *Beautiful Enemies*, Andrew Epstein makes a compelling argument for why avant-garde communities might not be considered a stable and safe resting place. He writes that 'these groups are often marked by fractious, lively disagreement and conflict rather than contented harmony, and by sexism, homophobia and power politics that are not so different from the dynamics of the mainstream they oppose' (Epstein 2006: 33). It is understandable, then, that while he invokes a number of friendships and specific artists, O'Hara might be reluctant to affiliate with any one group above another. As quoted in my introduction, Ahmed summarizes this problematic of avant-garde communities very well. While they might pride themselves on resisting convention, they often come to reflect the systemic exclusions of wider society. She writes that the perceived freedom from normality can quickly become 'freedom to exploit others, to engage in behaviours that are almost exact approximations of the normal that subjects think of themselves as opposing' (2014: 172). Similar to Epstein, Ahmed identifies that avant-garde communities' insistence on freedom from traditional social constraints creates a different social space in which there is nonetheless still freedom to exploit. While the avant-garde might have seemed to resist much of American culture in the 1950s and early 1960s, that did not necessarily mean it was always a welcome resting place for those who chose to inhabit it. Subjects, as a result, would have to be continually aware of the emergence of the 'normal' or any standardizing behaviours that demanded the same type of adherence as wider society.

Within this context, it's useful to think about O'Hara's collection under the general title of the 'New York School'. In the introduction to the poet's collected work, Ashbery writes that the term 'applied to poetry isn't helpful, in characterizing a number of widely dissimilar poets' (1995: x). Instead of standardizing, or establishing a 'normal', for a disparate group of poets including Ashbery, Kenneth Koch, O'Hara and James Schuyler, the New York School actually fails to accommodate the range of difference at work. All of the poets inhabited different spaces at different times; not all of them were in New York, in the same way that not all of them shared the same sexualities, in the same way that O'Hara died young while the others continued to write for some time. However, an earlier anecdote from Ashbery and O'Hara's friendship explains why the category, or collective itself, might be a productive way of addressing the difficulties of group identity. In *City Poet: The Life and Times of Frank O'Hara*, Brad Gooch describes the encounter between the two poets as follows: 'In the din, Ashbery heard a flat, nasal voice, sounding much like his own, making an offhand pronouncement that he could imagine himself making in one of his more tendentious moments' (1993: 136). Ashbery is not only able to recognize himself in O'Hara, through both the voice and the provocative way of speaking, but also able to recognize O'Hara's particular motive in making pronouncements at the centre of a party. Ashbery claimed O'Hara believed 'art is already serious enough; there is no point in making it seem even more serious by taking it too seriously' (1995: 136). The seriousness of art within this context lends credence to O'Hara's claim that 'it's all in the poems'; if the poems themselves work seriously, then it's better that the manifesto not make them seem even more so by taking them too seriously. The poems have to be treated flippantly because in and of themselves they are serious enough. It is perhaps the two poets' similarity that initially led to friendship and then a relationship that was very much informed by the discussion and sharing of poetry. Ashbery was able to recognize a wilfulness in O'Hara and an impulse that he shared to use lightness and unseriousness as provocatively as possible. While the poet rejects the New York School as a formal mode of organization, it is clear that the two poets met over a flippant act, where O'Hara acknowledged the seriousness of art through a not taking it seriously, and Ashbery nodded.

This kind of relationship does not call the individuality of 'Personism' into question. The title focuses on the singular; it places a sole person at the centre of the poetics that follow. Sedgwick writes that 'the emergence of the first person, of the singular, of the active, and of the indicative are all questions rather than presumptions of queer performativity' (2003b: 71). Here, the use of first person throughout the manifesto, in conjunction with O'Hara's deliberate framing of the singular, raises questions about the way in which the poet interacts within wider contexts. Much like Sedgwick suggests, the importance of the individual serves as a stage from which the manifesto's dialogue and socialization is able to take place as inherently performative. O'Hara rarely uses a collective pronoun, refusing to conflate himself with an audience or wider poetry community through the unity of 'we'. In fact, he constantly makes distinctions between the 'I' and the 'you'. When determining structure 'you just go on your nerve', and when considering reception 'you just let all the different bodies fall where they may'. At times the you of the manifesto seems to relate directly to O'Hara's own practice, as if he is using the second person as a means by which to communicate a poetics; in shifting from the first person he creates a way of working that could be imitated by others but is still inherently his own. This is problematized later in the manifesto when O'Hara writes that because Personism is so recently founded, he will 'give you a vague idea' of its key premise. This shift to an audience moves the second person away from the poet himself and into a far wider-ranging category – that of the reader. When the manifesto finally does resolve in a collective gesture, O'Hara asks, 'What can we expect from Personism? ... Everything, but we won't get it.' Similar to the promise of Personism, the manifesto's tone seems to propose an intimacy that is continually thwarted, with the reader only being resolved or dissolved into a relationship with the 'I' in an acknowledgement that neither will get what they want.

O'Hara's care/care not attitude, his flippancy, mitigate the potential damages of exclusion while ensuring that he never seems loyal to a particular ideology or group. O'Hara's need to keep emerging, in part fuelled by an insouciant attitude that in some ways pre-empted rejection, suggests that he is always running from an armed assailant, all the while narrating the process. Even when a poet identifies with a counterculture, there should still be some restraint in regard to total affiliation. Ahmed writes that this form of restlessness is inherently queer: 'Queer feelings may embrace a sense of discomfort, a lack of ease with available scripts for living and loving, along with an excitement in the face of uncertainty of where discomfort may take us' (2006: 155). Even if O'Hara's attitude was cultivated purely to respond to the exclusivity of certain kinds of groups, the discomfort with affiliation ensures that his work and life avoided the available scripts for living and loving. Instead, he deviated, creating friendships, lovers and literary communities (both immediate and international; contemporary and past) that generated enthusiasm and excitement through uncertainty. Forever turning away and towards objects, creating a poetics that is vital and 'on the way' but never quite arriving, O'Hara turns what seems like a deliberately cultivated attitude into a political poetics, in which faithlessness actually creates a radical openness to everything.

This kind of radical openness – the queer performativity that asks questions instead of making presumptions – is enacted through the way in which the manifesto shifts and moves, establishing all of its key ideas as highly relational to external sources. Allegedly, throughout the process of creating Personism, O'Hara was physically in the company of one friend, while thinking about his feelings for a lover. The very techniques and structures of poetry are also established through relationships, albeit confrontational ones. It would not be possible to express the technical elements of poetry were the speaker not being chased, in the same way that distribution and reception could not be discussed were O'Hara not to describe a particularly indifferent lover. Similarly, if the speaker of the manifesto had felt no desire or sexual attraction, the poet would not know that the poem needs to be as alluring as a tight pair of trousers. The poem, at its best, is also described as the sex position 'Lucky Pierre'. Desire, love, sex, rejection and poetry are all treated interchangeably, but all entirely linked to engagement with other people. This is the crux of the difficulty of Personism; the individual needs to maintain relationships of all varieties in order to bring such a poetics into existence.

The manifesto, then, continually addresses discomfort with co-option and participation, without ever directly rejecting the stability of fixed communities. It is necessary to retain a level of distant criticality in order to resist being fully assimilated into groups that, as Epstein claims, may reproduce wider power structures. The foregrounding of aloneness and separate thinking places some ethical onus on the individual to trouble categories and communities. In 'To the Poem' (1995k: 174) O'Hara addresses this concept of responsibility, locating possibilities of openness and resistance within the poem and the poet. The work, while creating a clear gap between the speaker and wider American culture, still places the work within that very context. Even if the poem is able to contest dominant and prevailing norms, it must do so from within their inescapable confines. Ahmed writes that 'willfulness can be required in order to persist not only *as* an individual but *in* one's very loyalty to a culture whose existence is deemed as a threat' (2014: 151). Demonstrating a loyalty to poetry and freedom itself, which is an inherently American concept, 'To the Poem' (O'Hara 1995k: 174) practices forms of resistance that at once allow the 'I' to persist while remaining partly loyal to a wider culture. The poem opens calling for a non-conformist act, in which the poet addresses the poem with: 'Let us do something grand/just for once' (ll.1–2). The use of this instance is not the collective or the community, but the writer in conjunction with their own writing. The grandness of the 'something' is soon undercut by the continued iterations of 'thing' throughout the poem. The possibilities for action are reduced to 'something', 'some fine thing', 'merely a thing', while the poem is ultimately resolved as 'a real right thing'. The non-specific thing-ness of the poem in some ways resists didacticism and a seriousness of tone, while also refuting the traditional ways a poem might draw on signifiers in order to make meaning. The repetition also queers the objects of orientation that might allow for the poem and poet to make their way towards a grand politicization. In orientating repeatedly towards 'thing', and a number of different 'things', the poem and poet are unclear as to where they should stick their commitment. It becomes apparent, then, that 'something' must happen, but that the very 'thing' of resistance might be hard to define. The opening of the poem suggests that the writer and text will collude to do something 'small and important and/unAmerican' (ll.3–4). This form of dissent is not only anti-nationalist but also indicates a will to resist homogenization through small acts that cannot be co-opted. That small act, the one that seems tiny and yet has significance, could even be the poem. The rest of the poem goes on to elaborate on these concepts, writing that 'Some fine thing':

> will resemble a human hand
> and really be merely a thing
>
> Not needing a military band
> nor an elegant forthcoming

to tease spotlights or a hand
from the public's thinking

But be   In a defiant land
of its own real right thing

The fact that this unspecified thing is likened to the human hand locates the possibility for action within the living individual. It also gestures to writing; if there is a capacity for the hand to write, and the poem to resemble that very action of writing, then small resistance becomes possible. The refusal to specify this action echoes O'Hara's refusal of didacticism within the manifesto, instead choosing to create spaces in which human autonomy beyond the space of the poem is assumed. 'Resistance is possible', O'Hara seems to say, 'but if that's not your thing, bully for you'. The unspecified thing finds itself, intact and integral, among the grandeur of a military band, a spotlight and the public thinking, locating itself within a 'defiant land', in which it is ultimately able to be both real and right.

'Where to love at all's to be a politician': The poem as love and sex

'Personism: A Manifesto' draws on sexual imagery throughout in order to communicate the operations of the poem. When considering the formal aspects of poetry, O'Hara turns to the image of desire writing 'as for measure and technical apparatus, that's just common sense: if you're going to buy a pair of pants you want them to be tight enough so everyone will want to go to bed with you' (1995a: 498). In this instance, if you are going to write a poem, the technique and structure need to accentuate the content, making sure that the reader is aware of what they're going to get if they decide to peel back the layers. Technique ensures that the reader wants to get at the content. The use of sexual analogy here undercuts poetry as a high art divorced from human experience, locating it instead not in seduction but as a light-hearted expression of desire in which the reader hopefully always wants to get into your pants. A similar image is used for O'Hara to elucidate the centrality of the telephone to his poetics. He claims that calling up a love object ultimately 'puts the poem squarely between the poet and the person, Lucky Pierre style, and the poem is correspondingly gratified' (1995a: 499). 'Lucky Pierre' was used to denote the middle-man in a three-way encounter; the one who is being penetrated, while simultaneously penetrating. The poem, and Lucky Pierre, is thus the site of total pleasure, where the interpenetration of writerly and readerly attention come to fruition. It seems important to note that O'Hara prioritizes the poem's gratification over that of the poet or the reader, making the text itself animated and alive in a way that can be heightened through attention.

In their dialogue, Berlant and Edelman think 'about the subject as that which is structurally nonsovereign, in a way that's intensified by sex, intimacy building, and structural inequality' (2014: 5). Having established poetic structure as entirely contingent on what a pair of tight trousers can do to increase one's appeal, O'Hara is embracing this nonsovereignty. Instead of discussing a rampant individualism, he uses sex as a means by which to establish relationality, intensifying the reliance upon the reader and the poem object through making their presence analogous to sex acts or sexual desire. The fact that Lucky Pierre relates to a specific subculture addresses the structural inequality of homosexual identities, while nonetheless using it to illuminate aspects of the poem. In *Queer Phenomenology*, Ahmed writes:

> Sexuality would not be seen as determined only by object choice, but as involving differences in one's very relation to the world – that is, how one "faces" the world or is directed toward it. Or rather, we could say that the orientations toward sexual objects affect other things that we do, such that different orientations, different ways of directing one's desires, means inhabiting different worlds.
>
> (2006: 68)

Within the manifesto itself, it is clear that the object choice for O'Hara is the poem. Through extending the poem in sexual analogy, the writer establishes a dynamic in which the poem affects how he addresses sex, and sexual tastes impact on the way he approaches the poem. Through establishing a queer orientation for the work, in which unzipping a pair of pants is ultimately a readerly act, while the poem sits at the joyous centre of a threesome, O'Hara creates a different way of directing desire. Desire is the poem, allowing the poet to inhabit worlds different to his own through a conflation of genre, sexuality and object choice.

However, the manifesto does not purely focus on sexual desire but also creates space where love can exist. Similar to sex, love works as a form of orientation: 'It is hard to simply stay on course because love is also what gives us certain direction' (Ahmed 2006: 19). O'Hara writes 'Personism' having just departed the company of a friend: 'It [Personism] was founded by me after lunch with LeRoi Jones on August 27, 1959, a day in which I was in love with someone (not Roi, by the way, a blond)' (1995a: 499). Much like the sex of the manifesto, love and friendship are not purely representative of the way O'Hara engages with the world and extra-poetic material but a means by which the reader can access the poetic work itself. While a number of poems allude to or directly address love, particularly in what LeSueur has categorized as O'Hara's 'Vincent Warren period', the emotion itself occupies a complicated position within the manifesto.[2] Firstly, the kinds of feeling that O'Hara expresses seem inappropriate for the genre, which is meant to be impassioned politically and poetically. Placing a lover at the centre of the manifesto, while dismissing both the poem and the manifesto, means that the traditional affects of the genre are wholly disregarded. There is no anger, righteousness and O'Hara's tone does not communicate a depthless passion but rather a light and inevitable orientation towards friends and love.

The poet writes that 'abstraction (in poetry, not painting) involves personal removal by the poet' before elucidating in the next paragraph that Personism is 'totally opposed to this kind of abstract removal' (1995a: 499). This asserts that O'Hara's poetry creates a new form of abstraction in which there is no attempt at personal removal; in fact, the person (but perhaps not the personal) is ever present. This is supported by the later claim that Personism is 'all art. It does not have to do with personality or intimacy, far from it!'. Seeming to mimic Oscar Wilde's infamous preface to *The Picture of Dorian Gray*, in which the writer claims that all writing is just in fact art, O'Hara then moves into a disavowal of personality and intimacy. Here, a tension arises between the persistent presence of the 'poet' and yet an alleged lack of personality, in a document that seems to draw on intimate anecdote and a forceful personality to communicate views on poetry. As Eileen Myles writes in 'Long and Social', 'let's face it, [the male New York School Poets] were just as New Critical as everyone else was in the fifties. They would all assert that the poetry was not about them. It's about skimming the surface of the self' (2004: 151). However, this is somewhat contested by Nelson, who writes that in 'Personism' 'an intimate relation with another person becomes the condition of possibility for a statement of relationship between poet and culture ... the statement of the relationship between poet and culture that O'Hara's poetry proposes is, I think, as personal as it gets' (2011b: 89). Instead of emphasizing the disavowal of the personal as New Critical posturing, Nelson sees O'Hara's work as using the intimate relationship to create wider links between the poet and their culture. While O'Hara's love objects might shift and change, they remain consistent in facilitating his movement from the internal to a wider culture, in which his speakers always thrive.

When discussing the reception of poetry in 'Personism: A Manifesto', O'Hara writes:

---

[2] See Joe LeSueur, *Digressions on Some Poems by Frank O'Hara*, for further details.

> Suppose you're in love and someone's mistreating (mal aimé) you, you don't say, "Hey, you can't hurt me this way, I care!" you just let all the different bodies fall where they may ... But that's not why you fell in love in the first place, just to hang onto life, so you have to take your chances and try to avoid being logical.
>
> (1995a: 498)

The process of writing is based on beauty and feeling, not the legislation of reception and distribution. The poem itself is the gesture of loving someone without hope of reciprocation or being treated well and, in accordance, the poet must just 'go on your nerve' rather than hoping for logical responses to life stimulus. While this might seem to counteract the reciprocity of the 'Lucky Pierre' position, the act of love refers to the writing of the poem itself. It is a risk that undoes the poet's ability to 'hang on', cultivating instead a culture of taking chances. Later in the manifesto, O'Hara states that the poem itself must evoke 'the overtones of love without destroying love's life-giving vulgarity, and sustaining the poet's feelings towards the poem while preventing love from distracting him into feeling about the person' (1995a: 499). The poem occupies a difficult position in which it must be reflective of real life and evoke a sense of love, but without diminishing the affirmative vulgarity that comes with the lived experience, an affirming vulgarity that is very much present through the Lucky Pierre invocation. Even more problematically, the poet needs to maintain his feelings towards the poem without being derailed into distraction through imagining a loved object. It would appear from 'Personism: A Manifesto', then, that a poem must draw on experiences of love, without that love detracting from the feeling imbued into the poem, creating a poem object that is not derailed by movement towards a real-life object. Much like Ahmed's queer orientations, this kind of relationship changes how the poet is able to face both the world and the poem itself.

Love as a trope can be identified in a number of O'Hara's poems, particularly in his 'Ode: Salut to the French Negro Poets' (1995l: 305). In the fourth couplet, the poem questions the political resonance of the act of loving: 'here where to love at all's to be a politician, as to love a poem/is pretentious, this may sound tendentious but it's lyrical' (ll.7–8). O'Hara uses 'love' in order to express the ways inequality has made human relation so fraught that the act of choosing a partner has itself become a political. He also writes that to love a poem is pretentious and, in doing so, parallels the two. To be a politician is also to be a poet, welcome pretention, and be lyrical. Despite the politicization of love, it is also the solution to inequality: 'for if there is fortuity it's in the love we bear each other's differences/in race which is poetic ground on which we rear our smiles' (ll.15–16). The poem ends with the statement 'the only truth is face to face, the poem whose words become your mouth/and dying in black and white we fight for what we love, not are' (ll.27–28). Black and white evidently relates to race, given the title of the poem, but could also be applied to the use of the page: white paper and black ink. The words that become your mouth convey both the message and the making of the message; the words become both content and form. The poem and the poet become mouthy; they express what often goes unheard or is perhaps deliberately unheard by a wider culture. While 'Ode' is, I would argue, one of O'Hara's few poems that engages explicitly with the political, the work is preoccupied with lyricism, love, the poem and poet as instrumental to an expression of thought and instigator of change. Throughout, affect and feeling are central to the way politics can be practiced. The poem takes an international problem, gesturing away from America to France, and places it within a more personal realm. This troubles the individual and the national, in the same way that 'To the Poem' does. It suggests that personal relationships can be mimetic of international ones, or alternatively, that the personal holds the same weight and significance as the national. In this sense, the lone poet advocating a certain form of bravery in love seems less dictatorial and more personally relevant to a reader. Narrowing the scope of a political problem to the forum of a lyric, love-orientated poem makes effective change seem possible. Through communicating feeling throughout the poem, moving from the glorious calling-upon Whitman in the opening lines to a denial of essentialism ('we are'), O'Hara makes evident that the political fight will ultimately centre around what we 'love'. It is in this sense that Personism's emphasis on love and dialogue is perfectly realized not in irreverent or flippant content but in a lightness of movement and mouthiness that conflates love and poetry together.

Conclusion

One of the key aspects of O'Hara's flippancy is the way in which he approaches and undoes genre. Taking a flippant approach to form, he positions both the manifesto and the poem as incredibly light, in a stance that suggests both genres as serious enough without his weighing in with gravitas. 'Personism: A Manifesto' instead of operating as a didactic document or a thorough statement of poetics continually undermines its own purpose. While O'Hara claims that he will probably have many adherents, his manifesto neither attempts to recruit nor set out a clear poetics for followers to imitate. His discussion of the poem is vague, with a number of analogies that serve to obfuscate understanding of the genre as opposed to clarifying it. The reader is expected to orientate their understanding through armed assailants, threesomes, tight trousers and being rejected by a lover. This approach makes the poems themselves seem unserious, which reinforces the flippancy of the manifesto when O'Hara claims 'everything is in the poems'. The manifesto, therefore, is a piece of work that denies its own seriousness, trying to divert attention from it onto the genre under discussion. However, the chosen genre of poetry is also denied seriousness, placed within a series of humorous and unenlightening scenarios in the manifesto such that levity pervades all aspects of the writing.

Both the manifesto and O'Hara's poems foreground an important mobility. As Herd states, the poet's work could be understood as constructed around the footstep, always light and in transition from one place to another. Although the manifesto is hard to keep up with, the reader finds themselves continually introducing a lightness into their own reading practice, such that they might be able to follow where O'Hara leads, even if their pace is slower. Mobility not only resonates with the nimble tongue of flippancy but also speaks to the non-committal aspects of the poetics. To remain forever moving means that there is no resting place, there is a continued irreverence and freedom that can be effected through a constant light mobility. This allows for O'Hara to traverse everything, creating a constellation of references including the city, his friends, his lovers, other writers and musicians, drawing them into a dialogue that he leaves in his wake. The manifesto itself makes great use of this particular mobility to run through a range of literary references, many of which O'Hara dismisses, invoking them only to drop them lightly without further elucidation. There are also explicit references to mobility in the form of running with your nerve when the idea of a poem arrives, as well as the walk through New York that O'Hara takes after lunch with LeRoi Jones. Importantly, this flippant mobility is integral to the way in which sexuality is realized through O'Hara's work. There are a number of instances in which movement is associated with homosexual identity. As I have explored within this chapter, lightness of foot is not always related to a lack of commitment but can sometimes be considered in dialogue with queer shame and self-protection. A number of O'Hara poems that directly address homosexuality do so in relation to his movement, whether he is moving towards certain signifiers, such as a gay bar, or away from interpolation, such as being called a 'faggot' while on the train.

The lyric 'I' is also integral to the way in which flippancy is realized within O'Hara's work. The speaker conveys a specific style and tone throughout the works I have examined, both of which thrive on the light and conversational. In this chapter, I have focused specifically on tone because O'Hara seems to emphasize the centrality of the voice in a way that he does not with the body. The 'I' works as a consistent figure, conveying a continued levity and irreverence in the face of serious subjects, whether that is the poem itself, the manifesto, politics or nationalism. O'Hara's focus on the 'person' within the title of the manifesto is important when considering the operations of his 'I'. His use of the first person allows for him to participate and then walk away from collectives, practising an air of what Nelson describes as 'not-caring'. The insouciance with which he engages ensures that O'Hara can maintain a continual movement that ultimately frees him from a constrictive commitment to certain groups. This sits in tension with the fact that O'Hara is considered as one of a collection of New York School poets, as well as written about as a coterie writer who was heavily reliant on community. However, O'Hara was the only one of the New York School who truly imagined the city through this work, something that Ashbery discusses in his 'Introduction' to *The Collected Works of Frank O'Hara*. Similarly, his coterie writing was facilitated by a range of different friends and people, as well as lovers, in addition to a self-created network of writers from other locales and eras. As such, the 'I' of O'Hara's work is able to focus on the person, keeping them slightly distinct from those who surround him.

Finally, O'Hara's work resonates with my understanding of the poetics of flippancy in that he uses lightness and irreverence in order to create space for himself. His focus on love and feelings in the manifesto, as well as a number of poems, allows him to be orientated through positive feeling. As I have discussed, O'Hara is a poet often on his way towards an object, always in flux and movement, as opposed to reaching his resting place. The mobility that accompanies this opens up spaces of possibility which allow for alternative ways of living. As Ahmed writes, possibility is light, allowing for one to be blown this way and that, moving in tandem with shifting contexts and surroundings. O'Hara's levity combined with his commitment to movement makes this form of possibility essential and central to his writing. Moving with poise, and a light step, while embracing the potentiality of the nimble tongue in both the space of the poem and across the wire of a telephone, O'Hara uses the poetics of flippancy to create possibility for both his 'I' and the reader of the work.

4

'Who Are These Idiots Writing These Poems?': Eileen Myles' Pornographic Tone and Mutable Categories

'There is an argument / for poetry being deep but I am not that argument' (ll. 53–54) writes Eileen Myles in their poem, 'A Poem' (1991a: 107–113). A second-generation New York School poet, self-identified lesbian and feminist, and recent rejecter of gendered pronouns, Myles has been both a tenacious and ferocious voice in poetry from the early 1970s. Producing a number of memoirs, including *Chelsea Girls*, *Cool for you* and *Inferno: A Poet's Novel*, as well as numerous essays, some of which are collected in *The Importance of Being Iceland* (2009), Myles has continually transgressed the genre of poetry while still holding onto the title of poet, grabbing the term, undercutting its sacred associations, positioning it instead as the ultimate badge of failure and obscurity. As Myles claims, there are a number of arguments for poetry being deep, but in direct contrast, they attempt a poetics of surface, movement and slipperiness. This focus on the superficial does not interfere with Myles' communicating a coherent identity across their whole body of work. In fact, their written voice is remarkably consistent with an 'I' that remains characteristic of their bombastic troublemaking across poetry, memoirs and essays. In spite of this, however, the poet actively acknowledges that the 'I' is in a continual state of becoming, where selfhood remains elusively caught in a process of development. So while it might be easy to identify Myles' characteristic tone, it is impossible to pin down the 'I' themself. The coherence of brash and unapologetic posturing very intentionally recognizes that the self – especially the poetic self – is forever locked within a process of becoming.

The possibilities afforded through 'becoming' in conjunction with Myles' emphasis on surfaces are central to the lightness of tongue and nimbleness of foot practised throughout their work. This sense of flux is extended both to selfhood and the poem, allowing for identity and genre to become conflated with one another. As Myles writes in 'The Poet' (2016a: 183), 'A woman made me ache, I was love on the page not yet I had always felt like a brick shit house. I was the poem' (ll.36–37). The speaker's body, aching for a woman and loving on the page, is finally resolved in the embodiment of poetry. 'I was the poem' suggests that Myles' speaker becomes the poem, but also that the poem becomes them, establishing a relationship in which the two are interchangeable and imbued with the qualities of one another. The space of the page, and the unit of the poetic line, allows for the speaker's brick shit house version of selfhood to emerge. It is simultaneously something tough and solid, built for the fight, but fragile through the ache of love. This voice is characteristic of Myles' writing, where conflict, shifting gender identity, sex and politics create a self in flux and subject to change. This flexibility is interestingly offset by Myles' consistent self-references to 'Eileen' often featuring within poems. It is almost as if Myles' naming of themselves serves to destabilize the traditional relationship between poet and lyric speaker, where the former becomes a tool of the latter, as opposed to the other way round. This speaks to Riley's justification for flippant doggerel in the face of serious subjects, where a light tone can be reconciled with the serious question of political subjects through 'calling out, calling myself out, and being called' (2000: 111). Each iteration of calling recognizes how the self can be constituted, through both the act of vocalizing, self-naming and then answering the call.

It is these experiments of calling that allow for Myles to confront both the self and the poem as unimportant. Just as the genre can be trashed for its irrelevance to the world at large, the figure of 'Eileen' can be continually marginalized and undermined. In one of their most famous poems, 'American Poem', the speaker makes the claim that becoming both a lesbian and a poet was the best two ways in which to find total obscurity. Poetry and lesbianism remove someone from the mainstream, undermining their importance and possibility to influence. Both, in some ways, are aligned with a lack of gravitas, positioning the speaker as the ultimate 'loser'. Where no-one wants to be the all-American loser, or the exemplification of a failure narrative, Myles embraces it throughout their work, drawing on the social irrelevance of the avant-garde poet's position to offer up critique of gender identity, sexuality, politics and poetry itself. All of these discourses shape the work but are not omnipresent; Myles does not remain faithful to any one of them but, instead, subjects them to the same process of becoming that they create for their unstable lyric 'I'.

This chapter, then, will focus on Myles' relationship with the all-American loser, that they take on narratives and discourses of their country in order to challenge them through a flippant self-positioning. By extension, I will also consider the lightness with which Myles treats their genre of choice, locating poems as losers, invisible in the face of significant historical change. This treatment of poetry sets Myles' work up as a conflict or tension of possibility; because the poetry is an unlegislated space of losers, anything is possible; but because anything is possible, poetry will always remain obscure, marginalized on account of its potential power. In order to approach these plays and sleights of selfhood, I will use Myles' promotional video for *Inferno (A Poet's Novel)* as a lens through which to extrapolate a flippant lesbian poetics. Channelling Myles' own rejection of depth, and echoing my approach to O'Hara's manifesto, the work will focus on an unserious document as a means by which to recuperate the poet's lightness as a deliberate political and poetic strategy. In *The Queer Art of Failure*, Halberstam writes that failure 'turns on the impossible, the improbable, the unlikely and the unremarkable. It quietly loses and in losing it imagines other goals for life, for love, for art and for being' (Halberstam 2011: 88). This strategy can be mobilized in regard to Myles' writing, which works with a lightness of touch and a deftness of tongue to critique gender normativity, offering a queer feminism that thrives within spaces of uncertainty.

'This is a way I could get what I want': The poetics of the promotional video

The promotional video opens with a close-up of Myles' *Inferno (A Poet's Novel)* with the title as the obvious focal point among the pattern of flames across the cover. The video cuts to Myles, in black and white, standing to the right of the shot against the backdrop of an industrial grey wall. They claim 'a lot of people are going to like this book' over the sound of guitar chords being played with distortion (OR Books 2010). The screen goes black and 'Eileen Myles' comes up in white, the font reminiscent of graffiti or stencil work that has not been allowed proper time to dry.

The 'E', 'L' and 'S' are all still dripping, while the 'Y' has a line above it that seems to gesture towards paint having been clumsily applied outside the lines of the original design. There are flecks of white around their second name, which make the work seem casual, immediate and quickly executed. The camera returns to Myles, who is now face on, claiming 'the tone is all over the map', as the video cuts back to *Inferno (A Poet's Novel)* in the same graffiti black font and then quickly back to the poet who states 'it's almost porn' (OR Books 2010).

Figure 1 Eileen Myles author attribution – *Inferno (A Poet's Novel)*.

After the same font has been used to detail where the book can be purchased and to convey a favourable review, Myles asks, 'How can it get any better than that?' and the music begins in earnest with a drum beat added to the guitar, as the screen lights up white with a copy of *Inferno (A Poet's Novel)* gyrating and shaking (OR Books 2010). Within 24 seconds of a 3:57-minute video, the poetics of the promotional video and Myles' performance of self have become apparent.

The aesthetic of the video is almost as 'all over the map' as Myles claims their tone is. Moving through black and white to colour footage, from interview to reading, captions against a black screen and *Inferno* itself against a white screen, the video feels like it is unable to remain still. The longest shots are of Myles reading and talking and, as if to compensate for the lack of movement in cutting, the poet themself is so animated that the space is imbued with a sense of mobility. The movement between white text on black background reverses the aesthetic of the page and converts the writing into bold and targeted pronouncements. The statement of white on black, coupled with the clumsy graffiti aesthetic of the font, seems to declare that, while the work and poet themself may not be polished, there's an instantaneous urban harshness to them that must be heeded. The video is also interrupted by black screen with white lines running through it, as if the footage has been recorded on old tape that occasionally becomes too faulty to run. There is a retro feel to the digital, making use of a scratchy aesthetic to interrupt the otherwise smooth and clean series of cuttings between multiple shots and titles. Once more, in line with the graffiti and stencilled text,

Figure 2 Eileen Myles reading from text – *Inferno (A Poet's Novel)*.

the roughness conveys a readiness and immediacy; the tape has been thrown together with material flaws and technological throwbacks.

Throughout, the rock music, scratched tape aesthetic and black screens work to punctuate the video. They create spaces in which the last sentence can ring emphatically, while offering a break to the audience before the video moves into a new element of Myles' character. Alternating between their appearing to answer interview questions (interestingly without any evident interviewer) and their reading from the novel, the video covers a range of the poet's modes of performativity. In the interview, the poet is performing themself in what seems like an earnest fashion, while during the readings they are the Myles performing 'Eileen Myles' performing their new novel. The multiple angles and different colour lenses used on the poet serve to foreground this performativity and artifice. The constant shifting prevents the audience from investing in either the intimate dialogue or the reading. Instead, a deliberate and considered conveyance of self is occurring: one that has been directed specifically to expose an audience to a poet who says: 'Like everybody else I really don't know who I am' (OR Books 2010). The black screens, music and pauses become a large part of the performance in the same way that, as I shall argue, the space of the page, syntax and use of the line are integral to an understanding of their poetry.

The video's final shot is of the notes from which Myles has been reading. The audience are exposed to a more intimate version of their book extract with annotated pages of A4 printed type. The microphone peers over the stand: an

Figure 3 Eileen Myles reading from text – *Inferno (A Poet's Novel)*.

important symbol of the necessity of tone and voice throughout the video. Myles' glasses sit on the lectern, facing the camera, giving the absent poet a position of scrutiny from which they are able to look out to their audience rather than being beheld. It is an uncanny moment of connectivity in which Myles looks directly into their audience through a series of props that seem to reflect their performance best. We are offered their eyes, or at least a symbol of their vision, the technology for voice and, finally, a page of their own book with handwriting all over it. These three props illustrate the way we have access to a deliberately mediated Myles. Instead of attempting to diminish the distance between poet and audience, the film suggests strategies of voice and writing that actually complicate how Myles as a physical presence can be collapsed with the lyric 'I' of their poetry, even their own character 'Eileen Myles'. After this final shot, the video returns to where the book can be bought, providing a website for OR Books. The video and Myles, themself, are framed by the information necessary for purchasing the book, lest the audience forget why they are watching.

This reading of the promotional video is key to the poetics of flippancy within Myles' work. The video foregrounds a playful relationship with selfhood in which the poet happily takes on the moniker 'Eileen Myles' while still questioning their own identity. Much like the way in which Stein relies on 'Gertude Stein' as an official title in *The Autobiography of Alice B. Toklas*, Myles uses the proper name to allow for slips, evasions and plays on identity. Their relationship with selfhood and self-presentation is flippant; it demonstrates a lack of fidelity, a levity in relation to what might be considered a more serious self-declaration. The promotional video also takes a flippant approach to the genre of poetry itself. Not dissimilar from O'Hara, Myles is keen to denounce the poem, positioning poems themselves as a bunch of losers. As opposed to demonstrating the expected reverence for the genre, Myles establishes it as the playground of the marginalized and failing. However, they do not consider these positions to be unproductive or negative, instead using them to create a symbiotic relationship with queer writing that questions establishments. Finally, the promotional video's approach to porn highlights a lightness of approach in relation to sex. Drawing on a mainstream and highly stylized depiction of sex, Myles aligns their work with an easily consumed and artificial product. Conflating porn with reading elides sex with literature, which ultimately introduces an element of irreverence to avant-garde writing. If it is closest in style to mainstream pornography, then its gravitas and seriousness are undermined. Suggesting that the audience is more likely to get off on the writing than comb through it, relishing the obscurity and difficulty, introduces a more playful possibility to reading. It is these aspects of the promotional video that can be traced throughout Myles' body of work, ultimately creating a poetics of flippancy that addresses identity, poetry and sex.

'I made myself into a poem': Myles' constructed selfhood

Myles' physical presence in the promotional video seems to imply that the poet is happy for their bodily self to be confused or conflated with the representation of themselves within the poet's novel and, by extension, their lyric poetry. In this sense, they take a greater risk than both Stein and O'Hara in terms of addressing the ostensibly personal and lived experience. In *New York School Women: Some Other True Abstractions*, Maggie Nelson writes that Myles 'consistently disallows the lethal breed of amnesia that ghosts the lesbian, especially the butch, body (whatever that might mean) by articulating (on the page) and actualizing (in performance) a poetry rooted in bodily presence' (2007: 171). Nowhere is this truer than the movement of the promotional video, where the poet uses their bodily presence to recontextualize the way in which a self participates in the production of work, claiming that 'Eileen Myles' is simultaneously a construct and a reality. It is possible that this is an inevitable result of the contemporary moment in which Myles is an active participant on social media, including Instagram and Twitter. In an interview with *the Paris Review*, Myles discusses that the relationship between their writing and new communication technologies is largely indebted to O'Hara. Speaking on 'Personism: A Manifesto', they state:

> What a transitional moment in the history of poetry, to be writing and to realize that now we have technology that's in the world and doesn't have anything to do with poems and writing – then suddenly it does. Suddenly the poem *is* the phone call. I think poetry was never the same … I think every kind of technology changes the entire structure of the culture.
>
> (Lerner 2015)

In a different interview with *The Rumpus*, Myles says that social media means 'you're always coming from behind, out of invisibility into visibility, on your own terms' (Tambling 2017). In this sense, Myles' presence in media – both the promotional video and online – directly addresses the importance of visibility. Claiming there is 'nothing falser than Eileen Myles', the video for OR Books nonetheless places Myles at the centre of everything, interrogating the way in which embodiment and the written 'I' can be constructed and lived. This shifting relationship between representation and actual experience articulates the difficulties and disjunctures inherent in using the 'self' as fuel for a body of poetic work. What does Myles stand to gain from conflating their embodied self with the poetic 'I'? The promotional video offers no insight into the identity of the poet, nor the identity which manifests within the poetic work. Instead, it offers insight into the way an embodied performance of the discursive construct of 'Eileen Myles' is central to Myles' work. This, as a series of sleights and gestures, automatically troubles the self's assimilation into poetry. Simultaneously, however, it troubles the existence of poetry beyond the boundaries of the present and energized body.

In the transcript of their talk 'The Lesbian Poet', Myles writes that 'we all write our poems with our metabolism, our sexuality … an imagined body of a sort, getting it down in time, it moves this way and that, it is full of its own sense of possibility' (1997: 124). This possibility, as suggested by Ahmed and Butler, is central to a queer politics in that it makes possible experiences and identities previously overlooked or marginalized. Including the essay within their *Revolution: A Reader*, Lisa Robertson and Matthew Stadler describe Myles as 'a scintillating mentor in the art of being lesbian and female in the body, the city, and the poem' (2012: 431). Both orientation and gender blur the distinction between the body, the city and the poem, all of which are realized within the space of 'The Lesbian Poet', which itself becomes poetically inflected and urbane through the pure force of Myles' own distinctive tone. This suggests that a figure, even a body, can emerge from writing poems; this body exists at the intersections and overlaps of sex, energy, words, imagination and temporality. It is a body-writing duality that the promotional video echoes, where the possibilities for poetics are located in the living body simultaneous to the produced text. While this might seem to create a symbiosis, Myles' refutations of a stable selfhood allow the poet and their work flux. It is through these movements, and slips, denials of certainty that the relationship between writing and the body becomes troubled. Thus, the figure of the troublemaker emerges twofold, in one sense written and in another sense lived, queering the distinction between these two very separate manifestations of 'Eileen Myles'.

'If I were to start unwriting myself, Eileen Myles, I would begin with my name,' states Myles. 'That's the title of the poem, I own her' (1997: 131). Eileen Myles, the proper noun, is seen as representative of the whole; the person, the poet, their public persona, their identity, how they appear on the page etc. The 'I' invoked, however, allows for greater autonomy; it is the I that determines the way to undo the self is to deconstruct the name. Eileen Myles is a title, is a poem, all of which fall under the ownership of Myles themself. The movement of the sentence makes it unclear whether Myles owns the poem or their own name or in fact just the process of the subject slowly and deliberately unwriting themself. This unwriting, a necessary gesture in the movement to poetry, is not dissimilar to Halberstam's 'unbecoming'. The unwriting is a form of unmaking and undoing in order to open up more creative and surprising ways of existing. The conditions, it seems, for Myles to practise this unmaking and undoing, are being a lesbian who writes poetry. From this position of obscurity, the poet insists on dismantling their own title while still claiming ownership of the poetic and political gesture. In this way, Myles demonstrates that the self can be written as a poem. Unmaking and undoing the dominion of the poet over the poem product actually results in an unbecoming; Eileen Myles is no longer Eileen Myles but an indeterminate, moving, metabolizing poet. Nowhere is this clearer than in their titling of *Not Me*, a 1991 Semiotext(e) Publication of poems. Nelson writes that:

> the phrase 'not me' could be read as an intentionally unconvincing disavowal of the personal, or as the assertion of something patently true – that the collection is 'not her,' as representation is always incomplete, identity always in excess of its performance, and self always larger than language, no matter how 'personal' the work.
>
> (2011b: 182)

Or as Myles themself puts it in an interview with *the Paris Review*, '*Not Me* is a book that is personal and dissolves the personal at the same time' (Lerner 2015).

In 'not knowing' themself, Myles points to a generative way of making work in which existing and writing can be simultaneously constitutive. Similarly, in positioning the work as 'Not Me', while elsewhere claiming 'Eileen Myles' is the title of their poetry, Myles' work is an unconvincing disavowal of the personal and also an acknowledgement that the page can only ever approximate what it means to be 'me'.

When discussing their new, poet's novel, in the promotional video, Myles tells the camera: The first fiction is your name ... Eileen Myles. Am I Eileen Myles?' They go on to clarify that 'there's nothing falser than Eileen Myles' (OR Books 2010). The poet's work is a series of attempts to undermine the stability of selfhood, wherein the identity associated with the poet is continually becoming and unbecoming. The only falsehood, therefore, is to take on the name as mantle or title that implies some kind of knowing or certainty. So, while fixed in place as 'Eileen Myles', a title and a name they cannot dispose of, the poet is still unable to, and unwilling to, explain what such a title signifies. While the status as a fully constituted person with a name is impossible to evade, Myles positions it as a way of denoting who they are while revealing nothing of their self, similar to the way O'Hara's writing included in the previous chapter invites an intimacy that he ultimately denies. Myles, nonetheless, is tied to 'Eileen Myles', even if it is not a self-determined identity in the same way that 'lesbian' and 'poet' might be. In *Impersonal Passion: Language as Affect*, Denise Riley writes that 'the real impersonality of the personal name is ... where the promise of intimacy has faltered, and where that share of language which is given a name functions much like a travel ticket or a luggage label' (2005: 115). However, Myles' use of the personal name does not seem to communicate a failure of intimacy. In fact, acknowledging the difficulty of the name in relation to a continually developing sense of self creates a closer relationship with a reader or audience. They too are complicit in the disjunctures created by affixing an impersonal personal name to an identity that continues to become and unbecome. This also communicates flippancy, where the writer insists upon foregrounding the self while stating the self is unstable and unknown. Myles dismisses their own identity very lightly, and in turn, the reader is expected to skate the surfaces of experiences with a speaker who does not know who they are.

That said, Myles does use their own name as ticket by which to explore multiple areas of possibility, including poetics and politics. By claiming that even they do not know who 'Eileen Myles' is, Myles turns the name into pure outwardness, harnessed to experience the world, which is shifting and uncertain. Riley writes, 'My name is sheer "extimacy." And it's something I pull inside me to make mine, drawing it from the outside' (2005: 115). Similarly, in Myles' work, 'Eileen Myles' is the proper noun Myles has adopted that, while it has a bearing on their interiority, is actually an expression of their own existence and movement within a larger social sphere. Even as their own name is used throughout poems and autobiographies, it reveals nothing of the poet themself; that has to be determined through metabolism, and a body, moving this way and that. Instead, what the title suggests is that the poet is a fully constituted subject, and an embodied figure at the centre of a constellation of referents, still unable to move away from the burden of selfhood. The lyric 'I' as a result is still tied to 'Eileen Myles', if only because the latter is intentionally positioned as the creator of the former.

Myles and Riley are useful counterparts through which to consider the lyric speaker within poetry. While both are resistant to category identifications, they differ wildly on which categories can be evaded and which are inflicted upon the subject without flexibility. Riley's *Am I That Name?' Feminism and the Category of 'Women' in History* and their essay 'Your Name Which Isn't Yours' both consider the potential for a subject to abandon a name in order to become entirely independent. Whether more widely applicable to category definitions, such as woman, or just the personal name, Riley explores the possibilities of a subject emerging from the inflexibility of 'being called' into a more autonomous state of self-definition. She writes that 'self-assertion is thwarted, and its frustration is just one aspect of the unfreedom which attends naming and being named' (2005: 116). Myles explodes this carefully plotted movement to create the nominal poet; going by name, they perform their identity while acknowledging its state of flux, all of which is best realized through their use of language. In the refusal to be invisible, foregrounding the butch body, and drawing on a class-inflected Bostonian tone, which lends each poem its rapidity and colloquialism, the imposed identity restriction of the name becomes one that is wholly generative. The falsity of the name and its refusal to map perfectly onto Myles' own development create a sense of 'not me' while 'still me'. The impersonality of the given name and the movement into the world that it facilitates allows for constant self-exploration, posturing, becoming and unbecoming.

This is in part made possible, or emboldened, by the way Myles conflates themself with the poem. In this way they are both me and not me; the poem and not the poem. 'The Poet' (Myles 2016a: 183) for example, resembles prose with the words ranging from both margins, making full use of the page and investing in the sentence as a unit of meaning. In the first line, they write, 'I made myself into a poet because it was the first thing I really loved. It was an act of will' (ll. 1–2). Throughout the poem, the role of both the genre and the poet changes and fluctuates. Having assumed the title of 'poet' for the speaker, Myles' work still allows for some flexibility in the formulations of their 'I' and the poem itself. The lyric speaker states, 'You see the page for me has terrific dimension. I can go into the white & I do. The lines are designs for something real' (ll. 20–22). This implies that, even if the page is covered, and the piece appears to echo prose structures, it is the fundamental considerations of space and line that maintain the genre of 'poem'. The dimension and the possibility for the expansive blankness of the page are realized within poetry. The poem progresses to the lyric speaker, claiming 'I have truly become my poems, but do note the sculpture of others, their obliviousness, like architects leaving crumbs' (ll.44–46). These sentences have a doubleness to them, suggesting possibilities for the way the poet self-constructs and the part a reader could play in permeating the poem. The sculptural and architectural analogies imply that, rather than a natural outpouring of feeling, the genre is a careful construction with an awareness of structure, both in regard to the presentation of self and page. Myles embraces the role of poet throughout the poem, considering the formal elements of poetry even while the lyric 'I' ranges through a number of different scenes and ideas. The work becomes a meta-poem, masquerading as prose, while asserting its genre status and the collapse of the poet into the piece itself. In this way, Myles and the text themselves are performing a disconnect in which the poet unbecomes from human to poem, while the poem itself unwrites itself as prose. These plays of genre and self are both light and unserious, forever in a flippant flux with one another.

'For Jordana' (2016b: 285) allows for the poem to become a similar space of embodiment and desire. Myles writes:

> I think writing
> is desire
> not a form
> of it. It's feeling
> into space,
> tucked into
> language
> slipped
> into time,
> opened,
> felt.
>
> (ll.24–35)

The line breaks of this particular poem allow for the work to reflect on the relationship between the text and poet, while also conflating aspects of those two separate entities. The 'thinking writing' seems to associate the act of creation with thought itself, which transmutes into a form of desire. The rejection of form as an organizing principle for writing means that the boundaries between the formal aspects of the poem and the actual feeling of the poetry are destroyed completely. Instead, what the text allows is for the feeling and thinking to be realized in space and time, slipped into language, and as such opened to wider possibilities. In contrast, 'April 5' (2016c: 291) works slightly differently in that it foregrounds physical experience external to the poem, but then shifts, such that the experience becomes integral to the making of the poem itself. These conflations open the borders between the poem and life itself, allowing for the progression of both to be seen as interchangeable. Myles writes:

> you realize you have no
> pants on as you're
> walking down to the
> pool
> I have no pants on I
> say
> in this very unattractive poem.
>
> (ll. 1–7)

A similar conflation is achieved later in the poem, when Myles writes, 'I have / no pen I'm / in bed' (ll.40–42), where the absence of a pen within the present moment seems incompatible with the writing of the poem itself. Without the implement it seems impossible that the poet could comment on being in bed, and yet, the poem still happens, as natural as everyday existence or action. In the same way that Myles has pants on outside of the poem, this pantless-ness also becomes within the poem. The two spaces are separate but also the same.

'We are the liars & thieves, we are the women': Identity categories and politics

Myles invocation of the self inevitably develops into a relationship with collectives and collective identities. Not dissimilar from the way in which Riley describes 'mutating identifications' as 'sharpened by the syntactical peculiarities of self-description's passage to collectivity' (2000: 1) Myles makes use of collective identities in order to allow for a poetic speaker who is simultaneously fixed and mobile. At the same time that they are clearly performing identity for the sake of the poem, and the sake of selfhood, Myles is also invested in category habitation, strongly identifying as both a lesbian and a poet. These categories, however, also manifest themselves as Myles self-describing as a dyke, as butch, as a man or a guy (in some of their work), and ultimately coming to apply a gender-neutral pronoun to themself outside the page. In a 2016 interview with *Vice* magazine, Myles reflects that:

> After years of hearing 'they', 'they this', 'they that', 'Miss', 'Ma'am', 'How are you ladies?' I just feel like, though I was born female and my destiny will follow to a great extent the female destiny, I always question what I get when I say 'I'm a woman.' I've had my bio tweaked so many times by people that feminize it. If it was some kind of relational thing, like 'She's a mother figure over a generation of younger females,' we are not able to have a relation that is cultural. It has to be a 'woman thing.' There are times I feel like 'he.' What I really like about 'they,' despite its initial awkwardness for some people, including myself, is that it's kind of baggy and loose, and there's room for all my selves.
>
> (Satran 2016)

This statement recognizes that while Myles does not necessarily see their body as untethered from the female experiences that have conditioned the way in which they live, there is a rejection of the societal manifestations of what it means to occupy a stable gender position. 'They' offers room for all the selves in the same way that Myles' identification with specific categories, and then their transgression of them, allows for the coexistence of multiple forms of selfhood. These are not contradictory or vying for attention against one another but rather coinciding within the body and work of the poet identifying as 'Eileen Myles'. The testimonies and recommendations included on the back cover for *Inferno (A Poet's Novel)* and *I Must Be Living Twice* are testament to the way Myles mobilizes identity categories if only to occupy and then escape. Occupation, in this instance, seems far more aligned with the Occupy movement in which the disenfranchised regain some power by taking up residence in the very infrastructures that support oppression. Recognizing the identity category for the edifice that it is, Myles pitches their temporary tent with an eye to the next fruitful ground of hegemonic contestation. John Waters writes, 'Is she a "hunk"? A "dyke"? A "female" I'll tell you what she is – damn smart!' (Myles 2010), while Lena Dunham claims that Myles' essential poetry is 'the hip kid leaning against their locker' and 'the smartest boy in class.'[1] Encountering Myles' work is to

---

[1] 'I Must Be Living Twice' on *Serpent's Tail* https://serpentstail.com/i-must-be-living-twice.html (accessed 26 April 2017).

recognize the lesbian poet, the dyke bravado, butch posturing, all of which create instability from which the poet is able to move elsewhere.

The promotional video itself mobilizes categories in precisely the same way as Myles' creative work. Myles establishes themself as a 'poet', while promoting a new novel. The caveat of 'poet's novel' suggests a hybridity in which the poet as figure has ownership of the prose text. What cannot be displaced is this mantle of 'poet', and so it has to transgress the genre of poetry, remaining as a title that can be applied elsewhere. This suggests two things: potentially, above all else, Eileen Myles is essentially a poet; and then perhaps, contrarily, that the category of 'poet' is capacious enough to extend to novels and other genres. Both of these possibilities speak to Myles' continual emphasis that any categories of identity can be positioned as essential and constructed, simultaneously. As such, the promotional video itself is framing a piece of writing that exploits the instability of categories, a work wherein a poet can produce prose, and promoting prose itself can become poetry. Myles' embodied presence also speaks to category transgression in which they clearly present as butch. In an interview with J.D. Samson, before drawing on the gender-neutral pronoun, Myles stated that 'in terms of gender and sexuality, it is such a changing, changing thing over time ... I am female but I feel butch. But I feel like my version of butch' (Sampson 2011). Where this has since extended into a rejection of the female pronoun at the same time as recognizing how being born female creates an almost inescapable female destiny, Myles' performance in the promotional video is of a butchness that inevitably punctures or destabilizes their seeming female-ness. In *Queer Phenomenology*, Ahmed writes that 'you can feel the categories that you fail to inhabit: they are sources of discomfort. Comfort is a feeling that tends not to be consciously felt ... Discomfort, in other words, allows things to move' (2006: 154). These slight failures to inhabit fully manifest in Myles' work as a multivalent slipperiness. This slipperiness is finally consolidated by Myles' promotional video announcing themself as a 'lesbian no-one' in an imagined scenario of presenting their work to publishers. The lesbian seems to be conflated with irrelevancy and obscurity. It is not purely that Myles is unknown but that their status as a lesbian consolidates that unimportance. All of this is communicated via the medium of a promotional video, hosted on YouTube and a publisher's website. Even while identifying as a 'lesbian no-one', Myles is clearly demonstrating how that self-designation can move from obscurity into something analogous to avant-garde fame.

In 'The Lesbian Poet', a work titled to reflect Myles' identification as both a lesbian and poet, the writer addresses how they navigate a multiplicity of identifications, drawing on intersections of categories in order to find a place in which they feel comfortable. They write: 'It was something about the area of feminism, gay or lesbian issues, something like that, that tradition ... that's it, my spot, but then I realized it was poetry or the poetics of it that I was needing to address' (1997: 123). Creating a crude Venn diagram of identity, a shape that already seems to defy the straight lines of categories, Myles establishes their poetics as answering to the intersection of poet, lesbian and feminist. The necessity of responding to this overlap having been established, Myles goes on to undo the 'lesbian' throughout the piece. In a gesture of unbecoming as outlined by Halberstam, Myles allows for the lesbian to become lost as an essential category, re-emerging as a term that has far more power for poetics. Myles states that 'a lesbian is just an idea. An aesthetic one perhaps' (1997: 125). If 'lesbian' is an idea, then all identity categories are determined solely on concepts. An idea is not a certainty; it is created in thought, through processes, and can often be subject to change. Is it that Myles' lesbianism is an idea, or is it that to be a lesbian is to occupy the space of ideas? This is further complicated by the elision of idea with aesthetics. If 'lesbian' is an aesthetic idea, then how should it look? Unlike the promotional video in which the audience is able to engage with an embodied Myles, 'The Lesbian Poet' offers up no such physically realized iteration of the lesbian aesthetic. This not only problematizes the stable category of 'lesbian' but 'feminism' and 'poetry' too. If sexuality can be an aesthetic or idea, then how do the more mutable identities of feminist and poet fare? One is not born into politics or poetics but rather constructs them. Where Myles' Venn diagram seemed to offer up a stable centre from which a poetics could emerge, their subsequent discussion of those very converging identities actually suggests a writing that breaks the intersection, both conceptually and aesthetically.

In *Gender Trouble*, Judith Butler writes:

> If to become a lesbian is an *act*, a leave-taking of heterosexuality, a self-naming that contests the compulsory meanings of heterosexuality's *women* and *men*, what is to keep the name of lesbian from becoming an equally compulsory category? ... And if it is an 'act' that founds the identity as performative accomplishment of sexuality, are there certain kinds of acts that qualify over others as foundational? Can one do the act with a 'straight mind'? Can one understand lesbian sexuality not only as a contestation of the category of 'sex,' of 'women,' of 'natural bodies,' but also of 'lesbian'?
>
> (2006: 173)

Here, Butler recognizes the performative essence of identifying as a lesbian. The act of self-naming, which proliferates through Myles' work, not only resists heteronormativity and the gender binary implied by it but also foregrounds the possibilities for acting out. In having established their lesbianism as fundamental to poetics, Myles goes on to call the sexuality and identity into question. It is just an idea – an aesthetic one perhaps. In so doing, Myles consciously troubles the 'lesbian' as category, problematizing sex, gender and body categories, while addressing self-determination. It also demonstrates a flippant approach to the identity in which the usually politicized lesbian becomes something that is more aesthetically orientated. Their performative accomplishment of sexuality, here, is to refuse the stability of all categories, ultimately applying this very anti-essentialism to their chosen name, 'lesbian'.

'The Lesbian Poet' also describes a moment in which Myles is standing atop a hill, looking at the landscape and realizing 'there was no thing of woman at all. I was standing in nature alone, this guy. It was a terrifically human feeling' (1997: 125). Here, albeit involuntarily, Myles seems to escape the gender they have established within the work, to become a 'guy', which they position as ultimately universal. This transition from woman to guy, in which the former is totally effaced from the experience, is something the poet describes as terrifically human. Myles treats the movement between the genders incredibly lightly, where without precursor or explanation, they shift to freedom and guyhood. In their short essay 'Iceland', the poet explains a similar sensation on visiting the country, writing 'I think a man is safe like this in the world and a woman never is. So it was a masculine feeling when I woke up. I opened my eyes. And there it was again. Magnificent' (2009: 44). This invocation of maleness is problematic in a number of ways. In 'The Lesbian Poet' it seems to suggest that total freedom is only made possible through the male gender. While 'guy' is colloquial, it still moves Myles out of a category of woman and into one that is approximating man. Furthermore, there is the suggestion that in order to access and represent human experience, one must be male. This, of course, speaks to a history in which the male is universal, while female experience is relegated to representations of messy subjectivity. This is reiterated in 'Iceland', where Myles describes appreciation for a landscape through a lens of masculinity. It is perhaps because they find the landscape expansive and non-threatening that they must be identified as a man. However, it is also possible, as Butler writes that the lesbian is 'a category that radically problematizes both sex and gender as stable political categories of description' (2006: 153). If this is the case, then Myles takes the act of problematization even further, not purely relying on lesbianism to trouble gender categories. Instead, they are simultaneously a lesbian (one who radically troubles the stability of sex and gender), a woman and a man. Myles rejects Butler's suggestion that a lesbian 'can, if one chooses, become neither female nor male, woman nor man' (2006: 153). Instead, they become both: they are this guy on the precipice of the universe, and they are this female lesbian considering the aesthetics of identity. What might be a choice determined by a binary is disregarded entirely, creating a lightness through which Myles is able to shift. Refusing the nothingness associated with the lesbian identity, Myles opts for everything, creating a fluid and difficult movement between all of these instable categories.

Myles' 'Promotional Material' addresses the problem of the category of 'woman' and 'lesbian' (1991b: 96–103). They write that women 'get / pushed / around. We / don't know how / to fight' (ll.159–163). Using the collective pronoun, Myles' line breaks give this statement solidity, rather than fragmenting the identification. Women become collective through the ways they are treated, pushed and denied the knowledge of how to fight. Myles then moves into a second-person address, when discussing the way in which their identity politics are approached by others. They write, 'people / say oh are / you a feminist' (ll.174–177) and 'are you a / loser?' (ll.181–182). The poem then states that if women resist this collapsing together of feminism and being a loser, 'they / think you're / a lesbian' (ll.27–29), and later, '& you are / a lesbian. / Which ruins / everything' (ll.243–245). Here, Myles uses woman, lesbian and feminist as categories in order to explore how such identities can play out, dangerously, within a public space. In spite of the warnings that seem affixed to each identification, whether that is being a loser feminist, or a woman incapable of fighting, there is a humour in the fact that the status of 'lesbianism' affirms everything. This extract is funny, and in fact, flippant in the face of potential violence. Myles rejects the way in which they are interpolated in public, resisting such a call, but nonetheless recognizes that the call is correct. As opposed to railing, Myles concedes with a shrug that reveals a levity even in relation to the way in which lesbians are uncomfortably called out when demonstrating a particular kind of politics.

Whatever fluidity that Myles allows for themself in 'The Lesbian Poet' and 'Iceland', both works strongly suggest that such fluidity cannot easily move beyond the texts into wider social contexts. As Ahmed writes in *Queer Phenomenology*, 'the politics of mobility, of who gets to move with ease across the lines that divide spaces, can be re-described as the politics of who gets to be at home and who gets to extend their bodies into inhabitable spaces, as spaces that are inhabitable as they extend the surfaces of such bodies' (2006: 142). Myles' continual movements suggest that there is not a home to be found anywhere. Spaces might be habitable for a short while, but movement is inevitable. This relates to the way that Myles occupies space, acknowledging the need to take up a challenging impermanent residence before inevitably moving on. In order to feel safety beyond the space of poetry, a masculinity or maleness becomes necessity. While Myles is unfixing gender categories, and certainly their place within them, they are also interrogating the way women can encounter the world. Gender seems to serve as a mediator for experience, where the transcendent and sublime is made impossible to women through danger. 'The Lesbian Poet' fluctuates between the biologically determined and the constructed, prioritizing neither over the other, ultimately suggesting that both can be subject to significant change. This demonstrates an unbecoming levity in which fluctuations of identity are unbecoming and then becoming, only to unbecome once more. The ease with which Myles moves, and the lack of hierarchy at work, approaches sex and gender with a lightness that is flippant.

Nelson writes that she 'can think of no other contemporary American poet who has wielded the power of the performative utterance as astutely and exhaustively as Myles' (2011b: 179). In their *Paris Review* interview, Myles makes a number of comments about the compulsive performance of selfhood. They say, 'It's very weird – I feel like I'm working for Eileen or something, like I have this job being their performer' (Lerner 2015). That Myles describes 'Eileen' as a performance job flippantly constructs selfhood as something that must be compulsively performed but does not have any essential realness. They then go on to say that 'writing is all performance ... The performance is us writing what's using us, remarking upon it' (Lerner 2015: 179). These performances are vital for Myles' engagement with, and transgression of, traditional identity categories. The performative utterance is one that seems to fix the poet in place, before the next exclamation allows for them to move completely and unexpectedly away from that which is established. Myles recognizes the centrality of performance to all of their work. Performance is not just a reading, nor presenting the self within the work; it is also the act of writing itself. Myles' work, as I will go on to explore later in this chapter, is obsessed with both the act of writing and the sex act. It is no surprise that the centrality of writing and sex are equated with the performative and the put-on; they are an act in the same way Myles' active interrogation of 'Eileen Myles' is an act. It is not, therefore, just a medium or a means of communication but a possibility of performance. Myles has stated that poetry can be deep, but they are not a good example of it, which is perhaps why their emphasis is on the performativity of the text and the surface. This rejection of depth is also widely applicable to their approach to gender, performance, selfhood and writing. They skate across the surfaces of each category, flippantly and lightly using and disregarding titles.

This intentional performance of both selfhood and creative writing speaks to the way Butler addresses Drag Queens as the best embodiment of gender performativity. She writes, 'If the anatomy of the performer is already distinct from the gender of the performer, and both of those are distinct from the gender of the performance, then the performance suggests a dissonance not only between sex and performance, but sex and gender, and gender and performance' (2006: 187). While Myles' anatomy, sex and gender are not clearly and deliberately different from one another, as in the role of Drag Queens, their presentation of butchness and intentional movements between male and female categories complicate the consistency of gender, sex and performance. Can butch be a gender? Can the anatomy of the butch raise questions about the gender identity of the performer, radically disrupting the coherence with which it has previously linked to performance and gender? Myles' understanding of poetry as performance, in addition to the performative aspects of their promotional video, demonstrates a knowing dissonance in the ways that gender, sex and performance can map onto one another. Even more significantly, Myles demonstrates that this dissonance can be especially productive within the performance space of the poem. Here Myles demonstrates a highly conscious performance in which self-representation is a very necessary affectation, all of which allow for them to move lightly among sex, gender, poetry and identity, using flippancy acts as a form of disruption and dissonance.

'I must get on & save myself': Community formations

Given Myles' approach to selfhood and identity categories, there are – understandably – numerous ways in which to approach their understanding of community. In *Getting Medieval: Sexualities and Communities, Pre- and Postmodern*, Carolyn Dinshaw writes that community is 'some sort of social grouping that is not a conventional kinship group; the term as I use it does not in itself imply unity or homogeneity' (1999: 22). In contrast, Ahmed understands that 'affective communities take shape by a shared orientation toward certain things', suggesting that the stickiness of affective bonds is created through collective movement in certain directions (2010a: 158). The 'things' might be ideas, values or objects, but they nonetheless orientate a group such that their affects and identities are consolidated through community ties. This is different to Heather Love's understanding of 'community not as constituted by a shared set of identity traits, but rather as emerging from shared experience of social violence' (2007: 51). Myles' understanding of community situates itself somewhere between all three definitions, resonating with each one in different terms. Through affiliating themselves with poets, Myles is redefining kinship groups such that they are based around shared investment. It is, perhaps, not conventional for poetry to be the 'thing' by which a group is orientated, as Ahmed outlines. However, this sharing does allow for a directed community to emerge which, in spite of its shared object, is not characterized by unity or homogeneity.

However, there is also an element of Love's definition of community that emerges throughout Myles' work. Unlike Ahmed's and Dinshaw's understanding, in which non-normative models of living and cooperating come together, Love's communities are predicated on shared experience – more specifically, the shared experience of social violence. As someone born female with a female destiny, a dyke, a poet and a no one, Myles inevitably experiences and engages with the negative affects that are associated with their identity intersections. Their book *Chelsea Girls* describes Eileen being gang-raped, to which their ultimate response is writing their name in the sand on a beach and then erasing it. Myles says that this moment exemplifies 'the precarity ... the precarity of the name and the self is so real' (Lerner 2015). The character is trashed by the group of men because Eileen Myles is young, working class and female. What Myles' writing does is not just create or describe communities in which objects are shared and affects are strong but also where the hurt and marginalized may be able to share those pains.

In *Inferno (A Poet's Novel)*, Myles writes, 'I understood community. Going to the place and standing around. Aiming for connection to bodies, language and the future' (2010: 41). This definition of community is preceded by Myles' claim that it was 'an artist's responsibility for a very long time to get collected socially' (2010: 33). The idea of 'collection' does not necessarily map onto finding a collective but, instead, onto being assimilated into a community. The social aspect of this is vital; poetry communities are not realized remotely, with an emphasis on shared objectives, but are instead an embodied coming together. That Myles understands the artist's prerogative as being collected speaks to Ahmed's community in which people adhere to one another through a shared orientation. Speaking about art, socializing around art, the artist is socially collected through this particular orientation. When reading this against Myles' definition of community as connection to bodies, language and the future, each of these possibilities constitutes a 'thing' that orientates the social groupings. What is interesting is that this almost noble formation of artist communities is undercut by the banality of 'going to the place and standing around'. Even while Myles seems to take the importance of community seriously, this is a flippant approach to groupings. They are made possible through the mundanity of hanging out in a specific location. This does not constitute a traditional kinship model, but it is a grouping that could exist without unity or homogeneity. Community, for Myles, seems part banal, part necessary, full of promise and also contingent, where embodied presence is a necessary prerequisite for the grouping. Yet all of these things are deflated so that the seriousness of community becomes light-hearted and flippant; as a queer poet, you don't have to look for sameness; you can just stand around.

'The Lesbian Poet' develops these unconventional kinship models through an invocation of other poets towards which Myles finds themself orientated. In outlining a poetic lineage for themself, in essence making family of those who have preceded them, they turn to both men and women, acknowledging that they emerge from a many-fathered tradition as opposed to one populated by maternal figures. Citing Jimmy Schuyler, John Weiners and Robert Creeley, all of whom were alive at the time of writing, Myles states that 'recently I began claiming men, a new idea. To not be ashamed of their influence on me' (1997: 127). Interestingly, what Myles does with their vocabulary is create a traditional kinship model that purports a non-normative mode of poetic engagement. Choosing a 'family' analogy, Myles refers to the male poets as uncles and then goes on to identify their mothers as 'Gertrude, Gertrude Stein, of course. And all the living women I know' (1997: 127). Myles identifies multiple mothers: Stein and then every woman whom they know. In doing so they queer what could be understood as a matriarchal lineage, drawing the role of mother into the realization of everyday contemporaries. While Stein has a weighty and canonical gravitas, certainly within the avant-garde, the 'living women' speak far more to people operating within the same space. Generation is irrelevant, and Myles is indifferent to hierarchies, while still acknowledging that they are begat of all the women whom they meet. In this way, the gender category informs their poetic work in a more slippery and digressive way than the cited male poets do.

Nonetheless, 'The Lesbian Poet' also recognizes the misogyny that circulates within both queer and poetry movements. Before constructing a rich poetic lineage of uncles and mothers (but, perhaps significantly, not fathers), Myles says that 'as a literary lesbian vis a vis gay men I'm more alone than ever before' (1997: 126). Invoking the AIDS crisis, Myles gestures to the fact that numerous gay men have died, often quickly, and with little warning. Poets had to address the need to remember these men, not purely commemorating them but to make their loss of life an active political tool. While Myles whispers that they are willing to continue naming these men, invoking them even after they have gone, they acknowledge that the necessary conversations between lesbians and gay men are not going on. In fact, they state, 'Men want to be remembered by men' (1997: 126). This statement ruptures two potential communities for Myles, wherein the poetic and the queer are dismantled through unequal gender relationships. Writers are not united by the fact that they share a similar object of orientation, as outlined by Ahmed. In fact, male writers want to be recognized by male writers; their community is determined through gender recognition. Similarly, gay men do not want to be remembered by lesbians, because actually, only other men can confer value on the dead. Unlike the groups suggested by Dinshaw and the shared orientations explored by Ahmed, women are blocked and rejected from both literary and LGBT communities. It is not purely that women lack worth but that the female gaze and female power are considered worthless. They cannot reflect greatness onto the men who desire it. This marginalization from both writing and queer communities, two of the circles of Myles' Venn diagram, resonates far more with Love's analysis of community as comprised of those who have shared experience of social violence. A woman's place in both queer and literary communities is undercut by their gender.

It is perhaps for this reason that 'The Lesbian Poet' calls for exclusively female relationships to establish themselves. Myles write: 'There is a word in Italian, *affidamento*, which describes a relationship of trust between two women, in which the younger asks the elder to help her ... Women I know are turning around to see if that woman is here' (1997: 130). Thus, while Myles is able to identify their male uncles and even address the fact that they are indebted to male poets for their influence, they also recognize the need for new female attachments. Women need to be reorientated towards one another, channelling energy into the turn. The revolutionary turn is a radical gesture; it is a turn away from what sits at the centre so that the rest of the room can come into play. In this sense it requires a commitment to unbecoming; becoming unbecoming through turning away from a world that rejects you, turning into a series of relationships that might actually form a successful model of kinship.

In their poem 'Keats & I' (1991c: 171–183) Myles gestures to wider community affiliations, having created a poem that moves through multiple locations, different forms of technology, such as the answering machine, and a number of temporalities, ranging from the weekend to specific times of day. Myles writes:

> I believe in
> a community of
> believers. It's
> the most believing
> I do which
> creates faith.
>
> (ll.278–283)

They then go on, 'Let's drink buckets / of coffee. Let's / imagine ourselves / all fired up / for once' (ll.292–296). The belief in the community is located, outside of the grandiose claims of faith, in the banal day to day of coffee drinking. Once more Myles' serious approach to communities is deflated with flippancy in which caffeine is as integral as belief, faith and being fired up. This seems to gesture back to Myles identifying all the women they know as mothers of their poetics; it is the quotidian that creates the community and allows for faith and belief to develop.

Myles makes similar statements, but specifically in relation to women, in their poem 'Basic August' (1991d: 73–95). They write:

> I believe
> all the women
> could be strong
> & stand up &
> lock hands
> & bond. We
> could save
> ourselves
> we could save everyone
> we could be
> here tonight
> & I am.
>
> (ll.218–229)

While these statements of community are embedded within longer lyric poems, their presence counters the individual and mobile focus that dominates the rest of the works. Interestingly, in both poems, Myles places emphasis on communities over categories. When they ask women to come together and lock hands and bond, the category of 'woman' moves into the 'community of believers' outlined in 'Keats & I'. Myles' work propounds that community has the capacity to move people together, create sticky affects and mobilize solidarity in order to effect change.

This, to some extent, explains the way in which 'The Lesbian Poet' concludes in a consideration of Getrude Stein. The return to Stein almost enacts the turn Myles wishes for all women; instead of progressing onwards, they look backwards to a poet who has already been referenced within the talk. 'It's a pity she's dead,' Myles says, before elaborating: 'yet the fact that our greatest poet of the century is a lesbian is nothing to sneeze at ... That a woman unwriting herself, flooding the world with her details, standing in such an endangered place could be free' (1997: 131). It is possible that Myles identifies something in Stein that seems applicable to their own way of working and being. Indeed, Nelson writes that Myles' writing 'balances a Stein-like conviction of her own genius and significance with a startling – indeed shameless – exploration of her powerlessness and shame' (2011b: 185). Stein is a lesbian and butch; she transgresses feminity while still retaining an ability to write the rhythms of the female body. This focus on the body is fundamental in terms of mapping onto Myles' ideas of presence and embodiment in which the poet is in some ways embodied through the use of their title (or name) and the lyric 'I'. The fact that Stein unwrites herself is what Myles aspires to; it is an unbecoming that allows for the subject to move in potentially new directions. Among a culture of shared violence, in which we can assume Stein had the same problems of marginalization as Myles, the former is free. Freedom is possible in spite of the endangered place, something that seems evident from Myles' poetry on perfectly realized female communities.

'I was the mouth': The pornography of poetics

Myles' work on sex is not purely to destabilize the relationships between gender and performance. Sex features heavily in every poetry collection, each memoir, and most vividly in *Inferno (A Poet's Novel)*, where there is a highly descriptive and slightly abstract section on the different vaginas of Myles' lovers. This sex writing is occasionally realized through Myles' direct references to pornography as a genre. In fact, in the promotional video, the poet claims that people are going to love the book because 'the tone is all over the map ... it's almost porn' (OR Books 2010). Linking voice to both consumption and sex, the energy suggested by such an analogy once more gestures to the performative nature of the poet's work. The energy is such that an audience can become aroused through the movement, shifting and unrepentant tonality of the text. How is it that traversing the map with tone becomes potentially sexual? And if not explicitly sexual, as compelling, addictive and consumable as pornography? Myles' embodied presence in the promotional video ensures that their voice remains the same throughout – a stable voice that is recognizable through all of their poetry and memoirs. Even if the register or tone shifts, the reader and viewer understand Myles and their lyric I as one and the same. This pornographic tone could emerge from the poet themself, the manifestations of their voice on the page, the page itself, or the reader's interpretation of Myles' performance of the writing. All over the map suggests a fixed sense of place that is, in parts, animated by the movement of the speaker. De Certeau defines place as an 'instantaneous configuration of positions. It implies an indication of stability' (1984: 117). What Myles is claiming for tone, however, resonates far more with de Certeau's definition of space, which is 'composed of intersections of mobile elements. It is in a sense actuated by the ensemble of movements deployed within it' (1984: 117). Somewhere between the place of the map, then, and the actual space that the mobile and fluctuating tone creates, we have the possibility for almost-porn to emerge.

While Myles often references pornography within their poems, essays and interviews, their work could not be said to constitute porn, a concept that I will return to later. Instead, the use of the term seems to suggest that a poetics of pornography could be traced through their writing, one that is inherited, changed and then redeployed within their own lesbian feminist context. In *Inferno*, Myles describes the work of Frank O'Hara as follows:

> the poems were queenie – slippery and fast like the city outside the store. You could hear it right on the page. I thought about Frank Harris who wrote *My Secret Life*, which was pornography. This was a little bit too. You had to close the book if you wanted it to stop.
>
> (2010: 40)

Porn, in this context, proposes both location and dislocation in regard to voice and embodiment. Myles discusses their relationship with two texts, which are audible from the page, slippery, fast and relentless. Nonetheless, the authors' bodies themselves are not present; the only mode of communicating pornography is the page. While the reading process is located within a bookstore, the voices themselves resemble the city beyond. As Myles stands still, engrossed in a reading process that seems to hold its own form of momentum, the pornographic happens around them, through the voices of the texts and the city outside. Both of these contributors to the pornographic speak to Myles' claim that their tone is all over the map. The reader is offered a place in which to locate themselves – Myles' writing – but no means by which to traverse the area. This disorientation turns the placeholder of page and voice into a mobile space of intersecting possibilities, one of which is arousal.

Pornography also offers a more complex approach to artifice and intimacy within the work of the poet. In porn, an audience is able to watch sex acts being performed. In that sense, the genre is both inherently concerned with performance and also the ability to act and act well. The participants must commit to their act, where what might be artificial in terms of narrative, setting and context becomes very real and embodied within the sex itself. This embodied, messy and necessary act of sexual intercourse within pornography almost queers how performance and acts can be understood.[2] There is a real underpinning the unreal of the artifice. However, this real does not necessarily translate into intimacy. To watch sex, or be a witness to the sex of others, within highly contrived situations for which the performers are paid, is not to engage in an intimate relationship with those involved. In spite of their bodies and in spite of the intercourse being represented, the spectator has no knowledge of the inner workings of the couple or even the individual's sexual preferences. Much like Myles' use of 'Eileen Myles' and 'I' throughout their work, the nakedness of porn does not automatically assume truth and intimacy. This, perhaps, offers a guide for the way in which the reader needs to think about Myles' own tone: we are given a map but no directions, encouraged to enjoy the artifice that, at times, resembles nakedness.

The feminist lesbian relationship with pornography is a complicated one, given the politics' history with the genre. In contemporary feminism, the pornography debate has been reignited with the publishing house Routledge producing a publication that supports and interrogates the industry from a pro-porn stance (Robinson 2013). Meanwhile, feminist activist Julia Long claims that this particular historical moment is seeing a re-emergence of the anti-pornography movement (2012). This is offset by more significant developments in the United States and Canada, particularly in the form of *The Feminist Porn Book* (2013). Combining writing from academics, activists, practitioners and performers, the book considers the possibilities for feminist pornography in a non-hierarchical text that privileges all forms of testimony and analysis. As such, I will focus on *The Feminist Porn Book*'s definition of the genre, given that Myles

---

[2] I use 'intercourse' here to denote any kind of sexual engagement intended to arouse or titillate an audience. Using intercourse here is necessary for differentiating between what the performers do to one another and then the more general idea of sex being understood as an 'act'.

seems to be deploying the terms in ways that are sex-positive and celebratory. Feminist porn generally:

> uses sexually explicit imagery to contest and complicate dominant representations of gender, sexuality, race, ethnicity, class, ability, age, body type, and other identity markers. As a result, there is no definitive stance on what 'porn' is, what it constitutes, who it subjugates and what its politics are. It explores concepts of desire, agency, power, and pleasure at their most confounding and difficult, including pleasure within and across inequality, in the face of injustice, and against the limits of gender hierarchy and both heteronormativity and homonormativity.
>
> (Penley et al. 2013: 9–10)

The editors of *The Feminist Porn Book* champion porn that 'creates alternative images and develops its own aesthetics and iconography to expand established sex norms and discourses' (Penley et al. 2013: 10). This particular porn seems very much defined through its ideological underpinnings, as well as its aesthetic possibilities. In this way it does not differ entirely from how Myles approaches the term 'lesbian'. Exploding the signifier into an aesthetic idea, the poet creates a sense of openness for identification. Similarly, feminist pornography is confounding and difficult but primarily concerned with agency and undoing gender hierarchies. Interestingly, in her anti-pornography work, Long writes that 'most people in a culture where pornography is available are able to recognise it without a consensus on a definition' (Long 2012: 58). Much like the tone that ranges all over the map and the Eileen Myles who doesn't know who they are, pornography should be immediately recognizable and affective, even if it cannot be clearly and coherently defined. Interestingly, this is not dissimilar to the figure of the Gertrude Stein butch, who is understood through the maxim 'You know one when you see one.'

Pornography's presence within the promotional video is both bravado and flippancy. Porn works as a flippant comment on how good and compelling writing can be, while the claim that their writing is so consumable demonstrates a great confidence on Myles' part. Porn's conflation with 'being all over the map' implies that narrative is not central to conveying meaning. Returning to the promotional video, it is easy to see that narrative is not central to Myles' projection of their work and self. Moving and cutting throughout, the video denies a linear progression, favouring disruption and digression instead. Tone follows a similar pattern. It does not move from point A to B in a solid and progressive journey forwards. The reader will be presented with a series of tangents, wrong turns, slippages, turning around, revising and reorientation. This implies an erratic mobility for the voice of the work, as well as the reader. It also suggests that the movement itself is central, as opposed to where the moving ultimately takes us. In a 2001 interview with *HOW2*, Myles says, 'I often think of sex writing – whatever that is – in relation to something like dance movies, where there is little plot going on, and then people break into a dance. Later, when I saw porn, I thought oh, that's the same structure' (Lamm 2001). Once more, Myles makes use of a flippant parallel to discuss their relationship to structure and reader experience. Sex writing is like porn, is like a dance movie, perhaps the only genre to be considered less vapid than the mechanical reproduction of sex for the purpose of filming. Movement without an overriding narrative arc, or without the normative usage of a map, requires the reader to appreciate the affective emersion of becoming willingly lost. Emphasis is placed on the sensational, the vivid and experienced, as opposed to communicating a lucid progression to a reader.

Myles is not using the genre purely to reflect or frame their impact on readership. The inclusion of pornography is also a gesture towards subversive, counterculture and avant-garde modes of engagement. In 'A Feminist Teaching Pornography! That's Like Scopes Teaching Evolution', Constance Penley outlines some of the central concerns and ideas of pornography, reassuring her reader that 'porn isn't lewd for nothing' (2013: 187). She elucidates further with the following question: 'Can we still recognize porn's historical continuity with avant-garde revolutionary art, populist struggles, or any kind of counterculture impulses?' (Penley 2013: 187). This points to the fact that pornography has a history associated with counterculture as opposed to our current mainstream understanding of the genre. This is reiterated by Laura Kipnis, who says that pornography can be 'a realm of transgression that is, in effect, counter-aesthetics to dominant norms for bodies, sexuality and desire itself' (Penley 2013: 187). Pornography then is not solely concerned with female subordination and capitalism but can actually be affiliated with revolution and transgression. In offering a counter-aesthetics that is reflective of its avant-garde potential, pornography is much like the lesbian of Myles' 'The Lesbian Poet' – an idea, and an aesthetic one at that, that both the lesbian body in poetry and pornography can create spaces in which identity normativity is interrogated and subverted. For Myles, equating their tone to pornography reads as a resistance to the appropriate, choosing instead to reframe lust and consumption such that it can represent a feminist, lesbian poet.

In 'The Lesbian Poet', the speaker briefly recalls a conversation with a male friend about the size of female genitalia. Their male acquaintance laughs about the size of female orifices, claiming that men leave women after they have had babies; birth makes vaginas too loose for male sexual pleasure. The explicitness with which Myles relays this conversation speaks to the titillation of porn but also distances the reader from the more mainstream ideas surrounding arousal. We are not presented with the well-kept and tight woman, whom we are invited to penetrate in the way a man might. Instead, the speaker states how such considerations differ in lesbian sex, when two women encounter one another. They write, 'It's different for us. We love it. Huge with desire. An incredible dripping cave' (1997: 126). Here, the sex act is pleasurable on account of the hugeness. The vagina becoming a dripping cave makes wetness and the cavernous space welcoming, almost desirous of being filled. Thus, Myles sets lesbian desire against heterosexual and normative expectations, giving the woman's body an autonomy that invites sexual encounter.

In their poem 'Untitled (I Always Put My Pussy)' (2016d: 150) Myles addresses the female anatomy and the genitals of their female lover. Using the colloquial 'pussy' and 'cunt', which in themselves are porn-like in tone, they work to demystify the female genitalia. They write:

> I always put my lover's cunt
> on the crest
> of a wave
> like a flag
> that I can
> pledge my
> allegiance
> to.
>
> (ll.6–13)

The lover's cunt is not simply an orifice to be penetrated but receives diverse and divergent treatment that is more nuanced and relational. The lover's pussy is later personified, given human qualities and interests. It 'has a sense of humour / has a career / has a cup of coffee' (ll.37–39). The speaker also states that the cunt of their lover 'knows my face / knows my tongue / knows my hands' (ll.43–45) but has 'lousy manners' (l.47). Here, sex is being invoked, not in a simplistic and one-directional sense but with intimacy and multiplicity. The personal is attributed to the sex organs. This poem works as a form of empowerment, where the two cunts claim one another as territory, in a relationship of fidelity and tenderness. However, this juxtaposes with a more flippant approach in which the pussy is attributed with liking coffee and having lousy manners. This brings a sense of restlessness to the work, which reads as an interrupted declaration of solidarity, where the seriousness is continually deflated through flippant asides. It is these shifts and juxtapositions that allow for a poetics of flippancy to come to the fore, enacting the unbecoming levity in the face of more serious subjects. The poem develops such that the pussies of both the speaker and the lover gain a depth of character, becoming autonomous parts of human anatomy. When stimulation is finally introduced, through the naming of hands, face and tongue, the lover and their pussy are established as full and rounded. While the whole poem has been located around two cunts, the cunts are used to orientate the reader and the speaker such that, ultimately, 'my lover & I / can be safe' (ll.58–59).

The placement of the pussy, whether in the middle of trees or at work, also speaks to the idea of map and tonality: sex is placed firmly all over a series of locations, and the tone is one of simultaneous lust and carefulness. The pussy is viewed in multiple positions, but these snapshots situate themselves outside a coherent narrative. Much like the sex writing, which is so reminiscent of a dance film's sudden snap into musical numbers, the poem moves between various poses. The focus on the pussy works as the close-up of a camera lens, allowing a reader to see a multiplicity of colours and experiences that are then mapped onto public and social engagement. Myles also comments in their *HOW2* interview that 'sometimes it [writing about sex] seems like an interesting thing to do, and sometimes it doesn't even seem to be on the map' (Lamm 2001). Using the same image as in their promotional video, Myles implies that a combination of tone, focus and movement is what constitutes the pornographic, but that sexual explicitness has to be located on a map, even if its coordinates are hard to follow.

Myles' five-line poem 'Porn Poems' (2016e: 198) also addresses this question of structure, subversion and sex-writing dance moves. Opting once more to convey a moment through brevity and movement, the poem seems to echo what Myles considers to be a 'porn structure': a series of shapes thrown together without plot or through line. The work reads:

> Her tongue & her
> > heart were
> > > throbbing
> > in the holster
> > > of her pussy.

The plurality of 'Porn Poems' points to the multiple in a way that is immediately negated by the existence of one stanza. The poem does not describe plural scenarios and, unlike 'Untitled (I Always Put My Pussy)' lacks a number of positions: instead, it presents the image of one woman. The line breaks work to fragment the poem such that, structurally, it is reminiscent of the operations of pornography. The reader is encouraged to focus first on a tongue, then a heart, then the action of throbbing, then a holster and, finally, the image of a pussy. The fact that the pussy is equated with a 'holster' is indicative of what the vagina is able to carry: it might, in fact, be a place for a gun, a locus of power from which the woman can draw at any point. This sense of implicit violence, in addition to the power bestowed upon the genitalia, glamorizes the throbbing that is sexualized by the potential for action. Furthermore, the poem seems to be suggesting that both voice – through this, words – and feeling can be located in the pussy itself. Speech and feeling become synonymous with the gun traditionally held by a holster, while the pussy is the site for communication and love. Despite the structure echoing the jumping from image to image of pornography, Myles complicates the presentation of divided and disembodied female anatomy through drawing them together as a space for communication and power.

'I am full of holes because you are': The queer art of failure

Having described themself as a 'lesbian no-one' in the promotional video, Myles goes on to position themself as a total loser. This loser status, however, is offset by the bombastic reading from *Inferno (A Poet's Novel)* and the assurance with which Myles states their book is as good as porn. Their comportment and the fact that they are the star of a promotional video juxtapose with the status they ascribe to themself and, in so doing, heighten the performativity of the video itself. The poet and lesbian is playing the role of loser; it is an act. Later in the promotional video, Myles goes on to say that their whole novel is about 'what losers we are – Americans' (OR Books 2010). Considering the American attachment to success narratives, being a 'loser' is entirely antithetical to the all-American ideal. It also conflates heterosexual, white, male, authoritative figures with the lesbian no-one who sits at the centre of the camera's focus. While they might be a no-one, a happily self-determined one at that, this category of 'losing' actually extends to the whole of the United States. This sits well with Myles' destabilizing of categories but also speaks to their wider preoccupation with the idea of failure, which they consider as fundamental to poetry. They write in *Inferno* that 'poetry really does require failure, because failure produces space that nobody else wants. Poets as a group hate success' (Myles 2010: 56). Once more, Myles draws on flippancy in order to deflate both poetry and poets. In spite of their attention to poetry, they suggest that poets are anti-success and keen to fail, while poems themselves require a true space of failure that no one else could want. Here, it is probably useful to distinguish between the no-one, the loser and failure as a more general way of being. Myles is no one because they are both a lesbian and a poet, negated through an affiliation with both categories. However, they are also a loser within the wider scope of American nationality, a quality that they are able to share with all of their countrymen. Failure is different and associated far more with the idea of a 'lesbian no one' because it is a space 'nobody' else wants. Poets need this failure though and thrive on it. It allows for space in which Halberstam's unbecoming can take place.

Halberstam writes that 'we can recognize failure as a way of refusing to acquiesce to dominant logics of power and discipline as a form of critique. As a practice, failure recognises that alternatives are embedded already in the dominant' (2011: 88). Myles exemplifies this refusal to acquiesce when they claim that all Americans are losers as opposed to latent successes pursuing the dream of consumption and capital. What is especially significant about Halberstam's quotation is that failure is positioned as a practice. It is not, in fact, passive or a case of bad luck but instead something that must be actively exercised and stretched. Much like poetry, then, failure is a practice in which alternatives are discovered within the dominant. This speaks particularly well to the avant-garde, which is continually looking for innovation and change with the dominant, all the while failing to reach widespread audiences. By positioning the poet, and the poetry, as a space of failure, Myles is denying normativity in such a way that maintains autonomy. Failing, failing to fit and the inability to align give a subject the distance and requisite discomfort to critique their social groups and categories.

Throughout the promotional film, Myles' presence and their speaking have a sense of bravado. Framed by loud rock music, with praise of the work included in text on the screen, they are surrounded by loud affirmations of themself. However, they still choose to foreground that they believe themself to be a member of a nation of idiots and that the work itself is about what losers the people are. To move from bravado to bathetic declarations is central to Myles' poetic work and allows them to style the self as a lesbian underdog despite evident success. Their writing career has been preoccupied with the way in which they can perform the role of the woman, lesbian, poet while acknowledging that as a woman they are disadvantaged, as a lesbian they are sexually alternative and as a poet, they will not garner any mainstream literary success. Despite having written a novel, their insistence on maintaining the category identification of poet is an ongoing insistence to practise their failure to be a novelist, or a man, or heterosexual. Instead, they use their position of slight deviation from normative success to question American social hegemonies and to trouble their position within the communities they do identify with. Myles seems to embrace the role of one who is willingly co-opted; they are the ultimate capitalist loser. Even while they reject that which seems to categorize America, they are still participating in the promotional video, still performing a version of themselves, that while allegedly no one, still claims to be as addictive as porn.

In 'An American Poem' (2016f: 134), Myles explores the successes and failures inherent within the American dream by positioning their lyric speaker as a member of the Kennedy family, who has given up fame and fortune in order to become an obscure and marginalized lesbian poet. As is typical of their work, the numerous shifts, reframings and repositionings ensure that the poem is a problematic representation of power and success, with the lesbian poet ultimately becoming a 'Kennedy' for the people. The title 'An American Poem' seems to suggest two possibilities for the work: either the piece has qualities that would result in it being defined as American in an adjectival sense or it indicates the poem is the belonging of, or a tribute to, the country itself. When the speaker in the poem decides they will reject their Kennedy family and embrace obscurity, they write, 'Well I'll be a poet. / What could be more / foolish and obscure' (ll. 41–43). The lyric 'I' moves from the all-American to the ultimate American loser, rejecting their status as a symbol of patriotism and nationalism in order to adopt a role that renders them entirely unknown. The poem appears, then, to operate based on the assumed binaries of success and failure with an established political family encapsulating the American dream, while the poet represents the nightmare.

The lyric speaker goes on to state that they further distanced themself from the Kennedy success by becoming a lesbian: 'Every woman in my / family looks like / a dyke but it's really / stepping off the flag / when you become one' (ll. 45–49). Despite adopting the position of failure, the embodied lesbian poet, the 'I' states that 'I am beginning to think / there is no escaping / history' (ll. 52–55). These lines suggest that, irrespective of the ways in which an American may attempt to embody failure, their bodies and failings still contribute to a wider national discourse. Failure makes up an important part of the national identity and needs to be considered as central to Americanism as success stories. Due to an inability to avoid fame, the 'I' makes a final admission: 'I am a Kennedy.

And I await / your orders' (ll. 85–87). This section works as a complete reversal in which the poet has come to a position of such importance that they can no longer deny their visibility and political significance. Interestingly, the poem proceeds to consider conditions for production and the ways the political can dictate the movement of art:

> If art is the highest
> and most honest form
> of communication of
> our times and the young
> artist is no longer able
> to move here to speak
> of their time…
>
> (ll. 105–111)

Myles seems to pose the question that if the artist is denied a voice and is not able to offer a representation of their time, then society needs to find a new way to encourage means of expression. The ellipsis is especially notable in the compacted, skinny poem, foregrounding the impossibility of answering. They write: 'Shouldn't we all be Kennedys?' (l.115) and describe those who cannot afford healthcare have bleeding gums, produce art, do not work in politics, are gay; all of these people are Kennedys. The lyric speaker becomes, ultimately, the leader of the losers and also the president of America; 'I am not / alone tonight because / we are all Kennedys. / And I am your President' (ll.155–158). The lightness with which Myles treats the identity of the Kennedys but also the roving losers of which they become a leader is flippant – a practice of flippancy, which here intersects with the practice of failure and critique of American culture. To adopt such a position is to embrace failure, practising a light-heartedness that seems almost contrary to any aspirations of leadership and certainly any revolutionary politics.

Conclusion

Myles' work thrives on unbecoming, using levity as a means by which to undo category distinctions and gender binaries. Using this flippant strategy, they are able to play with titles, names and identities such that all of them become mutable and surface orientated. Myles shares the same genre irreverence as O'Hara, determined to keep their title of poet while moving into the form of the novel. However, they also openly acknowledge the writing of poetry within poems themselves, creating self-conscious constructs that make the process part of the discussion. This commentary introduces an element of levity and artificiality in which the poet very comfortably foregrounds writing, their body, their experiences, revealing to the reader that the poem sits performatively within a chain of communication, as opposed to emerging neatly, in language, untethered from life. This sense of play is also extended into the way in which Myles approaches selfhood. In this aspect, they overlap significantly with Stein, particularly in the way they use the proper name. Where Stein created space for Gertrude Stein, as allegedly written by Alice, in *The Autobiography of Alice B. Toklas*, Myles directly considers what it means to be 'Eileen Myles'. They even go so far as to say that performing Eileen Myles feels like their job. This goes beyond poetry, novels and promotional videos to suggest that identity and names necessitate a subject performing themselves continually. The fact that Myles addresses these various forms of performance, calling their genre, their poetry and themselves into questions demonstrates an unbecoming levity in which they wear all signifiers lightly.

This levity extends to the way in which Myles approaches identity and community as a whole. In *Inferno*, they discuss standing around and waiting to be collected. While Myles is clearly willing to participate in poetry communities, they nonetheless reduce such participation to total banality. There is not a sense of shared identity and investment but rather a feeling of being in the right place in front of other people who also happen to be there This makes community a series of arbitrary connections orientated around place and time, as opposed to occupation, gender or sexuality. 'The Lesbian Poet' critiques community further, stating how men, even gay men, only want to be respected by one another. In fact, there are few places for women to be considered on equal terms, which leads to Myles calling for every woman in the room to turn. Myles demands a reorientation of bodies within these spaces and times to create further possibilities for women. The poems I have examined here also seem to explore some of these ideas of community too. The structures of the works, with their rapid movement and short lines, facilitate a continued sense of lightness. This unbecoming levity allows for Myles to call for communities to come together against shared violence, for example, while still maintaining separateness. Myles exercises this when it comes to identities, too. While they call their name into question, they also interrogate the category of woman as well as that of lesbian. Moving easily between genders within some of the texts I have discussed, they show a levity in relation to binaries and categories. That Myles positions being a lesbian as an aesthetic choice but argues how it ultimately makes them obscure flippantly approaches difficulties surrounding orientation. Through declaring marginalization, while simultaneously undoing the category as anything essentialist, Myles makes space in which they are able to move. In this way, numerous terms proliferate through Myles' texts, one of the most interesting of which is 'loser'. Myles flippantly invokes this particular identity in order to describe their marginal position as both a poet and a lesbian. The social irrelevance of both roles, one of which is ultimately a profession and not related to any identity politics, is freeing in that Myles is able to turn, change direction and orientate themselves in ways that are less linear and heteronormative.

Myles also uses flippancy as a means by which to trouble any lazy associations and assumptions their readers might have made about communities, both poetic and political. Calling poets a group of failure who congregate around non-success contrasts strongly with Myles' reputation as the rockstar of poetry. It also demonstrates an irreverence in relation to their contemporaries, where whatever their success, they are ultimately drawn to the loser allure of poetry. The fact that Myles continues to write poems, and self-identify as a poet even within the space of the novel, demonstrates a disregard or disinterest in what might be defined as success. More politically, perhaps, is the way in which Myles mobilizes porn as part of their feminist politics. In spite of the anti-porn history in feminism, Myles happily draws on the genre to discuss their poetics as well as the way in which they approach the representation of sex. In some instances, porn is deployed with great levity. That Myles thinks their poems are like a dance movie, which is also like porn, sets up an interesting and complex analogy for the text. It becomes posed and postured with very little narrative and moments of great spectacle. That Myles believes their writing can operate with the same structures of porn, and that *Inferno* will be almost porn to the readership, suggests a particularly provocative relationship between the reader and the text. The written word is able to be sexy, but also highly artificial, animated by the desire to get the reader off. Linking their work to this genre places poetry, which is high culture, with the low culture and mass-produced artifice of sex for the camera. In this sense, they reiterate the claim that there are many arguments for poetry being deep, but they are not one of them.

5

'Was Harry a Woman? Was I a Straight Lady?': Tensions of Heteronormativity, Assimilation and the Second Person

Maggie Nelson seems a logical end point for this scrappy and irreverent lineage. She is good friends with Myles; is considered as the final generation in a New York lineage that includes Myles and O'Hara; and has written critically on Myles, O'Hara and Stein. As such, she rounds off this self-selected grouping, clearly influenced by the poets previously discussed in the development of her unique approach to identity and writing. Nelson's own book *Women, The New York School, and Other True Abstractions* pulls the three writers together in order to consider how Stein influenced the NY School, before exploring how O'Hara's poetics informed the writing of a next generation of women poets. In teasing out a heritage originating from Stein, Nelson seems to suggest that there is a relationship between high Modernism butchness and an urban, American camp. However, Nelson does not just reflect critically on these poets. She is the executor of Myles' estate and moved to New York purely to study under the poet. In a tribute for *Poetry Society*, Nelson writes 'after you hear certain voices, the direction of your life is changed, and there's no going back. That was what hearing the voice of Eileen Myles was like for me' (Nelson 2014). Nelson also refers to Myles as one of the 'many-gendered mothers of my heart' (Nelson 2015) in *The Argonauts*, in a gesture that both destabilizes gender and expands the possibilities of maternity. These modes of describing Myles are not dissimilar to the way that Myles approaches Stein in 'The Lesbian Poet'. In that essay, Myles defines Stein as one of their literary mothers before later going on to meditate on the Modernist's brilliant butchness. It is apparent, thus, from the work of Nelson that she associates her writing with that of Stein, O'Hara and Myles. While her relationship with Myles might be more intimate and immediate, akin to a friendship and maternity, her triangulation with Stein and O'Hara is achieved through her critical reflection on New York School poetry.

Nelson is a poet, critic and prose writer, and has expressed hesitation in regard to identifying her texts. As such, she often creates hybrids, teasing and testing the boundaries of demarcated genres. Her work *Bluets* is elegiac prose poetry meditating on the colour blue and a devastating break-up, while *Jane: A Murder* combines extracts from her aunt's diaries, with a heavily lineated poetry meditating on what it means to investigate the murder of a close relative. *The Argonauts* is perhaps Nelson's most genre-defying piece of writing, combining autobiography, memoir and literary criticism with a style that seems shaped in many ways by a background in poetry. When pushed to identify the text, Nelson has eschewed genres that speak exclusively to personal experience, such as autobiography and memoir, settling uncomfortably with autotheory. In an interview for *Book Forum*, she says that 'I realized you could name a book not with a genre but with a noun or even a verb. That was freeing to me, and so *Jane* became "a murder," and *The Art of Cruelty* became "a reckoning"' (Prickett 2015). Nelson says that while *The Argonauts* is lacking in a subtitle she does not mind it being classified as autotheory – 'I allowed that to go on the jacket copy' (Prickett 2015). These forms of titling are an important framing device for Nelson's work as a whole. She becomes almost restless in the naming of things, instead moving away from genre into nouns and verbs. Both 'murder' and 'reckoning' diverge from the terms of the titles and into the methodologies for the books themselves. We, as readers, are not caught within the fixity of the name or focused on the subject of the text, but rather directed to the processes of construction. Nelson's discomfort with naming her own works speaks to the key concepts within *The Argonauts*, a text that is concerned with transgressing the amorphous boundaries of genre and gender. Her titles demonstrate the ways in which our attempts to define language, including genre delineations, can fail to accommodate the mobility and movement necessitated by life.

In this chapter, I will be focusing on *The Argonauts* to consider some of the ways in which the poetics of flippancy can be both traced and problematized through Nelson's work. Again, I will be turning my attention to a new facet of queer culture, one that differs from the butch-camp of Stein, the light-footed posturing of O'Hara and the performativity of Myles into a more uncertain and resistant form of engaging with identity. As with the other writers I have considered in the book, not all of Nelson's work could be said to resonate with a poetics of flippancy. *The Art of Cruelty*, for example, shifts away significantly from the light-hearted into an exploration of dark subject matter. Of course, there are moments in which Nelson maintains an inappropriate levity, drawing on tone to communicate an irreverent approach to the subject matter. In her discussion of the horror film *Captivity*, for example, Nelson pillories the producers for saying that after hosting a focus group they decided not to kill their protagonist but conclude the movie with "'as much of a positive situation as the situation would allow'" (2011a: 51). Nelson wryly comments this 'means her stumbling naked out of a cellar with about a quarter of her internal organs intact' (2011a: 59). In spite of the darkness of death and disembowelment, Nelson makes space in which she can use the flippancy of part-mutilation to throw the aims of the movie producers into stark relief. They may claim to be moving away from the trope of killing beautiful blonde women, but it's only slightly improved into part-mutilation and eventual escape. Similarly, Nelson's memoir *The Red Parts* and *Jane: A Murder* address themes of sexual violence and the wider social problematic of women as idealized victim. Both digressive and interrogatory, restless and probing, these books share characteristics with *The Argonauts*, even if they could not be said to draw on the same dichotomy and juxtaposition of lightness among heavy material.

Nelson's work engages with a number of key themes for both the poetics of flippancy and the queer troublemaker. *The Argonauts* as a text almost seems to offer a critical framework for its own analysis, with citation in the margins creating a dialogue with other thinkers. They are not the afterthought of footnotes but always existing on the edge like a form of conversation. Introducing a range of voices, from poets to social theorists, cultural critics and her husband, Nelson creates a polyvocal text in which her voice mediates and moderates. Placing quotations in the text itself, mostly in italics, Nelson cites the authors or writers in the right-hand-side margin, such that the source can be easily traced, even read in conjunction with the body of the text as opposed to being sought after in footnotes. Occasionally, when reporting the speech of more familiar figures, such as Harry or her friends, Nelson will use speech marks or italics, but no citation. There, the body of the work itself gestures to the person, allowing a space for them to enter before the primary voice continues. This format creates a non-hierarchical textual experience, in which the words that emerge from intimate relationships and the words that emerge from theorists are considered equally. Nelson's work allows for the speaking self to be constellated and constituted by reading and relationships, creating a lyrical prose that moves between and outside the words of others. *The Argonauts* very structure creates a polyvocality in which there is no othering, so that the use of other voices creates an intersectional text in which the whole can demonstrate a consistency or even solidarity. Nelson does not speak for anyone else but rather aims towards a form of inclusivity.

As a result, there is a literary intimacy between Nelson and the critical writing she reads and then cites. Gender and cultural criticism are not seen as separable from life but rather integral to it, integrated within a body of work that meditates on personal experience. This was particularly evident in a recent conversation between Nelson and Judith Butler hosted by Berkeley Arts and Design (2017). Before reading from *The Argonauts*, Nelson spoke about how formative *Gender Trouble* had been for her life, as well as her critical thinking. This kind of recognition importantly demonstrates that critical theory, particularly gender theory, can have real, lived and human repercussions. Butler's theory has allowed for unbecoming, where sex and gender are considered as performative, which opens up the possibility for different and new identifications or, indeed, a simple rejection of such identifications. In the same dialogue about the importance of Butler's work, Nelson tells an anecdote in which a reader of her writing says 'it must be so hard that you have to deconstruct so many things but still live a life' (Berkeley Arts + Design). This statement is interesting because it raises two difficulties that Nelson's book works directly to counter. It seems to suggest that thinking may be incompatible to living; to deconstruct and analyse is a form of inertia, incompatible with moving through the world in an everyday existence. It also implies that deconstruction itself is not, therefore, freeing. In fact, it is stasis, rendering the thinker incapable of productive action. *The Argonauts*, by contrast, integrates theory into an exploration of love, gender identity and maternity, making it central to life and experience. As such, deconstruction is not turgid, but rather freeing. It creates space for movement and change, as well as possibilities for difference.

Nelson is the only parent I survey in this book, a qualifier which I do not believe makes her any less of a queer troublemaker or, in fact, any less flippant. However, where maternity and reproduction are central to the operations of *The Argonauts*, Nelson also faces and discusses matrophobia within queer culture. While she recognizes disdain for mothers is a wider and more general cultural problem, she directly addresses the non-reproductive futurity that has been seen as so radical within queer theory. As such, *The Argonauts* does important work in opening up the category of both queer and radical, creating a space in which reproduction does not counter queerness but instead becomes a part of it. Nelson recognizes that the pregnant body is one that is inherently queer, changing and becoming unrecognizable, before finally surrendering to the overwhelming physical sensations of labour. Eliding aspects of carrying a child and child birth with sex itself, Nelson makes the former appear open, transgressive and part of a spectrum of human experience that does not conform to heteronormativity. In focusing on feeling rather than categories of gender, sex and experience, Nelson allows for maternity, love and marriage to become both of the establishment and out of the establishment, creating queer relationships between feeling, experience and the theory with which she surrounds herself.

'Skimming the surface of self': Irreverent nonchalance

In her critical book on the New York School poets, Nelson considers the way in which the male, queer poetics of the first generation have informed and influenced a second generation of feminist writers. Noting some overlaps in approach and strategy, Nelson also comments on how the different social positions of the various writers invariably lead to different realizations of levity. She explains 'Mayer, Notley and Myles have combined this irreverent, nonchalant "skimming the surface of self" with feminist urgency, political conviction and literary bravado', resulting in 'some of the most alive and necessary poetry to date' (Nelson 2011b: xxvi). Surfaces and irreverence were pioneered by the first generation of the New York School and then complicated and enhanced through the work of the female writers within the second generation. These aspects of the writing sit in a troubling tension, where lightness and levity must be reconciled with the seriousness of the politics that informs Mayer, Notley and Myles. That the poets write with both urgency and conviction suggests a certain gravitas. Urgency is action that is intrinsically linked to temporality; it is vital that the writing happens now or comes into being through a necessary response to some event or feeling. Conviction, which is a demonstrative strength of belief, seems even more antithetical to flippancy, which I have been characterizing in some cases as a lack of fidelity or commitment. However, as Nelson suggests, these characteristics of urgency and fidelity are combined with the irreverent and the nonchalant. Rather than creating works in which wildly divergent poetics clash against one another, this combination allows for a skimming the surface of self that maintains its lightness while still communicating the serious-informed feminism. That all of the writers identified by Nelson draw on 'literary bravado' suggests that this swaggering certainty is also a necessity of a poetry that combines the irreverent with the urgent, the flippant with political conviction. These aspects of the second-generation New York School poets are carried throughout *The Argonauts*, where queer urgency is combined with irreverence, and commitment to ever-changing self-description is paired with a nonchalance of expression.

During the time *The Argonauts* relays, Nelson's husband undergoes a transition, in part facilitated by hormones and in part by surgery. When considering Harry's identity, and that he is located somewhere between the gender he was assigned at birth, but still not entirely comfortable with the male gender bestowed on him by the state, Nelson writes 'in a culture frantic for resolution ... sometimes the shit stays messy' (2015: 53). Transitioning is not always a movement from one gender to another, reifying the binary system, and in Harry's case it is the irresolution that is freeing. The very vocabulary that Nelson uses to express this lack of resolution is ultimately condensed into a very immediate and colloquial phrase – shit stays messy. The abruptness of this, as well as the general catch-all qualifier of 'shit' used to express LGBTQ+ experience, reads flippantly among Nelson's more expansive description of what it means to transition. Here, urgency and conviction are combined with a lightness that is almost akin to skimming the surfaces. Instead of attempting to detail all of the reasons for mess, Nelson reduces it to an expansive phrase, one that seems at odds with traditional academic language and the loquaciousness with which she considers identity. The text as a whole returns to this idea, that in spite of scene, scenario, interpersonal relationships and politics, sometimes language can be used for reduction, or generalization, ever so slightly ill-fitting for that which it describes.

In the early pages of *The Argonauts*, Nelson describes the early stages of falling in love with Dodge, a feeling that leaves her vulnerable. In the opening of the book, as Nelson is being fucked in the arse, feeling her face smash against the concrete floor of Harry's apartment, she opens her mouth and says 'I love you', entirely without forethought or intention (Nelson 2015: 3). It is immediately apparent to the reader that Dodge has turned language into a fugitive, escaping and eluding Nelson's desire for precise or controlled expression. Telling her friend about the intensity of her love, Nelson also confides that she is not entirely sure of Harry's gender and so has become a quick study in pronoun avoidance. The friend offers to do a search, 'to see if the Internet reveals a preferred pronoun for you' (Nelson 2015: 7). While neither falling in love nor gender identity are treated lightly throughout the book, this is a moment of unexpected irreverence, exploiting both the awkwardness of falling in love and not having asked a partner for their preferred way of being called. That Google might be the solution is wholly flippant; the irresolution of love, gender, the potential violence of misnaming can be simply answered by a search engine. Of course Harry's chosen pronouns and Nelson's knowledge of them cannot be resolved through Google; and of course the intimacy of what they are doing together cannot be elucidated through the top-ten search hits. Considering her newly developed use of pronouns to describe love, Nelson thinks, 'I want the you no one else can see, the you so close the third person need never apply', before her friend interrupts with '"Look, here's a quote from John Waters", saying, "She's so very handsome." So maybe use "she". I mean, it's *John Waters*' (Nelson 2015: 8). Nelson moves between the serious and the light at such rapidity that she creates an irreverence whiplash. Deviating from the act of googling Harry's gender, Nelson makes great use of the second person to address her beloved directly; she wants the intimacy of the second person to be so great that gender identity and preferred pronouns can be obliterated; who needs him or her, when I have you? The conviction of this statement is then juxtaposed with the friend's interjection, who has found a statement from John Waters gendering Harry as female. The lightness also arises from Waters, where celebrity is positioned as an authority on a beloved's gender identity. The emphasis on Waters, who is considered the Queen of trash and queer grotesque, moves the conversation away from the intimacy of you and I and into celebrity reference points.[1]

There are moments within the text in which seriousness prevails. Nelson acknowledges that she was reluctant to support Harry in starting T. She also states her unwillingness to write about Iggy, her son, falling ill following his birth. While she tells the reader about the illness, she does not describe elucidate, elaborate or deconstruct. There are some moments that are perhaps too fraught with feeling to be contained within language. However, concepts of sexuality, sex and unity are approached with a certain amount of irreverence and seriousness combined. This is especially evident when Nelson and Dodge make the decision to marry one another, a final resistance to Prop 8 which was beginning to roll through the country. Marriage, as an institution, is much contested within queer cultures, where in some instances it is viewed as positive assimilation, and therefore, equality, and in others, a perpetuation of heternormativity. The latter argue that gay marriage cannot be a radical act because it undoes queerness, allowing sexuality to be organized in state structures that centre around monogamy and property. Recognizing this, Nelson writes, 'poor marriage! Off we went to kill it (unforgivable). Or reinforce it (unforgivable)' (2015: 23). Nelson combines the two great resistances here, expressing the heterosexual worry that a queer union will destroy the institution of marriage and the queer anxiety that marriage should not be reinforced but destroyed. In spite of their knowledge of

---

[1] John Waters is an American screenwriter and director known as the 'King of Trash'. His films have a cult following and are known for their shocking and transgressive content.

these various resistances, Nelson and Harry say their vows. Turning her address outside of the text, Nelson writes 'reader, we married there, with the assistance of Reverend Lorelei Starbuck' (2015: 24). The Reverend for the wedding is a drag queen, who insists on Nelson and Dodge going through the motion of giving vows to one another. In spite of the subversive potential of Nelson, Dodge and the drag queen Reverend all coming together, Starbuck still adheres to some traditions of marriage, in this instance, the exchange of words. This moment encapsulates some of the tensions at the heart of *The Argonauts*, in which Nelson's choices could be seen as incompatible with some radical queer politics. It also encapsulates the movement between the irreverent and the urgent. Nelson approaches queer marriage with flippancy, in spite of the fact that she has been spurred to such a union by the government introducing legislation that discriminates against LGBTQ+ people. This is demonstrative of Nelson's commitment to probing and exploring queerness in such a way to open up the category's possibility, while still attempting to queer more heteronormative institutions.

The concept of shit staying messy and the irreverence whiplash are carried through the very structures of the writing. While *The Argonauts* moves with an exceptional fluidity, it continues the juxtapositions of focus, temporality and theory, mixing highbrow theoretical writing with the simplicity of everyday language. There is an open use of colloquial language, with the occasional pithy statement on the difficulty of complex experiences, for example, 'shit stays messy'. This contrast does not exist because Nelson is attempting to make the theory accessible to the reader, but rather demonstrates the easy incorporation of these complex thoughts into everyday language and life. The movement between colloquial and theoretical, as well as the intensely personal and the political, demonstrates how skimming the surfaces facilitates a fluid textual progression. The reader orientates themselves through the text in such a way as to appreciate there can be no purity of approach, no single position. Instead, forms of commitment can emerge from nonchalance, and urgency is not antithetical to a lightness of approach. While the text itself is not messy, it makes a mess of distinctions and differentiations, pulling on a range of different genre characteristics to create a poetic meditation that has repercussions far beyond the family unit Nelson creates for herself. In 'A Rough Geology of New Narrative', Jason Morris considers some of Bruce Boone's work, writing that 'by melding categories (poetic, theoretical, biographical, etc.) the writing registers as true to life: not exactly "codeswitching," but more a cross section of thought's sedimentary layers' (Morris 2017: 177). In some ways, this melding also demonstrates a lack of fidelity, where multiple genres unbecome in relation to one another. Placed together in an unexpected dialogue, Nelson's writing does seem true to her life in that the movement between poetic language, prose, deconstruction and theoretical analysis reflects the skimming of categories she explores within queer identity. Morris goes on to say that melding categories 'captures the way lived thought, thought moving through time, can form itself into a set of interlocking, adjacent layers: the poetic slanted and abutting a piece of gossip, an idea about Marx, a memory' (2017: 177). This analysis reflects the construction of *The Argonauts*, which practises lived thought, demonstrating how theory can reflect life and life itself can allow insight into theory.

'Sometimes the shit stays messy': Gendered labour, categories and not-caring

In an interview with Sarah Nicole Prickett for Book Forum, Nelson uses the women of the New York School as a means by which to discuss ambivalence. She says 'I was really interested in how certain women poets in the 1970s had heavy interests and heavy shit going on, so they couldn't perform the same kind of ease, or irreverence, as was being praised in the work of the New York School writers' (Prickett 2015). As such, the poets were required to find

> new ways to perform not caring. Because, in a way, not giving a shit about patriarchy, about getting into its clubs, is also a very profound form of not caring. I think there's a kind of a feminism not caring which is a little different from a campy not caring which is different from a nihilistic not caring.
> (Prickett 2015)

Nelson recognizes that the work of the poets is inherently performative and that the poetry expresses not just a resistance to assimilation but a very deliberate act against caring. Nelson's supposition is that while the campy not-caring might have arisen from poets such as Frank O'Hara, the same performance of not-caring is evident within the women poets for different reasons. It is not purely camp response but rather a feminism that attempts to reject the patriarchy while recognizing patriarchal structures will not necessarily make space for them. Preoccupied with her own forms of not-caring, Nelson states that with *The Argonauts*, 'I do care about the assimilation/revolution debate. I do care about homo- or heteronormativity. But on the other hand, I really don't care, if caring means that you have to buy into the terms of the dichotomy that has been presented to you' (Prickett 2015). Tracing a lineage of non-caring through camp poetics to feminist agendas, Nelson finally locates the same performance within her own queer politics. Her queerness fluctuates somewhere between caring and not-caring, a movement which reflects her rejection of the dichotomies she outlines for queer identity. There is both a seriousness and flippancy at work here, the flippancy finding itself in Nelson's lineage of not-caring, while the seriousness is located in the way she positions herself against the patriarchy, participating within the debate while rejecting its terms.

In the face of serious subjects, Nelson is both bothered by the topics and also willing to dismiss them if required to place herself within a set of impossible binaries. Within *The Argonauts*, there is a heaviness occurring around her: the impending Prop 8, the difficulties of fertility, Harry's mother dying, a reflection on her own father having passed away when she was very young. Nelson never enacts a form of not-caring towards the people and personal experiences detailed within the book, but she does maintain a levity of approach, in which she probes and questions what it means to commit and what the terms of her commitment are. There is both an irreverence and seriousness in her reporting of events, which places the two in dialogue with one another, much the same way the text considers what it is to both care and not care, to be heteronormative while also being incredibly queer. Throughout *The Argonauts*, Nelson's tone is light and irreverent, sometimes dismissive, but the terms that circulate around her life are always given due consideration. One of the terms that preoccupies Nelson most in this dialogue of caring and not-caring is heternormativity. The text as a whole seems to be in a constant tension of the normative and the anti-normative with examples from Nelson's life used to contest and blur the distinctions between the two. For example, Nelson falls in love with Dodge before being certain of his gender, a detail which continues to remain intentionally elusive; the two undergo fertility treatment in order to conceive, a process that queers the heterosexual assumptions of reproduction; Nelson supports Harry through top surgery and taking testosterone, while she is on her own hormone supplements to facilitate conception. This expands even further when Nelson considers the biological aspects of motherhood. In discussing the process of giving birth, she likens it to rough, intensive sex. Considering that birth often results in women shitting themselves, Nelson writes that 'did not strike me as exceedingly distinct from what happens during sex' (2015: 86). Here, unexpectedly, the more seemingly 'embarrassing' aspects of birth are elided with the excellent aspects of sex. If the latter is good enough, then a woman should be brought to the threshold of losing control of her faculties. Later in the book, Nelson writes, 'I had always presumed that giving birth would make me feel invincible and ample, like fisting' (2015: 86). Once more, labour is placed in dialogue with a particular kind of non-reproductive sex. It is significant here that Nelson is not invoking heterosexual penetration, an act that might result in pregnancy, but more diffuse and diverse acts. As such, birth is not purely associated with heterosexual sex, even while the bodily experiences labour necessitates might be similar to the surrender of sex that Nelson demands. It is also important that Nelson is not considering her maternal body as desexualized; she does not transition from a sexual woman into an asexual carer, instead focusing on the body's capacity for simultaneity. While some might consider the merging of sex and motherhood to be inappropriate, the lightness with which Nelson moves between the two and the irreverence with which she approaches labour allow for her to be multiple as opposed to reduced to her body's current function.

These parallels are especially significant in relation to the discourses surrounded non-reproductive futurity and queerness. Nelson takes what might be considered as significant in relation to a woman's experience and associates it with sexual acts; this immediately lightens the seriousness of labour, but also makes sex itself appear to be more serious and all-encompassing. While Nelson does not associate having a child with any form of essential womanhood, she rejects the concept that having a child will make her in any way less queer. Reproduction is not a form of assimilation, but it might be a form of fisting, defecating through pleasure, and surrendering 'with no safe word to stop it' (2015: 134). In placing labour in dialogue with fisting and total surrender, an experience without safe words, Nelson defies any expectation of motherhood as desexualized or, indeed, heteronormative. One of the key concepts of the text is that motherhood might be able to situate itself on a spectrum of queerness, rather than reifying a heteronormative society that uses the figure of the child to impose morality. Lee Edelman writes in *No Future*, the child 'marks the fetishistic fixation of heteronormativity: an erotically charged investment in the rigid sameness of identity that is central to the compulsory narrative of reproductive futurism' (2004: 21). Edelman's text outlines the way in which the child has become the centre of all investment in morality and a better future. Identity and actions are policed now in the hope that they might secure a better life or safer existence for children who do not yet exist. He writes:

> For politics, however radical the means by which specific constituencies attempt to produce a more desirable social order, remains, at its core, conservative insofar as it works to *affirm* a structure, to *authenticate* social order, which it then intends to transmit to the future in the form of its inner Child. The Child remains the perpetual horizon of every acknowledged politics, the fantasmatic beneficiary of every political intervention.
>
> (2004: 3)

As such, Edelman calls for a queer politics that 'fucks' the child, a more radical approach that does not affirm current structures nor authenticate social orders that are reliant on the figure of youth and innocence. If each political intervention is directed towards the young, or yet unborn, then there is no politics in existence that engages with the immediacy of now or the experiences of already constituted political subjects. Edelman's queer politics, thus, calls for a rejection of the child, both as a figure and in a more literal sense, associating queerness with death drives as opposed to the rejuvenation of life and family lines.

Nelson is very aware of this approach to queer politics and the resistance with which some approach the child, even while she is desperately undergoing fertility treatment in the hope of conceiving. She resists the concept that to want a baby, and have a baby, is antithetical to queer politics. Directly addressing Edelman's work, Nelson writes 'why bother fucking this Child when we could be fucking specific forces that mobilize and crouch behind its image' (2015: 76). Non-reproductive futurity, Nelson argues, makes an enemy of the symbol of futurity, the child, as opposed to addressing the powers which have emphasized the child's importance in relation to specific institutions and structures. Rejecting the child as symbol does nothing to counter global capitalism and the unfair distribution of wealth, in the same way that embracing no future allows for a complacency in relation to the economy, environment and climate. However, Nelson's rejection of non-reproductive futurism is also closely tied to an embodied queerness. On viewing A.L. Steiner's *Puppies and Babies*, Nelson is confronted with a series of intimate portraits of subjects holding either their dogs or their children, in which the non-human and the child can participate in the making of queer families. The titling of the exhibition itself is flippant, a seeming cutesy approach to queer relationships that focuses on the vulnerability of the baby and the appeal of the puppy. However, the exhibition reminds Nelson that 'bodily experience can be made new and strange, that nothing we do in this life need have a lid crammed on it, that no one set of practices of relations has the monopoly on the so-called radical, or the so-called normative' (2015: 73). Instead, the body and its relationship with others, whether dogs, lovers, ex-lovers or children, have the capacity to queer experiences, as well as be queered by experience.

In *The Art of Cruelty*, Nelson writes that 'not all boundaries or mediating forces are created equal; not all serve the same purpose. Neither politics nor art is served if and when the distinctions between them are willingly or unthinkingly smeared out' (2011a: 47). In her discussion of motherhood, Nelson is significantly smearing boundaries, blurring distinctions between maternity and queerness. While *The Argonauts* considers parenthood as a whole, Nelson's experience is very much tied to her position as a mother, as well as culture's tendency to vilify or disregard 'the mother', both as a figure and in reality. This suggests that Nelson is engaged in the same kind of gendered labour and issues as her New York School predecessors and that this specific gendered position might allow for her to perform not-caring but not the same kind of not-caring as O'Hara. Instead, her irreverence and lightness of foot must emerge from her caring about heteronormativity, as well as her not-caring if such a category is continually applied to her life. This not-caring also happens with less ease, necessitated by the heavy subjects and the heavy shit going on within the text itself; Nelson is dismantling gender, undoing a queer rejection of maternity, as well as telling the reader a love story primarily written in second-person address. This is not to say that the work itself is not flippant, or definitely flippant in spaces, but that the kind of lightness Nelson performs is very specific to her contexts and the lineage she has drawn up for herself. The lightness and rapidity with which she moves between subjects, the nature of her prose writing and past as a poet, do enable her to work around boundaries, easing their edges until they exist without certainty or clarity. Both her politics and art are served by this re-imagination of not-caring and the wilfulness to position the mother as inherently queer, if she so wishes, in spite of the queer theory that precedes her. Through this, Nelson performs a rejection of non-reproductive futurity and instead places the experience of having a child alongside other similarly queer experiences.

Nelson also teases out ideas of both hetero- and homonormativity with examples from her domestic space, examples that are flippantly constructed such that queer identity can hang or seem dependent on the thoughtless minutiae of everyday life. Early in *The Argonauts*, Nelson relays the story of her friend finding a specially made mug, with a picture of her and her family dressed in their Christmas best, ready for a pantomime. Nelson's friend says it is the most heteronormative thing she has ever seen. Having been accused of owning a heteronormative coffee cup, Nelson asks 'but what about it is the essence of heteronormativity? That my mother made a mug on a boojie service like Snapfish? That we're clearly participating, or acquiescing into participating, in a long tradition of families being photographed at holiday time?' (2015: 13). In taking on the term 'heteronormativity', Nelson relocates the meaning of the phrase, making it both expansive and multiple. In so doing, she also calls the concept of queerness into question, where certain acts or behaviours as a couple might render the relationship less queer. For example, is it heteronormative if one's relative buys a novelty piece of china with your photo on it? Can such an act be reduced down to the couple's own lack of queerness, and if so, can heteronormativity take hold through association? Or is it perhaps that Nelson's pregnant body in conjunction with Harry's suited one implies heterosexuality itself? Ostensibly, they are a couple in their Christmas best, where the woman is pregnant and the man is handsome. Is such a traditional image of heterosexuality enough to confer normativity on a couple that are trans, queer and indeterminate? That all of these questions arise from the flip comment of the friend, and the even more laughable novelty mug bestowed upon the household by her mother, demonstrates the fluctuations of flippancy and seriousness. The lightness of one-off comments can be used as the basis for a discussion of heteronormativity within queer families in the same way that serious subjects can inspire a lightness of tone and irreverence of response.

'Each word can fly': Performing strategic identification

The Argonauts opens with an argument between Nelson and Harry Dodge about language's ability to express thought, action and identity. The book as a whole asks whether we are able to express everything with a limited vocabulary and whether experiences which elude our language can still be communicated implicitly or inexpressibly. There is, of course, from both Dodge and Nelson specific and different investments in language's possibilities. Nelson is a theorist of language and a poet, wanting to believe in communicative powers, while Dodge is forever in flight, evading names and the categorization that language imposes on the lived. Nelson reports 'once we name something, you said, we can never see it the same way again. All that is unnameable falls away, gets lost, is murdered. You called this the cookie-cutter function of our minds' (2015: 4). It is not just the case that the names we have in place are inadequate but that the very act of naming, giving definition to, is a limitation. Our reliance on naming means that everything elusive, known but not interpolated, disappears or, more actively, is killed. *The Argonauts*, as a result, seems to be in both love with language and fighting against it, recognizing the difficulty with which it maps back onto life and experience. The text dwells on moments of linguistic mishap, like when Nelson first blurts an unexpected 'I love you' or sends Dodge an extract from Roland Barthes that is interpreted as a form of rejection. Language throughout the text works as a form of incompleteness, an approximation at description and communication but never quite satisfactory. While this has some limitations, resulting in misunderstanding or certain experiences remaining beyond the realms of expression, it also creates possibilities.

These possibilities are particularly important when it comes to the people who populate Nelson's private life. Love is able to change and evolve, retaining its integrity, while people in love can develop and alter, defying categories but still remaining in union with one another. Nelson writes 'one must also become alert to the multitude of possible uses, possible contexts, the winds in which each word can fly. Like when you whisper, *You're just a hole, letting me fill you up*. Like when I say *husband*' (2015: 8). These two italicized terms, presumably taken from Nelson's own life, are significantly different to one another. Husband is a role, or a legal title, whereas Dodge's whisper is an extended description. That said, husband is an identity that can only come into realization through the existence of the wife, while Nelson can only be a hole in relation to Dodge's capacity to fill her up. In spite of their different constructions, both are constituted through their relationality and contingency. It is not just the words themselves but their uses and their contexts that make meaning. When Nelson quotes Dodge whispering, there are multiple possibilities within the two phrases: that it might be a form of sexual intimacy or that it might be entirely based around emotional connection. When Nelson uses a word that appears more simple to understand, 'husband', the term itself is exploded. It expands and abolishes gender, where Dodge, identified as 'on his way' as opposed to resting within a set gendered position, can become a husband. Similarly, Nelson is defined entirely out of gendered terms; she is not even a body, just a hole, made full by her partner. Finally, it also queers marital relationships where the two are not reproducing forms of heterosexuality or capitulating to the pressures of assimilation. These readings and possibilities emerge not only from the language that is being used but from the contexts and the uses of *The Argonauts* itself. Here, language is not limited but open.

In *Gender Trouble*, Butler writes 'one might wonder what use "opening up possibilities" finally is, but no one who has understood what it is to live in the social world as what is "impossible," illegible, unrealizable, unreal and illegitimate is likely to pose that question' (2006: x). One might assume that existing within language, or assuming an identity that can be named, is a means by which to counter the impossible and the illegible. However, as Dodge states, language actually works to shore up boundaries, becoming ultimately a space of exclusion. Not only does naming constrict, but it also lacks the capacity to encompass everything; the unworded experiences and identities are murdered through their lack of representation in language. Through acknowledging that language itself is inherently flawed, Nelson opens up the medium. Shooting it through with holes demonstrates that there are gaps and spaces, areas of inexpressibility that still require our attention, even if they cannot be captured by our language. Recognizing the illegible and unreal and drawing their inexpressibility into the writing itself, *The Argonauts* creates an openness in approach to identity and our very use of language itself.

Language's possibility is not always deployed with seriousness. In fact, there are juxtapositions of lightness throughout, where an intimate insight into Nelson's relationship might then be replaced with literary gossip. When she and Dodge experience a hard time, she becomes obsessed with George and Mary Oppen, seeking out their marital failures to reassure her of her own. Nelson happily admits to engaging in a gossipy search for a literary relationship gone wrong. She also indulges in gossip on Alice B. Toklas and Gertrude Stein, considering that the latter refused to make a formal identity of sexuality, instead just declaring herself wedded to Alice. Nelson writes, 'I get why it's politically maddening, but I've always thought it a little romantic' (2015: 9). The language choices reveal feeling to be at the centre of Stein and Toklas' union, as opposed to rigid lesbian identities that require entry into a particular category of sexuality. Having considered the way in which the couple refused traditional terms as well as the vocabularies of queerness in their day-to-day life, Nelson goes on to say that Stein's biography makes it clear that her sexuality was not determined purely in relation to Alice. In fact, before Alice, she had a tumultuous affair with a woman named May, who Alice then jealously expunged from *Stanzas in Meditation*. Again, there is a movement between seriousness and lightness, in which Nelson can remove the categories from her own life through exploring language's possibilities, then turn to great literary precursors, and then meditate on the gossip and scandal that ripped through their relationship. Her vocabulary choices, such as describing Stein as politically maddening but romantic, have a particular flippancy to them, especially when considered in conjunction with the anecdote about May. *The Argonauts* relishes both its specificity and digression; or rather, it attempts specificity while recognizing language and identity's limitations and still finds space for moments of digression and anecdote. These moments are not irrelevant to the politics of the text but, as Morris suggests, a crossing of sedimentary layers, all of which make up lived thought. As such, Nelson maintains a lightness of foot throughout where her focus can shift and change, all the while foregrounding her consideration of words, gender and maternity.

This commitment to openness and resistance to categories also extend into Nelson's relationships with specific groups and political affiliations. In two instances within the book, she resents the belonging being bestowed upon her by others. Uncomfortable with her friend's interpretation of the mug, Nelson firmly rejects being placed within a heteronormative culture. This causes Nelson to reflect on the way that the pregnant body is interpreted, as well as the way in which her family might seem to conform to a heteronormative model. Pregnancy is seen as a heterosexual phenomenon, while Harry's handsome masculinity makes him seem like the perfect male companion for her fertile female body. Nelson also resents one of Harry's friends making assumptions about her when they first meet at a dinner party. Initially, the friend asks, '"Have you been with other women, before Harry?"', quickly followed up the statement 'straight ladies have always been hot for Harry' (2015: 10). This prompts Nelson to ask, 'Was Harry a woman? Was I a straight lady?' (2015: 10). Nelson calls into question first the assumption that she is straight and secondly that she conforms to a kind of category of women who would find Harry attractive, as if he is a general catch-all partner for a type. However, she does this questioning away from the social space, relegating the deconstruction to the space of the text.

In both instances, the mug and the party, social interaction places Nelson within a rigid category or type, which ultimately serves as the basis for an in-depth consideration of relationships, relationality and particular terms, such as straight and heteronormative. Throughout *The Argonauts*, Nelson writes towards finding a way to evade such categorizations, imploding them from within or exploding them from without, while still recognizing particular embodied experiences. For example, Nelson might resist the heteronormative reading of her pregnant body, but still has to heed and respond to what it means to give birth to a child. She can also critique the way in which Harry is positioned by his friends, but this is tied up with the pain of genderlessness and the materiality of his transitioning. Her critical work on the New York School resonates very strongly with these concepts. Nelson discusses the 'not-caring' because it allows for the poets to escape particular categories or at least disregard societal expectations and judgements. In championing not-caring, Nelson would be able to emerge unscathed from the interpretation of her family as heteronormative or her relationship with Harry as a straight woman's experimentation. However, these judgements are all bound up with the very difficult and material experiences of the couple, much in the same way that the 'not-caring' of the New York School women is inflected and changed by their gender identity. Campy levity so appropriate to O'Hara cannot work in the same way for female poets, especially those who are mothers. They not only have a responsibility to their children but have a challenge in facing culture that would marginalize or deride them. It is these particular factors that influence the faithless way with which Nelson moves among and between different types of communities, refusing solidarity built on the concept of 'radical' and seeking instead a form of 'openness'.

In her discussion of 2012 Pride, Nelson considers a group of radical queer activists who are calling for the parade to end its relationship with large corporations. One of the rallying cries of the groups is to 'fuck shit up', a queer objective that is also reflected in Halberstam's *The Queer Art of Failure*. The fucking shit up is a way of queering and resisting the way in which capitalism is being reified in LGBTQ+ communities. Queerness needs to continue as a repudiation of capitalism and state control if it is to remain distinct from heternormativity. Nelson celebrates a queer politics of refusal and resistance, but nonetheless finds herself unable to be called to arms with radical language. She writes, 'I've never been able to answer to *comrade*, nor share in this fantasy of attack. In fact I have come to understand revolutionary language as a sort of fetish' (2015: 27). In encouraging and accepting a certain form of queer politics, Nelson is also making it evident that she cannot be interpolated as a comrade. While she might support resistance to capitalism and support fucking shit up when it comes to heteronormative order, there are specific kinds of vocabulary that serve as a call she will not answer. In fact, comrade to her suggests a form of attacking that is almost fantastical; the way in which revolutionary people speak is a fetish for the language, and perhaps a fetish for the originators of the language, but not for the action itself.

Nelson states throughout the book that in meeting Dodge, she finally found someone with whom her perversities were compatible. However the fetish of 'comrade' is one Nelson does not enjoy; it is a word that removes her from the site of activism or at least inspires resistance. She extends this consideration to the idea of the radical, writing 'perhaps it's the word *radical* that needs rethinking. But what could we angle ourselves toward instead, or in addition? Openness? Is that good enough, strong enough?' (2015: 27). It is perhaps the case that radical, particularly in conjunction with comrade, is failing Nelson. It does not create a cohesive and coherent politics against heteronormative capitalism, but rather seems to necessitate a shared fetishization of the language of revolution and its history. The 'instead, or addition' implies that Nelson recognizes the gap that 'radical' fills in our language, and so if she is not able to replace it, she can at least augment it. Openness runs throughout the book, where Nelson is evidently hesitant about the categories she might inhabit, in addition to the fixity which some others might bestow upon her. She critiques heternormativity not purely because she does not want herself and Dodge to appear as a heterosexual couple but because the term itself seems ill-fitting or misplaced within her own personal narrative. Instead of purely dismissing terms throughout the text, Nelson searches for alternatives or supplements, more vocabulary that might in some way unlock the rigidity we understand through such definitions. Nelson is precariously positioned throughout the text; part of a non-normative family that might be read as heteronormative; someone who comes to distrust language's capacity to express but also has to continue with it – there is nothing else; someone who feels a strong longing to have a child even in the face of anti-reproductive queer theories; a woman who has never been more pro-choice as when she was pregnant. That the words 'radical' and 'comrade' are not enough for Nelson is perhaps then no surprise. They are bound to dogma and the fantasy of a single attack, one in which the unity of the attackees is apparent both within and without. Her favouring of openness is in some ways an attempt to undo both the radical and the comrade. It is a position that will change, a slipperiness that cannot be pinned, and a series of possibilities that will not be aligned or ironed out by participation within a very specifically directed collective.

This, importantly, has gone on to create a necessary solidarity with those who read *The Argonauts*. In an interview for *The Fader*, Nelson states:

> My experience with *The Argonauts* was really gratifying because, in a world which acts like we can't have solidarity or sociality without fixed identity, I've only met people through the book [who were] excited about all the space they felt, about unfixed identity. Many people will say that that's how they experience their life, that's how they live – [t]hey perform strategic identifications, but mostly they're in flight.
>
> (Saxelby 2017)

Nelson suggests that the book has brought her into contact with people who only make their identifications strategically, as opposed to be based on any form of essentialism or strong sense of belonging. However, they are primarily people in flight, always moving beyond categories, positions and stability, existing against the fixity that we might project onto people's lives and relationships. *The Argonauts*, which while queer, feminist, maternal, among other things, is calling all of these categories into question, vexed with the conflict of claiming and disengaging. In *Gender Trouble*, Butler writes that it is feminism's search for a stable subject of the politics that has led to difficulty. She writes 'the premature insistence of a stable subject of feminism, understood as a seamless category of women, inevitably generates multiple refusals to accept that category' (2006: 6). As readers, we see this practised within every identity and category invoked within *The Argonauts*. To be a mother does not render Nelson any less sexual nor does her pregnancy result in an inability to discuss cruelty and violence during her book tour for *On Cruelty*. Being a cisgender woman does not render Nelson's take on gender and trans invalid, but allows for her to refute the stability of subject positions in approaching feminism. In spite of being read as part of a heterosexual couple Nelson does not accept heteronormativity, but rather actively works against it, creating space in which she and Harry can be forever in flight. The refusal of the stable subject allows possibilities not only for Nelson writing herself, but for her address of Harry, for her relationship to maternity and, finally, in her interactions with the people who have orientated themselves around her finished text.

'It's of course about me': Lyric shame and selfhood

In this final section of the chapter, I want to consider the ways in which the queer and shameful lyric might be useful for approaching Nelson's use of the first person. In order to do this, I will use a framework of New Narrative, a movement which most simplistically creates openness for poets to move into prose, particularly prose that is critically, socially and politically inflected while maintaining aspects of the intimacy of lyric writing. Nelson began her career as a poet, publishing a number of collections of lyric writing, moving into prose for her first memoir *The Red Parts*. As such, Nelson is not dissimilar from the New Narrative writers who found themselves moving beyond the realms of poetry and into prose work while still retaining some aspects of the former genre. This framework enables a consideration of Nelson's use of pronouns throughout the text, including her shifts between the first and second person. Her relationship with Harry demonstrates a discomfort with third person, favouring the 'you' against a backdrop of rigid gender categories. Ultimately, this will lead me into a consideration of queer and lyric shame, and how both can be realized in the form of Nelson's autocriticism.

Although New Narrative will be elaborated on in the conclusion to this book, I want to offer a brief background here in order to contextualize the relationship with Nelson's writing. New Narrative emerged in the Bay Area within a similar timeframe to Language Poetry, responding to and rejecting the emphasis on impersonal experiments with language. Taking the Berkeley Renaissance poets, including Robert Duncan, Jack Spicer and Robin Blaser, as their precursors, the New Narrative writers favoured genre hybridity, experimenting with identity and lived experience. In the recently published *From Our Hearts to Yours: New Narrative*, editors Rob Halpern and Robin Tremblay-McGaw ask, 'What is the relation between formal innovation and socio-political urgency? How does a writer realize the body in one's work in light of this urgency?' (2017: 17). Although not dissimilar in their aims to unpack the relationship between experimental writing practices and politics, New Narrative writers were also concerned with how the body and lived experiences could be incorporated into the relationship. Emerging from primarily gay men, New Narrative writers had a different embodied experience of the world, one that was marginalized at the time of the movement's origins and decimated in the wake of the AIDS crisis. This understanding of the embodied writer and their place in relation to the work opens up possibilities for gender, sex and relationships to be reconfigured. In 'New Narrative Remix: "Not Resembling the Face in the Mirror"', Robin Tremblay-McGaw writes 'individual pronouns and their con/fusions re-contextualise and re-frame discourses and speakers. They provide a public space for staging multiple (mis)identifications and (mis)recognitions; they mean more than the speakers know, uncover the social conditions undergirding who speaks how' (2017: 126). *The Argonauts* explicitly addresses pronoun confusion, as well as the ways in which a wider society responds to gender instability with an emphasis on the established categories. Recognizing the limitations of language in addition to its problematic relationship with experiences and identities, Nelson creates a text that acknowledges pronouns and names may have greater power than she is able to describe, that her attempts to unpack language's limitations alongside gender's need for openness do not even begin to uncover the full social conditions of those who speak.

Tremblay-McGaw's essay goes on to quote Butler, a thinker pivotal to Nelson's writing on gender and sex within *The Argonauts*. From *Undoing Gender*, Tremblay-McGaw quotes 'the "I" that I am finds itself at once constituted by norms and dependent on them but also endeavours to live in ways that maintain a critical and transformative relation to them' (2017: 130). This is not dissimilar to how Nelson parses her caring and not-caring position. She is invested in debates around assimilation and non-assimilation, as well as hetero- and homonormativity, but not if there is no possibility for transformation. If she is trapped purely within the terms of debate, unable to move beyond the binary relationship that they dictate, then Nelson classes herself as 'not-caring'. Like Butler's 'I', Nelson's stance is determined by norms and to some extent dependent on them, but her 'I' is also restlessly seeking ways out of the dichotomies, deconstructing and criticizing as a means by which to create openness. Interestingly, Butler chooses to use the personal pronoun instead of 'self'. This suggests that the 'I' is neither internal nor personal but a means by which a person can enter and engage with the world. The 'I' is formed and realized through their relationship with the norms while simultaneously able to perform a resistance to these forms of constitution. The pronoun Butler uses is not dissimilar to an understanding of the lyric from my introduction, which is a highly performative means of exploring how an individual can be constituted within wider social and political contexts.

Nelson does not identify the 'I' of *The Argonauts* as a lyric, but using the political possibilities under discussion here, I want to argue that her personal pronoun is an extension of the 'I' of lyric writing. Altieri states that the lyric foregrounds artifice, communicating to the reader that the first person represented through writing is not an essential nor genuine reflection of the self. He writes, 'the "sincere" self, then, is one poets are tempted to posit as always beyond language' (1984: 22). This resonates with Butler's use of the 'I', which she treats as a vehicle through which to engage with the world at large, both drawing on and refuting specific discourses. Butler is not referring to a 'sincere self' through her use of the first person, but rather how the 'I' allows us to become a figure of pure externality, constituted by our relationships with social and political norms. Nelson's preoccupation with the limits of language and her playful approach to all pronouns resonate with both Altieri and Butler's discussion of the first person and lyric. Through foregrounding a debate on whether language can ever actually be good enough, and whether the inexpressible can be somehow communicated through what is expressed, Nelson suggests an insincerity within our very forms of relating to one another. When Nelson first questions Harry's pronoun choice, she states that she wants the relationship between 'you' and 'I' that need never open up to a third person. While the I and you sit within a matrix of romance and sex, the spectre of the third person brings a political dimension to the use of pronouns. Nelson and Harry can be constituted through the second and first person, but there is the societal demand that gender become concretized through the use of third person. As with the lyric and Butler, the 'I' in this particular example is one constituted through their relationship with an other, Harry, but also in some way constituted through the social expectations of how 'I' can refer to others. In spite of the personal relationship held in place by the first person, they are still very much caught within social norms, even while choosing a critical and transformative relationship to them.

Jason Morris claims that New Narrative's best first-person work 'reveals the lyric as ... the crushed moment, the liminal reaching-for unachieved mid-act' (2017: 178). Morris believes that the lyric can be realized in prose writing. It creates a liminality, an in-betweenness similar to affect's movements, as well as a sense of process that resonates with Riley's understanding of becomings. However, the fact that this lyric 'I' is realized outside of its traditional genre and is associated with the unachieved mid-act also aligns it with Halberstam's unbecoming. It is the mid-act, the forever in transition, failing to reach a destination. This is exacerbated through the lyric's relationship with temporality or 'the crushed moment', as Morris calls it. The momentary offers up an intensity of focus while also suggesting a structure that skips between moments, ultimately drawing them into a wider prose work. The crushed moment, then, serves as a mode for high lyricism, but also facilitates its existence within a longer autofiction. Morris goes on to quote from George Albon's book *Aspirations*, writing 'the lyric is emergent – gestural and suggestive – rather than substantive or complete ... The lyric is an intermediate world that shows itself fugitively' (2017: 179). This seems wholly applicable to the 'I' of *The Argonauts*, who explores identity through the crushed moments of anecdote and encounter. In this way, the lyric gestures to the scene while also suggesting readings or interpretation. Refusing completeness, the lyric of *The Argonauts* engages in world making and unmaking, challenging America in its current incarnation, resisting the inevitable Prop 8 through marriage and gesturing towards a future without fixed identity binaries. This is achieved through world making and unmaking, where the main argument about the insufficiency of language suggests that what Nelson has been able to convey to us is only a fraction of what she wishes to express. As such, the inexpressible is a fugitive remnant throughout the text, partially read in the gestures and suggestions, but also partly obscured through language's incapacity. Where the lyric 'I' can be understood as fugitive, it is also important to recognize that this is echoed through 'you', who is specifically Harry, described by Nelson as forever in flight. In spite of the different identifications and imperatives of both characters, Nelson and Dodge are positioned as insubstantive and incomplete. Even when their personal happiness is complete(ish) with Iggy, they are still reaching forward and for the unachievable society. In the final passages of *The Argonauts*, Nelson reworks a letter to her son Iggy, telling him that he was always thought of as possible. She writes 'two human animals, one of whom is blessedly neither male nor female, the other of whom is female (more or less), deeply, doggedly, wildly wanted you to be' (2015: 142). While the movement and flux of the book seems to treat identity and love lightly, and the irreverence of the text is a lack of stability, there is also a depth of seriousness that offers the reader a more open and possible future.

Nelson's use of the 'I' throughout *The Argonauts*, one that I am understanding through the lyric, also opens the text up to the possibility of shame. While Nelson evades the concept of pride and shame within her book, clearly refuting binaries, there is a sense that the autobiographical material and her foregrounding of the first person could be seen as shameful. As my introduction states, the lyric was historically associated with the highly feminine and feeling-orientated and as such was anti-masculine and almost embarrassingly personal. This is a concept that Perloff reiterates in her writing on contemporary poetry, in which she dismisses lyric work alongside the poet's attempts to communicate that they really *feel* something. White writes 'given that "expressive lyric" is the chief abjection of a powerful and increasingly canonical avant-garde antilyricism now forty years in the making, it is an identification that opens these poet's work to shame' (2014: 2). While Nelson's work does emerge from a relationship with the avant-garde, it is interesting that her critical work is drawn to the lyric of the queer and female New York School writers. In fact, Nelson seems comfortable using the 'I' and details from her own life so as to challenge the usual associations such a form might have with shame. She refuses both a female and a queer shame, within *The Argonauts*, foregrounding her first-person relationship with her chosen second person, Harry. In the text itself, Nelson writes 'if I insist that there is a persona or a performativity at work, I don't mean to say that I'm somehow not myself in my writing, or that my writing somehow isn't me. I'm with Eileen Myles – "my dirty secret has always been that it's of course about me"' (Nelson 2015: 75). Here, Nelson directly acknowledges the performativity of her work and that in some instances, her writing will be performing identity. The mediation of identity and experience through writing necessitates a certain form of artifice, where the real is flattened or deconstructed to fit on the page. However, this does not mean that Nelson's work is not about her – that the performance in some way negates her own selfhood and personhood. Rather, the difficult relationship between the performativity of the 'I' and the real self beyond the pages is one that continually navigates affectation and performance. Interestingly, Nelson associates this with both Eileen Myles and shame. Both poets share the dirty secret of writing being about themselves, but this is stated openly and clearly, shifting our focus onto the interesting textual realizations of 'I' as opposed to the shame of female feelings and personal material.

Conclusion

Nelson is situated at the end of a queer and flippant lineage, beginning with Gertrude Stein in Paris, moving to Frank O'Hara in New York, then on to Eileen Myles and finally to the Bay Area and L.A. One of the aspects shared by all of these writers, with the exception of Stein, is that they are fans of one another (and Stein was a fan of herself), which allows for a more informal and celebratory relationship with the lineage I am tracing here. In both her autocriticism, *The Argonauts*, and her critical writing, Nelson recognizes the importance of Stein, O'Hara and Myles to her own development as a writer. While O'Hara and Myles are very prominent throughout the critical work on the New York School, Nelson makes a strong case for their having been influenced by Stein. My chapter on Stein commented on her significance for the Language School, but Nelson makes it clear that this Modernist precursor was just as useful to New York School poetics. Myles and Stein both feature in *The Argonauts* as reference points for both sexuality and writing practice. Stein and Alice are discussed in relation to sexuality, where the former's refusal to adopt a category definition is both frustrating and romantic. Nelson sets up the two as beyond gender and sexuality through their love for one another, before problematizing this by reminding the reader that Stein had same-sex relationships in advance of Alice. By contrast, Myles' writing is a useful means for Nelson to discuss the performativity of selfhood and the relationship between her textual 'I' and the I of her lived experience. Not only do the three previous writers, therefore, inform Nelson's work in a critical and poetic sense, but they also allow her to consider sexuality, categories, affects and queer shame.

The Argonauts is more explicitly engaged with some of the ideas of this book than the work of the other three writers I have considered. While Nelson is not considering flippancy, her work discusses categories of sex and gender, the problematics of identity and where it might be possible to find space in which to remain forever in flight, or as Harry puts it, 'on my way'. Nelson's exploration of mobility, gender and sexuality, particularly with her emphasis on doing away with traditional identity categories, means that her work resonates perfectly with the results of flippancy that I have outlined in my previous chapters. Interestingly, *The Argonauts*' opening pages quote Riley, Ahmed and Butler, three theorists key to my considerations here. The content of the work, thus, is not purely anecdote and experience, the story of falling in love and then a narrative around queer maternity. It is also continual analysis and deconstruction of love, maternity, queerness and experience. Nelson does not purely discuss her context, focusing on the animated aspects of life, like O'Hara, but instead uses the autocriticism as a space in which autobiography can collide with analytical and critical writing. Nelson's analysis is informed heavily by gender theory, but she also makes space in which gender theory can become key to life. Her combination of the genres as well as the movement between critical thinking and experience ensures that all of these elements are inseparable. They coexist and, in fact, offer a model for queer living that is engaged, joyous, resistant and critical.

It is for these reasons that Nelson's text is also the most overtly engaged with contemporary queer movements. While Myles' career has been incredibly political, with them running for president as well as becoming a vocal supporter of Hillary Clinton, it is Nelson who really considers queer activism and its contemporary effects. Addressing activism in an explicit way allows for Nelson to consider what constitutes particular forms of resistance and how might they be best realized. In so doing, she considers no futurity and the difficulty of queer maternity, what it means to give talks at anti-LGBT Christian universities when the pay cheque would be helpful for childcare and how to fuck the right shit up if you want to challenge the hetero-patriarchy. Nelson also considers how her identity, and the identity of her family, must also suggest a certain kind of politics, particularly given that it was formulated in the shadow of Prop 8. Of the work I have examined in this book, Nelson's is the most tethered to actual incidents, actual policy, real campaigns and various iterations of queer activism. In this way, she differs fundamentally from Stein and O'Hara, neither of whom could be positioned as queer activists. However, Nelson's work also rehabilitates these kinds of figures, celebrating Stein for challenging category definitions and O'Hara for initiating a not-caring that is important to a range of genders and sexualities. Nelson distinguishes her work through calling for openness in contrast to radical, making space for different types of resistances that may or may not link directly to activism. This stance enables Nelson to consider collectivity and reject the term 'comrade', maintaining the autonomy of the 'I' in a way that is absolutely central to both Myles and O'Hara's work.

Conclusion

Throughout this book, the poetics of flippancy manifests differently in each chapter, introducing a lightness of approach in relation to particular modes of writing and historical contexts. However, there are shared characteristics throughout that suggest a coherent form of poetics, that while adaptable, is recognizable. Flippancy is borne of a combination of tone, style, affectation and performance, as well as the synthesis of form and content.

It could be aligned with ugly feelings, in that it does not have overwhelming affective power, and it could be considered in conjunction with minor aesthetic categories, which eschew the sublime and the beautiful in favour of the small and insignificant. In the work of Stein, flippancy is realized through the combination of butch and camp styles, both of which allow an affected performance to emerge. Toying with identity and zones of indeterminacy, Stein's babe talk communicates irreverence, playfulness and levity. Frank O'Hara, by contrast, while drawing on elements of camp, shifts the focus back onto tone through his emphasis on replacing the poem with the telephone. His insistent chattering elevates the poem and manifesto to a light skating of surfaces, in which both genres' potential seriousness are undermined through his deflation of them. Myles has overlaps with both O'Hara and Stein in their use of flippancy. Through the exploration of 'Eileen Myles' and their embodied presence within the promotional video, Myles experiments with the significance of naming and the ways in which we can undo self-representation. Their approach to the self has a great sense of lightness and irreverence, with them claiming both oblivion and failure, while conveying success and confidence. These juxtapositions create a poetics of fluctuation and flippancy, in which indeterminacy and openness can thrive. Maggie Nelson is perhaps the least flippant of the writers under discussion. Her work creates a poetics of flippancy through juxtaposition, in which the serious queer contexts and politics of *The Argonauts* are offset by lightness of tone and the nimble tongue of commentary and retort. Similar to

O'Hara, Nelson practices a lack of fidelity to communities, calling particular shared politics into question.

In spite of the differences evident between the poets, the poetics of flippancy throughout the work demonstrates some shared aspects of writing practice. While Nelson is perhaps the poet who creates the greatest sense of juxtaposition, all four write quick shifts that betray a lightness of foot. They move rapidly from one topic to another, skating the surfaces of experience and text so as to communicate a fast-pace and nimbleness to the reader. Each writer I study here seems to position the text as a place in which to talk a lot, whether that is Stein's grandiose self-reflection in *The Autobiography of Alice B. Toklas*, which is also shot through with anecdote and light asides; O'Hara's manifesto focusing on conversations with friends, talks with lovers and ultimately the telephone; Myles' Bostonian tone and speed of delivery, all of which are clear from the brevity and lineation of their poems as well as their embodied performance within the promotional video; and Nelson's self-description as a student who talked too much, a lecturer who is happy to interrupt and a lover, who discloses private details within their writing. If these poets were not talkative, there would be little space in which the poetics of flippancy could emerge.

The writers also share similar approaches to hierarchies, creating texts that ultimately reject authority. Significantly, the writers not only create non-hierarchical spaces within their writing but also undo the authoritative position of the 'I', who sits at the centre of the majority of their texts. Stein achieves this through her gossiping about a number of artists, happily revealing that the Futurists were boring and that Ezra Pound was a parochial over-explainer. *Lifting Belly*, too, in its invocation of proper names and use of pronouns, complicates the relationship with 'I' and 'you' such that they seem equally configured among a clamour of others. O'Hara's manifesto similarly plays with authority, undermining the poem as a genre by suggesting people would prefer to go to the movies. He also blasts through canonical references, placing them in dialogue with conversations with friends, such that the former and latter seem to be of equal significance within the process of writing. Myles reads a poem on Robert Lowell in the promotional video, dismissing the man as an old coot following his death. By positioning themselves as a loser, lesbian poet, Myles also undermines their own authority, communicating to the reader that while they might shape the text, they are able to do so because of their irrelevance beyond it. Nelson creates this non-hierarchy through her formal choices. *The Argonauts* quotes critical theorists and friends alike, without making distinctions between either. While Nelson attributes her quotations, she subjects all of them to the same process of consideration and deconstruction, such that the boundaries between the colloquial and the academic become increasingly porous. This approach to authority and hierarchy shows an unbecoming levity in the face of serious subjects. All four poets refuse to give weight to subjects that may become heavy, choosing instead to prioritize quick movement and a nimble tongue to serious consideration. As such, the poets seem to refuse depth. This is not to be confused with a lack of thought or analysis but rather that the skating of surfaces can reveal specific queer ways of being in the world. Foregrounding lightness and levity, all four writers reject hierarchies in favour of the open text.

Nelson discusses the importance of 'not-caring' in relation to the New York School, but notes some vital differences between the way O'Hara can practice such a position versus the way in which women might be able to adopt a similar pose. While Stein is not included within this analysis of not-caring, I see this particular mode of operation as incorporating the following: a faithless movement between subjects, a skating of surfaces in opposition to depth of analysis and an undoing of the self that decentres the lyric or autobiographical text. The not-caring, which in some senses is camp, or butch, and in other examples informed by living under the patriarchy, feeds into the key concept of 'unbecoming'. Unbecoming is realized in two senses throughout the work of the writers, the first of which is linked to the queer art of failure, while the other is linked more explicitly to flippancy. Given the way in which the texts I have examined focus on selfhood, unbecoming is a way for the writers to question identity and the coherence of the self. In spite of my focus on a coherent self-presentation across each of the poets, all of the works go to some efforts to consider how the self is made, how it is represented and how it can be undone to facilitate greater freedom of movement. As such, the works are focused on an unbecoming that creates openness. Rather than becoming being a way of following the clear lines of culture and social expectation, Stein, O'Hara, Myles and Nelson all unwrite themselves and their 'I's. Such unbecoming allows for deviation and resistance, wherein the speakers are not required to align themselves with those who are already lined up. They can deviate, transgress, turn and call themselves into question. By contrast, flippancy is defined as 'unbecoming levity in the face of serious subjects'. Here, unbecoming is not so much a process, as a lack of appeal; an inappropriate irreverence. When combined, however, the unbecoming that allows for a process of constructing and deconstructing selfhood as well as the unbecoming of irreverence allow for a queer subject who is active in their self-representation, and willing to be uncomfortable within the spaces and contexts they occupy.

Queer troublemaking

Each poet's use of flippancy allows for a particular consideration of aspects of queer culture, all of which trouble identity stability, gender normativity and understandings of sexuality. With each writer, there is a collision of performances and affectations, some of which intersect with drag acts, butch posturing, campness, transitioning and the more generalized queerness. These are all united through the way in which the writer draws on levity and flippancy to move through facets of queer culture, mobilizing them more generally as a critique of heternormativity. Flippancy, at heart, is anti-authoritarian. Even while it requires a poetic subject to manifest, its very nature rejects seriousness and hierarchies. As such, the poetics mobilized by the writers not only unsettle our understanding of sexuality and gender but also trouble wider social demands and expectations. The poets as a whole call into question their chosen mediums and immediate communities: Nelson is reluctant to name her genre-defying style and refuses to answer to comrade; Myles will not lose the mantle of poet even when writing novels and aligns themselves with bands of losers; O'Hara dismisses both manifesto and poems, practising a constant mobility that prevents him from participating in any club; Stein writes an autobiography that is not one, configuring a 'you' and 'I', 'Gertrude' and 'Alice' within a network of gossip and judgement. It is these aspects of the writing, all of which have wider social resonances, that I want to examine within this section, making a case for how each of the writers could be considered a queer troublemaker.

In *Lifting Belly*, Stein moves between sex and the everyday, positioning the two in continual dialogue with one another. The text has moments of innuendo, some of which are specifically gendered such that the male figure diminishes in contrast with the sexual superiority of two women together. The sometimes-innuendo, and sometimes-not, leads the reader to look for clues of sex and sexuality throughout the text, something which they are often denied. *Lifting Belly*, in its surfaces and suggestion, continues a mobility in which the 'I' and 'you' sometimes configure one another and sometimes collapse together. The use of terms such as 'husband' ultimately queer the text further, untethering particular masculine roles from maleness, opening them up for all gender and sexuality. This same playfulness and lightness is also carried through *The Autobiography of Alice B. Toklas*, in which Stein writes an autobiography from the perspective of her life partner. In becoming 'Alice' Stein unbecomes herself, creating a series of postures and poses that also undo the genre as we understand it. *The Autobiography of Alice B. Toklas* does not read as if Alice is writing an autobiography but rather as if she is writing a biography of Stein. Once the end of the book makes clear the ruse of authorship, where Stein unveils herself without changing the tone or style of the writing, our understanding of genre and authorship change once more. Stein has written an autobiography, ultimately, but has just positioned it as a biography written by Alice, who claims to be writing her own autobiography. Throughout both of the texts, Stein foregrounds her contingency; she is defined through Alice in *Autobiography*, just as the 'I' is constituted through the 'you' of *Lifting Belly*. The endless use of pronouns in the latter, and quick movement of the former, ensures that Stein is able to unbecome through the text while still drawing on the forcefulness of her own character and voice. The fact that this identity contingency coexists with a range of gendered pronouns, proper names, artistic groups and plays on the union of marriage troubles the stability with which we might approach heterosexual unions. Both texts made apparent their attacks on heternormativity, through taking the very union of marriage and reconfiguring it beyond heterosexuality. That Stein makes use of terms that are traditionally gendered, and then undoes them, suggests a non-essentialism within the texts that creates space and possibility for two women to live as a genius and her wife.

Ashbery described O'Hara as trying on knuckle dusters to see which one fitted best. The manifesto and poems I have examined are clearly provocative – O'Hara uses irreverence and a lightness of tone to undermine his own writing, in addition to the whole of literature. Ashbery's statement makes this provocation more explicit, suggesting that O'Hara was always preparing to swing the best punch possible. While this might seem acrimonious, given O'Hara's self-presentation such a punch is not necessarily the result of overt and uncontrollable masculinity. Rather, the knuckle dusters fit in with O'Hara's camp posturing and lightness of movement, all of which operate as a form of aggravation. Although Nelson describes some of O'Hara's more explicitly gay poems staying unpublished until after his death, the poet still incorporated shame and queerness into the poems themselves. A number of his writings make references to homosexual identity, as well as the difficulty of being called out or interpellated within a public place. 'At the Old Place' exemplifies this perfectly, where the lightness of foot and ecstatic mobility are realised through the guilt and shame of the final stanza. As such, the poet uses his lightness and mobility to address queerness and the concurrent negative affects associated with an identity that is necessarily closeted by the wider social context. Thus, while the poet writes a number of romantic lyrics in which the love object is a second person, as opposed to gendered, there are moments of defiance in which O'Hara clearly responds to homophobic culture. O'Hara then, while seeming light and unseriousness, is ready to trouble such a perception of himself, working through levity and irreverence as a form of knuckle-duster provocation. This troubling also extends into O'Hara's approach to authority, particularly within the form of the poem and the manifesto. His manifesto rests on a number of disavowals of the manifesto form. He takes a genre associated with radicalism, politics, didacticism and masculine poetics, and undoes all of these assumptions. 'Personism' is neither radical nor didactic, and O'Hara specifically warns against any movement that attempts to force-feed its adherents. Most of his advice surrounding the poem is related to sex, where casual pickup language and threesomes are used as a means by which to sell the genre to the reader. In spite of his making the poem sexual and sexy, O'Hara simultaneously dismisses the genre, suggesting that the movies or the telephone might be better outlets for enjoyment and expression. Thus, O'Hara approaches sexuality in such a way as to trouble the social mores of his own time, while allowing for the negative aspects of shame and concealment to enter the space. He also troubles the genres he chooses, denying any form of authority or superiority for writers and writing.

Similar to O'Hara, Myles makes trouble in relation to the poem itself. They state that poetry has to be a space of failure, because no poets like success. By extension, the genre itself becomes marginalized and unsuccessful, a playground for losers, which ultimately enables poetry freedom to move without mainstream restrictions. Interestingly, Myles also extends these ideas to Americans themselves within the promotional video for *Inferno (A Poet's Novel)*. By labelling all Americans as losers, Myles is directly contradicting American narratives of success, narratives that seem foundational to the country's identity. Not only does this undermine and trouble associations we might make with the American dream and the land of opportunity; it creates a space in which an American poem can emerge that champions the underdog and opens alternatives to the more rigid lines of national success. Through this very rejection, Myles creates a power for poetry, in which the genre of failure can speak to the American losers in such a way as to alternate, deviate and turn away from a heteronormative and staid engagement with the world. These ideas are also reiterated through the way in which Eileen Myles uses their own name. Through taking on the title 'Eileen Myles', as well as using the self-referential lyric 'I', Myles continually undercuts the stability of self. They perform the disjuncture between the forward-facing Eileen Myles and the performative 'I' who uses the name as a passport to the world and experience. While the name might remain stable, Myles describes performing

Eileen Myles as their job, something that continues and must be done, but belies a fluctuation, changing and uncertain identity underneath. This rejection of stability is a further rejection of American ideals, in which an obscure lesbian, loser poet and self in crisis can offer up commentary on sexuality, identity and nationalism through the form of failing poetry. Troubling the stability of identity also allows Myles to critique the patriarchy and patriarchal society. In both 'The Lesbian Poet' and 'Iceland', Myles writes about moments in which they engage with the open landscape and become male, or a guy. They demonstrate that some experiences can transform the gendered way in which we engage with the world. As such, gender and sex are not innate or essential, but rather become in response to the environments we occupy and the people we engage with. This is confirmed by the interview Myles gives on their shift to genderless pronouns, writing that while they might have lived a female life and have a female destiny, 'they' allows for more space, movement and freedom. It is important to address this idea of female destiny in relation to the masculine position Myles adopts in certain landscapes, because it is revealing of the poet's understanding of wider society. While they have refuted gendered terms, they recognize that their way of moving in the world will still be determined by wider society's perception of their gender. Thus, their destiny will inevitably be female. This removes the autonomy from Myles themselves and suggests that it is the social construction of gender that is especially restrictive and insidious. Not only does Myles trouble gender identity, they also recognize that gendered identity is itself troubling to the independence of the individual.

Myles does not purely critique America and patriarchy but also troubles our understandings of feminism. A self-declared feminist, Myles writes in ways that might seem to refute or complicate the politics. For example, in *Inferno (A Poet's Novel)*, the chapter on their lovers' genitals could be seen as extreme objectification, almost porn-like in the close-up view it offers the reader. However, it is also a celebration of the female genitals that refutes and denies the male gaze. It creates space for bodies that would be considered imperfect in pornography, paying homage to the diversity and multiplicity of the female body. Myles also troubles feminism through eliding her work with the genre of porn. Radical Feminism in its original second-wave iteration was proactively opposed to pornography of all kinds, while Myles draws on porn as an image and a possibility for the way in which their work is read. As such, Myles troubles both patriarchal expectation and a feminism that in some senses could be deemed to have a puritanical approach to sex. The poet, therefore, troubles everything, including themselves and their work, as well as wider discourses of feminism, capitalism and nationalism. They are irreverent when it comes to poetry, dismissive of poets as a category, light in their invocation of selfhood and flippant in regard to American success narratives. In taking on traditional radical feminist politics, Myles demonstrates that their restlessness exists in all areas, where an inability to sit still or hold one position necessitates the light footedness of flippancy. Through troubling stability and stillness in discourse, politics, friendship, poetry and even selfhood, Myles creates space in which movement, and therefore resistance, is possible.

Nelson's *The Argonauts* is perhaps less overtly flippant than the other works I have looked to but nonetheless draws on elements of the poetics to communicate a specific form of queer politics. Nelson builds on Myles' willingness to trouble everything refusing stability and security in the positions that she occupies. Like O'Hara and Myles before her, Nelson seems restless within her chosen genres, creating hybrids and uncertainties through her published work. That Nelson feels more comfortable attributing her texts with verbs or processes such as 'a murder' or 'a reckoning' demonstrates that she wishes to shed the limitations of genre, instead creating a direct relationship between her writing and her chosen areas of exploration. This uncertainty, and Nelson's deliberate attempts to create space for freedom, is carried through the themes and content of *The Argonauts*. The text very intentionally troubles sex, sexuality, gender and maternity, allowing all four of these areas to bleed into one another. As a result, at times they take on specific prominence, which is then deconstructed by Nelson, while at other times they fade into irrelevance. This demonstrates how all aspects of sexed existence can be analysed and considered, but also that there are times in which gender and sex can be blissfully escaped in the throes of intense feeling and experience. The movement between these subjects creates a lightness of foot and an unbecoming levity in the face of serious subjects. For example, Nelson queers maternity throughout her text and places it in an interesting dialogue with extreme sex experiences. She considers labour as a form of surrender, something she has previously enjoyed, and talks about how she had imagined giving birth as akin to fisting. The movement between sexuality and maternity shows that these aspects of existence are not separable but rather can be addressed within the same space. Similarly, gendered pronouns are forgotten within the sex acts, where the physical sensations take precedence over minor considerations such as 'he' and 'she'. However, elsewhere they exist in the text as burdens to be considered and considered again.

Nelson primarily addresses themes of transition throughout her text, considering her partner Harry undergoing surgery and starting on T, as well as her own transformation through maternity. The process of change is, in some ways, presented as troublesome. Nelson makes it clear that to reject pronouns, to move from one gender to another, is socially encoded as trouble. She cites a few instances of this, such as when Harry hands over identification alongside a credit card and is suddenly read as female in spite of presenting as male. She also recognizes that her indeterminate sexuality causes trouble, which is typified by Harry's friend asking Nelson about her history of dating women, before assuming she is heterosexual. At the time, within a wider social and political context, Nelson examines how LGBTQ+ parental rights are being pushed back in concurrence with Prop 8 attempting to undo gay marriage. While Nelson resists all of these things, she also recognizes how a number of her choices might be seen as troubling to the LGBTQ+ community. She acknowledges that in getting married, she and Harry could be perceived as reifying a heteronormative state institution. In choosing to have a child, she is also aware that her maternal wishes might seem counter to the no future that is central to some radical queer politics. Nelson is aware throughout the duration of *The Argonauts* that a number of her choices and positions create trouble both within queer cultures and wider heteronormative cultures. Equally significant is that Nelson's text creates a blurring of boundaries between academic, critical thought and lived experience. She draws on theorists in the same ways that she reports conversations with friends, troubling the clear hierarchies of high theory and personal information.

All of the poets included within this book draw on a poetics of flippancy in order to create trouble that is inherently linked to queerness. While Stein uses strategies of butch camp, O'Hara favours a camp mobility, Myles draws on gender shifts and bravado and Nelson deconstructs identity to create further spaces of openness. These different strategies inevitably have some overlaps, but primarily work towards creating further possibilities for existence. O'Hara, Myles and Nelson express greater worries about community and nationality than Stein does. O'Hara considers what it means to be American and how one can counter the grandeur in a small but significant way. He also maintains a continual sense of mobility such that he can always stay one step ahead of his readers, his attackers and his friends. Similarly, Myles positions all Americans as great losers and poets as people who only occupy spaces of failure. While they emphasize the need to go to places and stand around in order to be collected and inducted into community, they recognize that there are some communities that still privilege men and male authority. Nelson remains restless through her text, *The Argonauts*, thinking through her position within a widely homophobic America, as well as her position within a queer couple who might be read as heterosexual. She resists affiliation to any kind of group, critiquing both queerness and heteronormativity with the objective of creating further possibilities for living. Stein, Myles and Nelson also trouble sex and gender to a further extent than O'Hara. As Nelson comments in her work on the New York School, such a challenge to gender might emerge within the work of the women (in Myles' case, female encoded) because their experience of a patriarchal world is different to that of a man. Stein uses her text to play with the concept of husband and wife, untethering the roles from the usual expectations of heterosexuality so a woman and a woman can come together in such a union. Stein also plays with negation, where the categories start to unbecome, such that a non-husband can also be a husband and a non-genius can also be considered under the umbrella of genius. Myles similarly experiments with what it means to be a lesbian, at times declaring it a political identity and in other moments suggesting it is just an idea or an aesthetic. That Myles also incorporates moments of maleness into their writing demonstrates the contingency of sex and gender and how a public perception might enable certain freedoms denied to others. Nelson explicitly makes these ideas part of her text, discussing her personal experience in conjunction with theory as a means by which to consider sex and gender. *The Argonauts* is framed with an opening uncertainty about Harry's gender pronoun and then a resolution that emphasizes the exciting capacity of such uncertainty. She directly addresses trans narratives and discourses, considering how becoming and unbecoming can be communicated as open, as opposed to radical. Nelson's emphasis on the family unit also enables her to draw on her current political climate, at the time of writing, as well as queer critiques of both marriage and reproduction. That Nelson explores maternity within her book foregrounds some women's transformative experience, while Stein, O'Hara and Myles not having children affords them a certain mobility when it comes to socializing, the text, and being in the world. Nelson by contrast is focused on children in a world in which such a maternal pull is derided, dismissed and positioned as uncritical. Interestingly, Nelson takes the maternal role and demystifies and expands it, such that it resists occupying simplistic categories, much like sex and gender.

More broadly, all four poets trouble the way in which we understand genre. While it is too easy to elide genre with gender, the fact that the poets resist fixity speaks to a mobility of expression, content and form that necessarily fuels the poetics of flippancy. Stein, as a poet, writes an autobiography from someone else's perspective; O'Hara writes a poetry manifesto that denies the manifesto's usual characteristics while also adopting a flippant position in relation to poetry itself; Myles mobilizes the term of poet so that they produce a poet's novel, which is actually more of an experimental memoir; Nelson hopes to animate her text with alternative subtitles, uneasily allowing the marketing people to use 'autocriticism' to describe her work. These moves through genres are not laboured and tortured but incredibly light. The poets flit, bringing aspects of poetics to their prose writing, as well as a consideration of juxtaposition, mobility and representation of the self. The poetics of flippancy, given its emphasis on a nimble tongue and lightness of foot, makes these movements possible. It also facilitates the blurring of boundaries, in which the serious is suddenly rehabilitated in lightness and irreverence is prioritized over gravitas. That flippancy is a form of non-commitment, as understood by Riley, also allows for each of the poets to make their way through various genres, while playing with different iterations or presentations of selfhood. The poetics of flippancy can be read as a form of rejection and resistance. It creates space in which alternatives can thrive, allowing the poets the freedom in which to deviate or to err. As opposed to following lines of appropriate seriousness, the poets can engage in an unbecoming levity that orientates them in new and different directions. The levity, and its relationship with unbecoming, allows the poets to question identity representation and self-presentation. Stein becomes Alice B. Toklas to become Stein once more, while she also trades places with Caesar, and at times could be conflated with 'you', 'he' and 'she'. O'Hara is so thoroughly constituted by reference points within his manifesto and so intent on unseriousness that it is difficult to pin him down. The coherence of his tone betrays a personality, but this is entirely surface, all suggestion and all movement. Myles declares that they are performing 'Eileen Myles' and have no sense of who they really are, while Nelson rejects and resists any constrictive identity category that might be applied to her and her relationship. These questions around selfhood also allow the poets to become distinct and separate from rigid social expectations. When viewed against cisgender and heteronormative discourses, the poets are unbecoming, ill-fitting and unseemly. However, they are also unbecoming in the spaces we might expect them to call home, such as writing coteries, feminism or queer radicalism.

Even while the four poets differ, with emphasis on different facets of queer experience, they all use the poetics of flippancy as a form of rejection and resistance. None of the texts under discussion attempt to follow clear lines of success, or even communicate linear narratives, but rather create spaces in which there can be deviation and misdirection. This is not purely to resist 'straightening lines' but also with the aim to create greater openness and possibility for the speaking subject. The poetics of flippancy enables each poet to perform identity through their work, such that it challenges a ready acceptance or understanding of gender performativity. While Judith Butler, through Maggie Nelson in *The Argonauts*, writes that a bad understanding of *Gender Trouble* is that one can wake up each morning and perform a gender of their choosing, there is an interesting tension between performativity and performance. While performativity is reiterative and a socially constituted act, the performance is far more conscious and deliberate, allowing the subject to toy with their self-presentation in a way that is more autonomous. For example, Stein's performance of Alice, serving as a drag act, highlights the different realizations of gender between the two, therefore destabilizing assumptions we might make. Thus, while I am not suggesting that the performance of the writers allows for them to become whoever they want to be, as well as thoroughly dismantling the gender binary, it does give them more space to play within societal limitations and norms.

Flippancy also engages with affect and affectation, trying it on and calling out. In affecting a certain kind of performance, an air of not-caring, an irreverence and insouciance, the speakers of the work position themselves as affect aliens. While they are not unfeeling, or not unmoved by the affect of particular contexts and experiences, the affectation allows for a more intentional and contrived engagement. Thus, there is an almost critical understanding of society and community, achieved through an affected not-caring. Both the affectations and performances of the speakers tie into Riley's concept of trying it on, in both senses. Affectation is a form of trying it on, choosing a particular way of engaging with the world that is slightly unnatural. In that sense, it could be considered as a costume or as a particular and well-coordinated performance. Trying it on, however, also relates to pushing a subject to see how far it can go. In some ways, the analogy of O'Hara trying on different knuckle dusters to see which fits best could be applicable to all of the poets under question. All of their works are provocations and deconstructions, texts that deviate from the norm and even push back against the communities and contexts which might be considered home. It is important to recognize that the performances and affectations are freeing not just in regard to gender and sexuality but a means by which to provoke, interrogate and question.

In my introduction I state that flippancy is not quite as anarchic a form of failure as Halberstam outlines. Here, I want to take an opportunity to elaborate on this, before considering how flippancy might be a softer and more open form of failure. According to Halberstam, when failure is done especially well (or successfully), it has the power to 'fuck shit up'. It is not purely that the person failing becomes a loser in the eyes of wider society but that their refusal to participate in narratives of winning calls standards of success into question. It also interrogates certain lifestyles, particularly ones that are propagated by the state as happy and fulfilling. This is not entirely dissimilar to how Ahmed understands the politics of happiness. While, admittedly, happiness and success are different to one another, we are often led to believe that success will lead to happiness and that happiness is its own form of success. Ahmed writes that the project of happiness works purely to sharpen the distinctions between the marginalized and the non-marginalized. It makes demands of happiness from those who cannot be happy with society as it stands. The emphasis on happiness allows for society to pass judgement in such a way that seems bound up with care and consideration, as opposed to being focused on discouraging than non-normative. To follow happiness and success, then, is to mimic heteronormative structures that work to eradicate difference, constraining existence to tried and tested, as well as narrow, paths. On account of flippancy's levity and lightness, it does not have the power to effect a total failure, especially one that leads towards the revolutionary. It could, therefore, be considered a gentle form of failure, a deliberate provocation that is aimed at affecting thought instead of riots. The problematic of the unbecoming levity is that it might be too light, ultimately, to have strong material impacts. However, the refusal of seriousness does have a greater significance than the nimble tongues and lightness of foot. It demonstrates a willingness to reject society as it is and particularly to accept what has been sold to us as beneficial, happy and successful. In so doing, it interrogates and dismantles ideas of patriarchy, heteronormativity and gender normativity, as well as any beliefs in stable subjects. The particular flippant rejection of seriousness that I am examining here ultimately creates spaces that might not be wholly radical but are open. The unbecoming levity cleaves areas in which the serious and expected are refuted, such that a more open and diffuse way of being becomes possible.

However, it is also worthwhile considering the ways in which flippancy sits in dialogue with privilege. It is not always the case that poets are able to respond to seriousness with lightness or deflate the severity of prejudice with levity. In fact, in some instances, unbecoming levity could have dangerous material and embodied consequences. I am not suggesting that the queer troublemakers considered within this book are only engaging in low stakes questions around sexuality and gender. Rather, that each one is privileged in their use of flippancy; they are able to draw on lightness as a mode of response without dangerous results. This is in part addressed by Nelson when she discusses forms of not-caring. While O'Hara practised a certain form of not-caring, this changes significantly when employed by women given their differing social positions. Flippancy, as a result, works along a spectrum, in which the poets are able to practice lightness even while at points a more radical engagement is required. It may well also be the case that to be able to affect unseriousness in relation to gender identity and sexuality is to occupy a space of security within contemporary culture. It implies each writer is not reliant on social acceptance, family ties or any other institutions from which homophobia and cissexism may arise. This kind of irreverence might only be practicable by people who sit in positions in which their approach, as well as provocations about their gender identity, and sexuality, will not prove fatal. O'Hara and Stein were securely placed among people with similar interests and investments, where sexuality was either shared or rendered irrelevant. Nelson is part of a university which allows her financial and institutional security. Myles is perhaps the most precarious of the poets, having discussed their class-related experiences of sexual violence, as well as their movement towards gender-neutral pronouns. Every one of the poets I have looked to in order to trace the poetics of flippancy is white, which given their different contexts, and the intersections with gender and sexuality, ensures them a particular privilege within both French and American society. I want to recognize, therefore, that flippancy might be made possible of a very material privilege that ultimately impacts on and facilitates the strategies one can use in order to undermine normativity. These privileges also enable the writers to engage with the wider world in a more secure and less precarious way, which also allows for flippancy as a response.

This is not to say that a poetics of flippancy is entirely without political ramifications, even if it might be facilitated by privilege. In *The Promise of Happiness*, Ahmed has done interesting work around the subject of lightness and how it might be rehabilitated for a feminist politics. In her discussion of Poppy, the lead character from the film *Happy Go Lucky*, she writes, 'she [Poppy] might seem light as a feather. She might seem careless and carefree. But freedom from care is also freedom to care, to respond to the world, to what comes up, without defending oneself or one's happiness against what comes up' (2010: 222). This consideration of lightness and care seems integral to the way in which Nelson discussed forms of not-caring within the work of O'Hara and then Myles. While Ahmed's Poppy might be careless and carefree, the troublemakers I have discussed here are defined by their 'not-caring'. This is different from careless, which is to be haphazard and lacking attention, and carefree, which is to be without care. 'Not-caring' is a posture of indifference, a deliberate and intentional rejection of care as opposed to the careless and carefree, which can be more accidental or circumstantial. However, this 'not-caring' as practised by Stein, O'Hara, Myles and Nelson allows for them to care in different directions. That Stein rejects other people's unhappiness, and does not care for particular characters or artists, creates space in which she is able to care about other things and elsewhere. O'Hara in not caring about which clubs he is able to join creates his own unique form of engagement with friends, lovers and the city. Myles not caring enables them to care about feminist politics and to continue on a political trajectory that might position them as outside and marginal. Finally, Nelson's not caring about how the terms of the debate around identity politics forces one into a binary position, allows her to refuse polarities and move in the open space of uncertainty. The lightness that inevitably comes with not-caring is not just a practiced levity but an ability to move with autonomy, as well as a willingness to create spaces for different forms of engagement and care.

The lyric I, self and New Narrative

In my chapter on flippancy, I considered the lyric 'I' in two different ways. The first is to associate the genre with shame, a shame that for the most part has been associated with femininity. To discuss oneself, or at least to use the personal pronoun, has been understood as reductive and simplistic, encouraging focus onto the subject as opposed to the material of language or the significance of politics. This, historically, has been elided with the 'feminine' will to speak up, as well as the 'feminine' impulse to speak only of one's experience. To use the lyric 'I' in this way is to open the poetry to the shame of self-exploration, where this focus is seen as microscopic and non-transcendent. I have also considered the lyric in relation to Narcissus, where the will to realize the poetic self in the form of the 'I' is the same as Narcissus beholding his own reflection in still water. To use the lyric is to work in a mode of self-reflection, as well as a form of self-love. Here I am using the self not to represent the poet but rather as a construct with which the lyric 'I' inevitably engages. Both the shame of the feminine and the shame of self-love create a strong relationship with queer culture. Not only are homosexual relationships understood to be driven by sameness, and thus Narcissism, but queerness is often bound up with gender attribution and misfits (such as the feminine) which are social constructs as opposed to essential identities. Throughout this book, I have explored lyric poetry of the poets, with the exception of Nelson, but I have also considered statements of poetics, advertisements, autobiography, memoir, all of which I believe mobilize the self in similar ways to that of the lyric. Given that the four writers examined here are primarily poets, or were poets before they moved into prose, there is a poetic haunting of all of their texts, which allows for selfhood to be constructed and toyed with in the same way as lyric writing. As Altieri suggests, the lyric communicates that there is an authentic self situated always beyond the artifice of the text. These writers mobilize the 'I' within their work to think how such artificial self-presentation might map back onto identity that is more in flux than authentic.

In 'Personism: A Manifesto', O'Hara claims that poetry 'does not have to do with personality or intimacy' (1995a: 499). He goes on to qualify that the focus of the poem is to sustain some of love's intensity, without being derailed from the poem into a consideration of the love object. This escalates into him proposing the poem as Lucky Pierre before concluding on the telephone as a happy technological substitution. In spite of O'Hara's claim within the manifesto, his work is about personality and intimacy, and simultaneously is not. The manifesto is framed in a tone that suggests complicity with the readership, an ability to read the humour, even if we are not able to keep up with the pace. The piece also communicates a forceful personality, which is light and irreverent at the same time as very well-read. However, instead of reading O'Hara's personality and creating an intimacy with the poet, as irresistible as this might be, it is important to read the text as conveying these concepts. The text itself is imbued with the aliveness and animation that is often attributed to O'Hara himself, when actually it is the construct of selfhood on the page that encapsulates the irreverence and lightness. 'Personism' is in many ways the personal, in that we are encouraged to have a personal relationship with the page, in the same way that the poem might be an intimate middleman for us and the writer. However, it also denounces the personal through presenting a voice that is at once compelling and elusive. The information divulged throughout the manifesto seems to offer us an insight into the poet himself, but actually is constructed such that we have no insight at all, just an appreciation of a web of relationships. The manifesto and the poems I examine use the 'I' to foreground contingency, in which without the presence of others, the writing could not have happened.

Myles' promotional video creates a similar effect in that the viewer is immediately aware of the mediations of self, even while the poet is physically present for us to behold. Through their use of first person, tone and posture, as well as reading from *Inferno*, and their own poems, Myles suggests a relationship between their embodied lived form and their use of the 'I'. However, this is paired with Myles openly declaring that they do not know 'who I am'. Myles' work is shot through with this question of 'who is Eileen Myles?' and by extension, 'who is I?', so even when we can see Eileen Myles themselves, in corporeal form, the question of selfhood still arises. This is not dissimilar to the way in which Stein plays with the first person, which skips and moves throughout *Lifting Belly*, alongside the second person and then gendered pronouns. However, it is the 'I' of *Alice B. Toklas* that most effectively resonates with the queer lyric of uncertainty and Narcissus. Stein uses 'I' when she writes from the perspective of Alice B. Toklas, who in turn is writing about Stein and her interesting life. That Gertrude Stein sits at the centre of the text, but that the 'I' is attributed to Alice, in spite of Stein being the author, creates a relationship with the lyric that is entirely reflection and performance. Nelson, once more, addresses these ideas far more explicitly in her work *The Argonauts*. At times, the text is frustrated by the need to pin down experience and concepts through language, which is realized when Nelson writes that her 'I' wants Harry so closely as a 'second person' that gendered pronouns are rendered irrelevant. Nelson recognizes that she and Harry are in a continual state of becoming, human animals that are in some ways configured through their love of one another, but also subject to change on account of that very love. She makes use of the 'I' to move through the text, her sexuality, sex, transition, recognizing that her medium is flawed and her 'I' is uncertainly constituted. All four of the poets are working with not just self-representation but the way in which the self can be constructed within a specifically queer framework. In this sense, the self is considered as existing within relationality, a matrix of people, conversations and relationships, as well as being highly contingent. While the speaking subject remains consistent throughout the works of each writer that I have examined, they each demonstrate a light approach to selfhood and the 'I'. The flippant approach to genre is echoed in the way the poets play with identity itself, which is generally carried with lightness, in addition to shifts, switches, plays or interrogation. As such, the poets all queer the concept of the stable subject, in addition to the stable genre, using self-presentation as a means by which to cultivate a flippant approach to sexuality, sex, gender and identity.

While the New York School has been useful in my discussions of O'Hara, Myles and Nelson, I want to use the space of the conclusion to turn to New Narrative. The resurgent interest in the group, which has resulted in collections of New Narrative writers, *Writers Who Love Too Much* (2017) and *From Our Hearts to Yours* (2017), being released within the last year has propelled the movement into my consideration of flippancy. In the introduction to *From Our Hearts to Yours*, editors Rob Halpern and Robin Tremblay-McGaw define New Narrative as follows:

> New Narrative aimed to straddle the distance between Language poetry (with its emphasis on the materiality of signification) and Movement writing (with its emphasis on the centrality of identity), while maintaining close ties to both its emphasis on construction *and* expression, artifice *and* selfhood. At the same time, New Narrative was close to Queer performance art as it mobilized an impure aesthetic, incorporating high and low culture, probing the collective fictions of the person and personality, while also foregrounding popular culture as a scene of social practice and politics.
>
> (Halpern and Tremblay-McGaw 2017: 8)

New Narrative, therefore, drew on the experimental bent of Language Poetry, with its emphasis on language while still attending to ideas and concepts of identity. Rather than creating experimental works that reified identity categories, New Narrative writers considered self-representation as a form of performance, one that might draw on impure aesthetics. In this instance, those aesthetics relate to the combinations of high and low culture, as well as popular culture and social practice, but in my work could be seen to relate to the cross-contamination of the butch and camp, the use of the promotional video for analysis, and in O'Hara's work, the serious treatment of a lightly written manifesto. In 'Long Note on New Narrative', one of the movement's originators, Robert Gluck writes about creating the original group with Bruce Boone over a shared enthusiasm for O'Hara. He states that 'Bruce [Boone] and I were poets and our obsession with Frank O'Hara forged a bond' (Gluck 2016: 25). O'Hara gave the two poets a means by which to play with high culture and low culture, as well as avenues to write about gay sexual experience and encounters. It was not just that experiment informed the writing but questions around representation and realization of queer identities. Gluck goes on to say that 'in writing about sex, desire and the body, New Narrative approached performance art, where self is put at risk by naming names, becoming naked, making the irreversible happen' (2016: 31). Throughout the works I have examined, the self is continually placed at risk because of the instability of its construction. Foregrounded in each piece of writing as performative and artificial, the self does take on a certain amount of risks through naming personal relationships and experience, but perhaps even more so from questioning whether the self as a construct is ever a stable and reliable one. This clash of experiments with form and genre, as with my queer troublemakers, and the performance of selfhood are both integral to the lightness that arises through the poetics of flippancy.

New Narrative, in spite of emerging in the Bay Area in the late 1970s, also has ties to Modernism. In 'Poetry with Feeling' by Kaplan Harris, an interesting distinction is made between the campaign of Language poets versus New Narrative writers. Kaplan writes, 'whereas Language poets looked to the past for linguistic innovators ranging from Gertrude Stein to Velimir Khlebnikov, New Narrative looked to the past as a *queer* recovery project' (Harris 2017: 158). A queer recovery project does not need to be understood as the poets of New Narrative identifying LGBTQ+ precursors, though this was an aspect of the campaign. The emphasis on queer, here, can also relate to poetics and narrative. Rather than considering work as exclusively experimental, or simply Modernist, New Narrative writers wanted to trace queerness within and as integral to this tradition. Harris also writes, 'New Narrative embraced a kindred experimental genealogy associated with some of the same modernists, but it ascribed as its *raison d'etre* to a very different reading of those forerunners. In the case of New Narrative, the imperative was to recover certain emotions in its precedents and sources' (Harris 2017: 158). This suggests that while this group of writers drew experimental practice into their own work, including aspects of Language poetry, which was in turn influenced by Modernism, there is also a more affective and queer objective. Not dissimilar to the way in which I have been tracing a poetics of flippancy, the aim was to look for certain emotions and a particular queerness within the Modernist precursors. Harris writes that 'New Narrative writers argued that modernist pedigrees were a liability if void of queer feelings' (2017: 159). As such New Narrative wants to create a lineage with queerness running through it, in which the emotive and affective might have resonance across time, as opposed to just pure writing praxis. It is for these reasons that I have chosen to focus on Stein's babe talk *Lifting Belly* and her popular *Autobiography of Alice B. Toklas*, both of which are structured around a queerness that is actually addressed within the content. Similar to New Narrative writers, I have been looking to discover a history that is not devoid of queerness but rather uses experimental praxis as a means by which to play with queerness, using affect and performativity through performance and flippancy.

Myles and Nelson have both been considered as tangential to, but still a part of, New Narrative. Myles' writing is included within some of the collected anthologies, particularly *Biting the Error: Writers Explore Narrative*. In spite of the fact that New Narrative is quite strongly situated in the Bay Area, and Myles is understood as a New York poet, there are significant overlaps in the objectives of each. For example, Myles has produced a number of prose outputs, including multiple memoirs. As such, Myles is invested in the idea of narrative, even if only as a means by which to explore queerness, sex and selfhood, all themes I consider within my chapter. Similarly, Nelson shares overlaps with New Narrative, in spite of her having written critically on the work of the New York School. In fact *The Argonauts* strongly resonates with Gluck asking 'how can I convey urgent social meanings while opening or subverting the possibilities for meaning itself?' (2004: 27). Even the vocabularies Gluck uses to consider the role of language within identity, politics and self-description are similar to the words chosen by Nelson. They are both focussed on what openness can achieve and how new possibility might be realized through playing with identity, while questioning language's very ability to do so. Through the poetics of flippancy I have attempted to identify a lineage of queer troublemakers who are not united by shared sexuality, in fact they cover too much of a spectrum for such a unity, and who do not share the same writing praxis. Rather, much like the New Narrative project of recovery, I have been looking for a legacy of queerness realized through flippancy. While this is not a particular emotion, I would argue that it is a queer strategy for engagement that facilitates their agitation of self-constructions in relation to wider social contexts.

Conclusion: Possibility

In this conclusion, I want to turn towards the politics of the poetics of flippancy. Although lightness and irreverence might be seen antithetical to political commitment, the unbecoming levity can be freeing within queer contexts. As such, I want to focus on ideas of openness and possibility to consider how the unbecoming levity frees the queer subjects to turn, reorientate, deviate and change direction in ways that are not facilitated by heteronormative culture. In her footnotes to *The Promise of Happiness*, Ahmed expands on her understanding of possibility in relation to lightness, writing 'possibility is light in the sense that in possibility one is open to being blown this way or that, to being picked up by what happens, which can include being picked up in a good or bad way' (Ahmed 2010a: 281). Levity, therefore, facilitates possibilities' existence at the same time that possibility allows for lightness. When things are possible, a subject can be moved about in multiple directions, influenced and affected by their surroundings, but forever responsive. This is not entirely different to the way that Myles describes writing a poem in 'The Lesbian Poet'. They write 'for me getting a poem has always been an imagined body of a sort, getting it down in time, it moves this way and that, it is full of its own sense of possibility'

(Myles 1997: 432). Both Ahmed and Myles see possibility as a form of lightness that allows for movement. The subject can orientate and reorientate themselves, made movable by the levity with which they engage with the world. Nelson also focuses on the benefit of lightness when it comes to language. She writes 'one must become alert to the multitude of possible uses, possible contexts, the winds in which each word can fly' (2015: 8). Not only are subjects carried this way and that through their levity, but words themselves do not have the weight and gravitas to stay always on course, consolidated in their one single objective or trajectory. In this sense, lightness is inherently linked to possibility, opening up spaces in which we are able to move and multiply.

In *Gender Trouble*, Butler also considered the importance of opening up possibilities. Here, she combines openness with possibility, reinforcing the need for space in which queer subjects can move, mobilize, become and unbecome. She writes 'one might wonder what use "opening up possibilities" finally is, but no one who has understood what it is to live in the social world as what is "impossible," illegible, unrealizable, unreal and illegitimate is likely to pose that question' (2006: x). Butler asks that we open spaces to accommodate those who have been previously marginalized, or more extremely, completely eradicated from any kind of public discourse. Butler's possibilities enable those who have been invisible to emerge in a meaningful political and social sense, such that they take on existence and presence that matters. This might seem to contrast with the potentiality that Halberstam outlines for failure. They claim that failure 'turns on the impossible, the improbable, the unlikely and the unremarkable. It quietly loses and in losing it imagines other goals for life, for love, for art and for being' (Halberstam 2011: 88) Where Butler asks for possibilities, Halberstam thrives on the impossible; where Butler calls for legibility and legitimacy (even if that is resistant and queer), Halberstam finds strength in the unremarkable and quiet. How is it possible for queer subjects to be brought into existence at the same time as seeking out different ways of living? I would suggest that Butler's call for further possibilities is not purely to allow for queer assimilation but to make space in which the non-normative can thrive as opposed to being endangered. Similarly, Halberstam is not calling for us to reject successes of the LGBT movement but instead to relish the alternatives. Both Butler and Halberstam make space in which the queer subject can be blown this way and that, moved by lightness that still has social repercussions. Nelson seems to summarize the tension of these ideas very nicely when she writes 'perhaps it's the word *radical* that needs rethinking. But what could we angle ourselves toward instead, or in addition? Openness? Is that good enough, strong enough?' (2015: 27).

So how does this ultimately relate to the poetics of flippancy, which is a textual realization of some of these tensions of queer identity? The texts I have examined here allow for a making and remaking of the self, in which unbecoming levity translates as a questioning and destabilizing of selfhood, in addition to creating possibility to be moved back and forth. The poetics of flippancy is, in some ways, a form of failure; failure to commit; failure to be taken and to take seriously. However, this kind of failure has lower stakes than that outlined by Halberstam because it still engages, using its contexts in order to emphasize its levity. As such, flippancy is an alternative to the straightening narratives, an engagement with assimilation, but one that both cares and doesn't really care either. It is juxtaposition, which can sometimes read as a whiplash in tone, but otherwise highlights the levity of the speaker in relation to their surroundings. Flippancy is also the turn away from, refusing to be orientated by the same goals and successes as heteronormative society, where to be taken seriously is analogous to following straight lines that are without deviation or possibility. The poetics of flippancy, finally, is a lightness within contexts that forever demand seriousness. This does not mean that flippancy is not a serious mode of engagement but that its very strategies are undoing the seriousness with which it approaches topics.

References

Ahmed, S. (2006), *Queer Phenomenology: Orientations, Objects, Others*, Durham, NC: Duke University Press.
Ahmed, S. (2010a), *The Promise of Happiness*, London: Duke University Press.
Ahmed, S. (2010b), 'Happy Objects', in G.J. Seigworth and M. Gregg (eds.) *The Affect Theory Reader*, Durham, NC: Duke University Press.
Ahmed, S. (2014), *Willfull Subjects*, Durham, NC: Duke University Press.
Altieri, C. (1984), *Self and Sensibility in Contemporary American Poetry*, Cambridge: Cambridge University Press.
Andersen, C. (2005), 'I Am Not Who "I" Pretend to Be: The Autobiography of Alice B. Toklas and Its Photographic Frontispiece', *The Comparatist*, 29: 26–37.
Ashbery, J. (1957), 'The Impossible', *UPENN*, 18 July 2007. Available online: http://www.writing.upenn.edu/~afilreis/88/stein-per-ashbery.html (accessed 11 September 2017).
Ashbery, J. (1995), 'Introduction', in D. Allen (ed.) *The Collected Poems of Frank O'Hara*, California: University of California Press.
Berkeley Arts + Design (2017), *Gender, Identity, Memoir: Judith Butler and Maggie Nelson in YouTube*, 15 June. Available online: https://www.youtube.com/watch?v=t-g9tKSy4WY (accessed 22 May 2018).
Berlant, L. and L. Edelman (2014), *Sex, or the Unbearable*, London: Duke University Press.
Bruhm, S. (2001), *Reflecting Narcissus: A Queer Aesthetic*, London: Harvard University Press.
Butler, J. (2006), *Gender Trouble*, London: Routledge.
Cleto, Fabio (1999), *Camp: Queer Aesthetics and the Performing Subject: A Reader*, Edinburgh: Edinburgh University Press.
Cooreal, A. (2016), 'How Eileen Myles, Poet, Spends Her Sundays', in *The New York Times*, 29 January. Available online: https://www.nytimes.com/2016/01/31/nyregion/how-eileen-myles-poet-spends-her-sundays.html (accessed 15 January 2017).
Cvetkovich, A. (2013), 'Personal Effects: The Material Archive of Gertrude Stein and Alice B. Toklas's Domestic Life', in *NOMOREPOTLUCKS*. Available online: http://nomorepotlucks.org/site/personal-effects-the-material-archive-of-gertrude-stein-and-alice-b-toklass-domestic-life-ann-cvetkovich/ (accessed 3 January 2018).

Davidson, M. (1984), 'On Reading Stein', in B. Andrews and C. Bernstein (eds.) *The L=A=N=G=U=A=G=E Book*, 196–197, Southern Illinois: Southern Illinois University Press.

Edelman, L. (2004), *No Future: Queer Theory and the Death Drive*, Durham, NC: Duke University Press.

Epstein, A. (2006), *Beautiful Enemies: Friendship and Postwar American Poetry*, Oxford: Oxford University Press.

Ferguson, R. (1999), *In Memory of My Feelings: Frank O'Hara and American Art*, London: University of California Press.

Glavey, B. (2015), *The Wallflower Avant-Garde: Modernism, Sexuality, and Queer Ekphrasis*, Oxford: Oxford University Press.

Gluck, R. (2016), 'Long Note on New Narrative', in *Communal Nude: Collected Essays*, South Pasadena: Semiotext(e).

Gooch, B. (1993), *City Poet: The Life and Times of Frank O'Hara*, New York: Knopf Press.

Gregg, M. and G.J. Seigworth, eds. (2010), *The Affect Theory Reader*, Durham, NC: Duke University Press.

Halberstam, J. (1998), *Female Masculinity*, London: Duke University Press.

Halberstam, J. (2011), *The Queer Art of Failure*, London: Duke University Press.

Halpern, R. and R. Tremblay-McGaw, eds. (2017), *From Our Hearts to Yours: New Narrative as Contemporary Practice*, Oakland: Contemporary Practice.

Hammer, K. A. (2015), 'Butch Life Writing: Private Desires and Public Demands in the Works of Gertrude Stein', *Feminist Formations*, 27 (2): 27–45.

Hampson, R. and W. Montgomery (2010), *Frank O'Hara Now*, Liverpool: Liverpool University Press.

Harris, Kaplan. (2017), 'Poetry with Feeling', in *From Our Hearts to Yours: New Narrative as Contemporary Practice*, 153–166, Oakland: Contemporary Practice.

Herd, D. (2010), 'Stepping Out with Frank O'Hara', in R. Hampson to W. Montgomery (eds.) *Frank O'Hara Now*, 70–85, Liverpool: Liverpool University Press.

Holbrook, S. (1999), 'Lifting Bellies, Filling Petunias, and Making Meanings through the Trans-Poetic', *American Literature*, 71 (4): 751–771.

'I Must Be Living Twice' in *Serpent's Tail*. Available online: https://serpentstail.com/i-must-be-living-twice.html (accessed 26 April 2017).

Lamm, Kimberly. (2001), 'Interview with Eileen Myles', in *HOW2*, 21 March. Available online: http://www.asu.edu/pipercwcenter/how2journal/archive/online_archive/v1_8_2002/current/workbook/lamm-interview.htm (accessed 14 March 2016).

Lerner, Ben. (2015), 'Eileen Myles, The Art of Poetry No. 99', in *The Paris Review*, Issue 214. Available online: https://www.theparisreview.org/interviews/6401/eileen-myles-the-art-of-poetry-no-99-eileen-myles (accessed 3 April 2017).

Long, Julia. (2012), *Anti-Porn: The Resurgence of Anti Pornography Feminism*, London: Zed Books.

Mark, Rebecca (1989), *Lifting Belly*, Tallahassee: Naiad Press.

Mark, Rebecca (1995), 'Introduction', in *Lifting Belly*, Tallahassee: Naiad Press.

Mikkelsen, K.A. (2011), *Pastoral, Pragmatism, and Twentieth Century American Poetry*, New York: Palgrave Macmillan.

Morris, J. (2017), 'A Rough Geneology of New Narrative', in R. Halpern and R. Tremblay-McGaw (eds.) *From Our Hearts to Yours: New Narrative as Contemporary Practice*, Oakland: Contemporary Practice.

Myles. E. (1991a), 'A Poem', in *Not Me*, 107–113, New York: Semiotext(e).

Myles, E. (1991b), 'Promotional Material', in *Not Me*, 96–103, New York: Semiotext(e).

Myes, E. (1991c), 'Keats & I', in *Not Me*, 171–183, New York: Semiotext(e).

Myes, E. (1991d), 'Basic August', in *Not Me*, 73–95, New York: Semiotext(e).

Myles, E. (1997), 'The Lesbian Poet', in *School of Fish*, 123–131, Santa Rosa: Black Sparrow Press.

Myles, E. (2010), *Inferno (a poet's novel)*, New York: OR Books.

Myles, E. (2012), 'The Lesbian Poet' in L. Robertson and M. Stadler (eds.) *Revolution: A Reader*, 431–440, Canada: Paraguay Press & Publication Studio.

Myles, E. (2013), 'Painted Clear, Painted Black', in *The Volta*, May. Available online: http://www.thevolta.org/ewc29-emyles-p1.html (accessed 12 May 2017).

Myles, E. (2016a), 'The Poet', in *I Must Be Living Twice: New and Selected Poems 1975–2014*, 183, London: Tuskar Rock Press.

Myles, E. (2016b), 'For Jordana', in *I Must Be Living Twice: New and Selected Poems 1975–2014*, 285, London: Tuskar Rock Press.

Myles, E. (2016c), 'April 5u', in *I Must Be Living Twice: New and Selected Poems 1975–2014*, 291, London: Tuskar Rock Press.

Myles, E. (2016d), 'Untitled (I always put my pussy)', in *I Must Be Living Twice: New and Selected Poems 1975–2014*, 150, London: Tuskar Rock Press.

Myles, E. (2016e), 'Porn Poems', in *I Must Be Living Twice: New and Selected Poems 1975–2014*, 198, London: Tuskar Rock Press.

Myles, E. (2016f), 'An American Poem', in *I Must Be Living Twice: New and Selected Poems 1975–2014*, 134, London: Tuskar Rock Press.

Nelson, M. (2011a), *The Art of Cruelty: A Reckoning*, London: W.W. Norton and Company.

Nelson, M. (2011b), *Women, The New York School, and Other True Abstractions*, Iowa: University of Iowa Press.

Nelson, M. (2014), 'Tributes: Maggie Nelson on Eileen Myles', *Poetry Society of America*. Available online: https://www.poetrysociety.org/psa/poetry/crossroads/tributes/maggie_nelson_on_eileen_myles/ (accessed 10 May 2017).

Nelson, M. (2015), *The Argonauts*, Minnesota: Graywolf Press.

Ngai, S. (2007), *Ugly Feelings*, London: Harvard University Press.

O'Hara, F. (1975), 'Statement for Paterson Society', in *Standing Still and Walking in New York*, Berkeley: Grey Fox Press.

O'Hara, F. (1995a), 'Personism: A Manifesto', in D. Allen (ed.) *The Collected Poems of Frank O'Hara*, 498–499, London: University of California Press.

O'Hara, F. (1995b), 'The Day Lady Died', in D. Allen (ed.) *The Collected Poems of Frank O'Hara*, 325, London: University of California Press.

O'Hara, F. (1995c), 'Autobiographia Literaria', in D. Allen (ed.) *The Collected Poems of Frank O'Hara*, 11, London: University of California Press.

O'Hara, F. (1995d), 'Poem (Now it is the 27th)', in D. Allen (ed.) *The Collected Poems of Frank O'Hara*, 345, London: University of California Press.

O'Hara, F. (1995e), 'A Step Away From Them', in D. Allen (ed.) *The Collected Poems of Frank O'Hara*, 257, London: University of California Press.

O'Hara, F. (1995f), 'Personal Poem', in D. Allen (ed.) *The Collected Poems of Frank O'Hara*, 335, London: University of California Press.

O'Hara, F. (1995g), 'Meditations in an Emergency', in D. Allen (ed.) *The Collected Poems of Frank O'Hara*, 197, London: University of California Press.

O'Hara, F. (1995h), 'Homosexuality', in D. Allen (ed.) *The Collected Poems of Frank O'Hara*, 181, London: University of California Press.

O'Hara, F. (1995i), 'At the Old Place', in D. Allen (ed.) *The Collected Poems of Frank O'Hara*, 223, London: University of California Press.

O'Hara, F. (1995j), 'Biotherm', in D. Allen (ed.) *The Collected Poems of Frank O'Hara*, 436, London: University of California Press.

O'Hara, F. (1995k), 'To the Poem', in D. Allen (ed.) *The Collected Poems of Frank O'Hara*, 175, London: University of California Press.

O'Hara, F. (1995l), 'Ode: Salute to the French Negro Poets', in D. Allen (ed.) *The Collected Poems of Frank O'Hara*, 305, London: University of California Press.

OR Books (2010). *Inferno (a poet's novel)* [video file] in *YouTube.com*, 28 July. Available online: https://www.youtube.com/watch?v=Yk_vryOmXLU&t=147s (accessed 10 May 2014).

Penley, C. (2013), 'A Feminist Teaching Pornography? That's Like Scopes Teaching Evolution!', in T. Taormino and C. Parrenas et al. (eds.) *The Feminist Porn Book: The Politics of Producing Pleasure*, 179–199, New York: The Feminist Press.

Penley, C. et al. (2013), 'Introduction', in T. Taormino and C. Parrenas et al. (eds.) *The Feminist Porn Book: The Politics of Producing Pleasure*, 9–22, New York: The Feminist Press.

Perelman, B. (1984) 'Untitled', in B. Andrews and C. Bernstein (eds.) *The L=A=N=G=U=A=G=E Book*, 199–200, Southern Illinois: Southern Illinois University Press.

Perloff, M. (1998), *Frank O'Hara: Poet among Painters*, London: The University of Chicago Press.

Perloff, M. (2012), 'Poetry on the Brink: Reinventing the Lyric', *Boston Review*, 18 May. Available online: http://bostonreview.net/forum/poetry-brink (accessed 13 June 2017).

Prickett, S.N. (2015), 'Bookforum talks with Maggie Nelson', in *Bookforum*, 29 May. Available online : https://www.bookforum.com/interview/14663 (accessed 12 April 2018).

Riley, D. (2000), *Words of Selves: Identification, Solidarity, Irony*, California: Stanford University Press.

Riley, D. (2005), *Impersonal Passion: Language as Affect*, London: Duke University Press.

Robinson, Mark (2013). 'Routledge to Publish First Porn Studies Journal' on *T and F*. Available online: http://www.tandf.co.uk/journals/press/porn-studies.pdf (accessed 12 January 2014).

Samson, J. D. (2011), 'Eileen Myles and JD Samson in Conversation', in *Recaps Magazine*. Available online : http://recapsmagazine.com/review/eileen-myles-and-jd-samson-in-conversation/ (accessed 10 January 2017).

Satran, R. (2016), 'Exclusive: Eileen Myles Explains Their Impassioned New Poem for Hilary', in *Vice*, 4 November . Available online : https://i-d.vice.com/en_us/article/exclusive-eileen-myles-explains-their-impassioned-new-poem-for-hillary (accessed 12 May 2017).

Saxelby, R. (2017), 'In Search of Nuance with Maggie Nelson', in *The Fader*, 8 December. Available online : https://www.thefader.com/2017/12/08/maggie-nelson-nuance-interview (accessed 12 March 2018).

Sedgwick, E.K. (2003a), 'Around the Performative: Periperformative Vicinities in Nineteenth-Century Narrative', in *Touching Feeling: Affect, Pedagogy, Performativity*, 67–92, Durham, NC: Duke University Press.

Sedgwick, E.K. (2003b), 'Shame, Theatricality, and Queer Performativity: Henry James *The Art of the Novel*', in *Touching Feeling: Affect, Pedagogy, Performativity*, 35–66, Durham, NC: Duke University Press.

Seigworth, G.J. and M. Gregg (eds.) *The Affect Theory Reader*, Durham, NC: Duke University Press.

Setina, E. (2012), 'From "Impossible" Writing to a Poetics of Intimacy: John Ashbery's Reading of Gertrude Stein', Genre, 45 (1): 143–166.

Shields, B. (2018), 'I'm the Marmalade: An Interview with Wayne Koestenbaum', in *The Paris Review*, 15 March. Available online: https://www.theparisreview.org/blog/2018/03/15/im-the-marmalade-an-interview-with-wayne-koestenbaum/ (accessed 12 June 2018).

Silverberg, M. (2010), *The New York School Poets and the Neo-Avant Garde: Between Radical Art and Radical Chic*, London: Routledge.

Sontag, S. (2009a), 'Notes on Camp', in *Against Interpretation*, 275–292, London: Penguin.

Sontag, S. (2009b) 'Afterword: Thirty Years Later' in *Against Interpretation*, 305–312, London: Penguin.

Stein, G. (1995), *Lifting Belly* (ed.) Rebecca Mark, Tallahassee: The Naiad Press Inc.

Stein, G. (2001), *The Autobiography of Alice B. Toklas*, London: Penguin.

Stein, G. (2004a), 'Poetry and Grammar', in P. Meyerowitz (ed.), *Look at Me Now and Here I Am: Writing and Lectures, 1909–45*, 123–145, London: Peter Owen.

Stein, G. (2004b), 'What Is English Literature?' in P. Meyerowitz (ed), *Look at Me Now and Here I Am: Writing and Lectures, 1909–45*, 31–57, London: Peter Owen.

Stein, G. (2004c), 'Composition as Explanation', in P. Meyerowitz (ed), *Look at Me Now and Here I Am: Writing and Lectures, 1909–45*, 21–30, London: Peter Owen.

Tambling, Zoe. (2017), 'The Rumpus Interview with Eileen Myles', in *The Rumpus*, 24 February. Available online: http://therumpus.net/2017/02/the-rumpus-interview-with-eileen-myles-3/ (accessed 12 June 2018).

Vincent, J.E. (2002), *Queer Lyrics (Difficulty and Closure in American Poetry)*, New York: Palgrave Macmillan.

White, G. (2014), *Lyric Shame: The 'Lyric' Subject of Contemporary American Poetry*, London: Harvard University Press.

Will, B. (2000), *Gertrude Stein: Modernism and the Problem of 'Genius'*, Edinburgh: Edinburgh University Press.

Winterson, J (2011), 'All I Know about Gertrude Stein', in *Granta 115: The F Word*. Accessible online: https://granta.com/all-i-know-about-gertrude-stein/ (accessed 29 May 2018).

Index

affect
    Eileen Myles 110, 120, 121, 124, 128–9
    femininity 13–15
    flippancy and affect 2, 7, 10, 22–8, 165, 169, 176–8
    Frank O'Hara 76–9, 87, 94, 95, 97
    Gertrude Stein 47, 48
    New Narrative 161, 163, 183, 184
    ugly feelings 29–32
affectation
    Eileen Myles 120
    Flippancy 7, 24, 27, 29–30, 32
    Frank O'Hara 77–9
    Gertrude Stein 41, 44–5, 48
    Maggie Nelson 162
    Trying it on 165, 168, 176
Ahmed, Sara
    In 'Happy Objects' 26
    In *The Promise of Happiness* 27, 72, 84–5, 120, 178, 184
    In *Queer Phenomenology* 42, 81, 91, 94, 96, 115, 118, 187
    In *Willful Subjects* 21, 31, 80, 89, 92
America
    anti-success 170–3, 178
    camp 139
    contexts 2, 3, 6
    culture 64, 75, 79, 81, 86, 89, 92, 97
    failure 102, 132–5
    homophobia 161
Ashbery, John
    On O'Hara 79, 89, 90, 99, 169
    On Stein 34, 35, 36, 37, 39, 42, 45, 56, 58

becoming
    anti-normativity 161, 167, 168, 174, 181
    flippancy 7, 10, 22–6, 29
    Frank O'Hara 81, 82, 83, 85
    Gertrude Stein 45, 52, 59
    identity categories 101, 102, 110, 111, 119, 123, 129

Berlant and Edelman 76, 82, 83, 94
butch
    authority 51, 53, 55, 57, 58
    camp 59, 65–8
    Eileen Myles 107, 111, 114–15, 120, 125, 128, 139–40
    identity 33, 35, 37–45, 48–9
    lineages 3, 5, 7, 9
    troublemaking 165, 167–8, 173, 182
Butler, Judith 27, 28, 42, 60, 108, 116–17, 120, 142, 153, 157, 159–60, 163, 176, 185

categories
    aesthetic 7, 24, 28–9, 34, 45, 165
    gender 9, 48–9, 56, 62–8, 87, 111, 122
    genre 5, 71, 89–91, 172
    identity 114–20, 132–7, 163–4, 174–5, 182
    irony 20
    openness 142–3, 146–7, 151–9
community
    Eileen Myles 120–4, 136
    Frank O'Hara 88, 89, 90, 92, 99
    Gertrude Stein 51
    irony 29
    poetry 3, 5
    queer 15, 16
    resistance 173, 176
care 90, 147–9, 177, 178–9, 186

dialogue
    In *The Argonauts* 141–2, 147–9
    In *Lifting Belly* 54, 56
    Personism 75–7, 94, 97, 98

echo 7, 19–21, 30
Edelman, Lee 149–50

failure
    camp 39–40, 43
    Eileen Myles 101, 102, 103, 110, 115, 132–5, 137, 154, 156

flippancy 21–2, 24–5, 28–9, 31–2
genre 16–17, 18
happiness 83, 86
identity 59, 66
strategy 165, 167, 170, 173, 176–7, 185–6
feeling
  affect 22–32
  avant-garde 11–18, 183
  Eileen Myles 112, 113, 115, 117, 132, 136
  Frank O'Hara 70, 71, 77–9, 91, 95–7, 99
  Gertrude Stein 46
  Maggie Nelson 143–5, 154, 162, 165
  ugly feeling 7
female
  category 171, 173, 174
  Eileen Myles 108, 114–15, 117–18, 120–1, 123, 125, 129, 130, 132
  Gertrude Stein 33, 35, 40–1, 43–4, 55, 61–2, 66–7
  Judith Butler 28
  lineage 4, 9
  Maggie Nelson 143, 145, 155, 161–2
  shame 12–13
gender
  butch/femme 41–5, 48, 55, 56, 59–68
  Eileen Myles 101, 102, 103, 108, 114–17, 119, 120, 122, 123, 125, 128, 135, 136
  Maggie Nelson 139, 140, 142–5, 147–8, 151, 153–5, 157–60, 162–4
  transforming gender 168, 169, 171–4, 176–8, 181, 185
  troubling gender 3, 4, 6, 7, 9, 10, 12, 13, 25, 27–8

Halberstam, Jack
  In *Female Masculinity* 41, 43, 65, 67
  In *Queer Art of Failure* 22, 24–5, 40, 103, 109, 116, 133, 156, 161, 176, 185, 186
heteronormativity
  alternatives to 170, 173, 174, 175, 177, 184, 187
  Eileen Myles 117, 128, 137
  Gertrude Stein 40, 65, 68
  Maggie Nelson 142, 146–9, 151–2, 155–8
  resisting 6, 15, 28, 31

identity
  Eileen Myles 101, 102, 106–21, 128–9, 134–8, 139
  flippancy 2, 3, 6–11, 14–18, 24–8, 30, 32, 34, 36
  Frank O'Hara 71, 79, 81, 86, 89, 98
  Gertrude Stein 41–5, 48, 49, 54–9, 62–8, 70
  Maggie Nelson 142, 144–59, 161–4
  troubling 165, 167, 168, 169–71, 173–5, 178, 179–82, 184, 186
irony 19–21, 23–6, 29–31, 64
irreverence
  discomfort 165, 167, 169–70, 172, 175–8, 180, 184
  Eileen Myles 135, 137, 139
  Frank O'Hara 71, 78, 97–9, 107
  Gertrude Stein 38, 51
  Maggie Nelson 140, 143–9, 151–2, 162
  poetics of flippancy 1, 5, 7–10, 30

levity
  Eileen Myles 107, 118, 119, 131, 135–7
  Frank O'Hara 69, 70, 71, 87, 98, 99
  Gertrude Stein 38, 42, 44, 45, 49, 51, 59
  Maggie Nelson 140, 143, 148, 155
  poetics of flippancy 1, 2, 4, 7, 9, 22–6, 29, 32
  troublemaking 165, 167, 168, 170, 172, 175, 177, 179, 184, 185, 186
lyric
  Eileen Myles Poems 96, 98, 102, 106–7, 111–12, 124–6, 134–5
  flippancy and the lyric 7, 8, 11–18, 22–3, 28, 30
  Frank O'Hara Poems 77, 81, 85, 86
  In *Lifting Belly* 56, 67
  shame and selfhood 158, 160, 161, 162, 167, 169, 170, 179–81
lesbian
  Eileen Myles 101–3, 107–10, 114–19, 122–30, 132–4, 136–7
  fluidity 154
  Gertrude Stein 33, 36–7, 41–3
  In 'The Lesbian Poet' 3, 4, 9, 139, 166, 171, 174, 184
  sex 15, 56, 60
labour 142, 147–9, 151, 172

masculinity 40–4, 53, 60, 66–8, 71, 117, 119, 155, 169
maternity 139, 142–3, 151, 154, 158, 163–4, 172–4
Myles, Eileen 2–9, 11–13, 15–16, 18, 23, 30–2, 95, 101–37, 139–40, 143, 162–8, 170–5, 178, 179–81, 183–4
    In *Inferno (A Poet's Novel)* 5, 8, 101, 103, 104, 114, 121, 125–6, 132, 136–7, 170–1, 180

name
    Eileen Myles 8, 103, 106, 109–11, 116–17, 121, 125, 135–7
    Frank O'Hara 71–2, 86–7, 92
    Gertrude Stein 36, 46, 49, 50, 53–5, 58, 59–60, 62, 64–6, 68
    Maggie Nelson 140, 152–4, 159, 166
    troublemaking 168–70, 182
Narcissus 7, 17–22, 179, 181
narrator 48–9, 52, 63–4, 66, 68
Nelson, Maggie 2, 4–6, 9–10, 11, 16, 18, 23, 30–2, 86, 88, 95, 99, 107, 109, 119, 125, 139–64, 165–9, 172–9, 181, 183–5
    In *The Argonauts* 5, 6, 9, 16, 18, 139–44, 146–8, 151–5, 157–63, 165–6, 172–4, 176, 181, 184
New Narrative 146, 158–9, 161, 179, 181–4
New York
    city 1–5
    Frank O'Hara 73, 77, 81, 82, 84, 86, 98
    Maggie Nelson 139
    poetic lineage 163, 183
New York School
    Frank O'Hara 99
    New Narrative 181, 184
    poets 1, 4, 5, 95, 101, 107, 151
    In *Women, The New York School and Other True Abstractions* 5, 9, 88–90, 139, 143, 147, 155, 162–3, 167, 174
nimble tongue
    flippancy 7, 22, 23, 30, 32, 175, 177
    Frank O'Hara 98, 99
    Gertrude Stein 44, 49, 53, 68
    Maggie Nelson 165, 167

O'Hara, Frank 1–4, 6–11, 16, 18, 23, 27, 30–3, 67, 69–99, 103, 107–8, 110, 126, 135, 139, 140, 147, 151, 155, 163–82
    In 'Personism: A Manifesto' 1, 16, 71, 72, 73, 78–80, 82, 88, 90–1, 93–7, 108, 170, 180
openness
    butch and femme 42, 46, 55
    Eileen Myles 128
    flippancy 165, 167, 173, 175, 184–5
    Frank O'Hara 86, 91–2
    as opposed to radical 10, 154–60, 164
    queer troublemakers 22
performance
    In *The Autobiography of Alice B. Toklas* 63–6
    butch 41–5, 48, 59, 60
    camp 39
    Eileen Myles 104–9, 115, 119–120, 125–7, 136
    flippancy 2, 7, 8, 15–19, 21–3, 27–9, 32
    Frank O'Hara 70, 78, 79
    Maggie Nelson 147, 162, 165–6
    troublemaking 168, 176, 181–3
performativity
    Eileen Myles 105, 119–20, 132, 140
    gender 7, 24, 27–8, 32, 44, 45
    Maggie Nelson 162–3, 176
    queer 32, 59–60, 119–20, 132, 140, 162–3, 176, 183
    In 'Shame, Theatricality, and Queer Performativity: Henry James's *The Art of the Novel*' 14, 87, 90–1
Perloff, Marjorie 6, 11, 12, 14, 15, 18, 162
pornography 9, 103, 107, 125–32, 134, 137, 171
possibility
    anti-categories 34, 57, 60, 86, 92–3, 173–5
    In *The Argonauts* 139, 142, 146, 152–4, 157–60, 184–6
    Eileen Myles 101–3, 107–13, 115, 117, 119, 122, 126–8, 134, 136
    gender 28, 62, 169
    Personism: A Manifesto 72, 74, 76–7, 95, 99
political 10, 14, 21–3, 42, 171

queer
    Eileen Myles 103, 107–9, 115, 118, 122, 123, 127, 132
    flippancy 21–4

Frank O'Hara 70–1, 81, 85, 87–91, 92, 94, 96, 98
Gertrude Stein 32–4, 36, 38–42, 44, 55, 58–9, 63
Maggie Nelson 140–3, 145–54, 156–8, 162–4
shame 14–19
troublemaking 165, 167, 168–9, 172–4, 175, 177, 179, 181–6
writing 1–12, 27–9, 32

radical
  failure 22
  flippancy 170–5, 177–8
  gender 117, 123
  levity 1
  queer culture 10, 91, 142, 145–6, 149–50, 156–7, 164, 185
Riley, Denise
  In *'Am I That Name?' Feminism and the Category of 'Women' in History* 111
  In *Impersonal Passion: Language as Affect* 110–11
  In *The Words of Selves: Identification, Solidarity, Irony* 19–21, 24, 25, 26, 29–30, 64, 79, 83, 102, 113, 161, 163, 175, 176

seriousness
  Eileen Myles 102, 107, 122, 124, 131
  female seriousness 143, 145, 148, 149, 152, 154, 162
  flippancy 1, 2, 5, 7, 9, 10, 12, 21–3, 25–6, 30–2
  Personism: A Manifesto 79, 81, 89–90, 92, 97–9
  readings of O'Hara 68–71
  readings of Stein 34–40, 42, 44, 45
  trouble 165, 167, 168, 172, 175, 177–8, 182, 186
  unbecoming levity 49, 51
shame
  lyric 7, 11, 12–14, 158, 162
  queer 29, 87, 98, 163, 169, 170, 179
  shamelessness 125, 158, 162
Sontag, Susan
  In 'Afterword', *Against Interpretation* 38
  In 'Notes on Camp' 2, 38, 39, 43, 67, 78

Stein, Gertrude 2–10, 11, 18, 23, 30–2, 33–68, 106, 107, 122, 125, 128, 136, 139–40, 150, 154, 163–9, 173–9, 181, 183
  In *Autobiography of Alice B. Toklas* 16, 18, 42, 44, 47, 48, 49–52, 59–60, 63–6, 67–8, 181
  In *Lifting Belly* 15, 42, 44, 47, 48, 52–8, 60–3, 67–8, 181
  In 'Poetry and Grammar' 46, 47
  In 'What is English Literature?' 46
style
  butch camp 40, 41, 48, 58, 67
  elippancy 165, 168, 169, 177
  emotion 12
  flippancy 23
  Frank O'Hara 71, 73, 78, 79, 98
  New York School 4, 8

Toklas, Alice B.
  Cult figure 6, 33, 58, 154
  legibility 10, 36, 42, 45, 53, 56, 66
  performance 16, 18, 41, 48, 51, 63, 64, 175
tone
  Eileen Myles 101–4, 106, 108, 111, 125–31
  flippancy 2, 7, 23, 165, 166, 169, 175, 180, 186
  Frank O'Hara 36, 41, 49, 67, 71, 72, 76, 77–80, 90, 92, 95, 98–9
  Gertrude Stein 36, 41, 49, 67
  Maggie Nelson 140, 148, 152
  Perloff, Marjorie 12

unbecoming
  becoming 7, 22–6, 42, 45, 47, 123
  Eileen Myles 109–12
  identity 125, 133, 135–6, 142, 161
  levity 1, 22, 29–30, 32, 38, 44, 49, 51, 59, 119, 131, 167
  queer 10, 22, 167, 168, 172, 174–5, 177, 184–6
unserious
  butch Camp 44
  flippancy 7, 8, 21, 32
  provocation 90, 98
  trouble 112, 170, 175, 178